Pathways to Marriage

Premarital and Early Marital Relationships

Dean M. Busby

Texas Tech University

Vicki L. Loyer-Carlson

Family Wellness Center, Inc.

Boston   New York   San Francisco
Mexico City   Montreal   Toronto   London   Madrid   Munich   Paris
Hong Kong   Singapore   Tokyo   Cape Town   Sydney

Editor in Chief: *Karen Hanson*
Series Editor: *Jeff Lasser*
Series Editorial Assistant: *Andrea Christie*
Marketing Manager: *Judeth Hall*
Production Administrator: *Anna Socrates*
Editorial Production Service: *Matrix Productions, Inc.*
Electronic Composition: *Peggy Cabot, Cabot Computer Services*
Composition Buyer: *Linda Cox*
Manufacturing Buyer: *JoAnne Sweeney*
Photo Researcher: *Helane M. Prottas/Posh Pictures*
Cover Administrator: *Kristina Mose-Libon*

For related titles and support materials, visit our online catalog at www.ablongman.com.

Between the time Website information is gathered and then published, it is not unusual for some sites to have closed. Also, the transcription of URLs can result in unintended typographical errors. The publisher would appreciate notification where these errors occur so that they may be corrected in subsequent editions.

Library of Congress Cataloging-in-Publication Data

Busby, Dean M.
    Pathways to marriage : premarital and early marital relationships / Dean M. Busby,
Vicki L. Loyer-Carlson.
      p.   cm.
Includes bibliographical references and index.
ISBN 0-205-33555-1
    1. Marriage. 2. Marriage compatibility tests. 3. Mate selection. 4. Courtship.
5. Couples. I. Busby, Dean M. II. Loyer-Carlson, Vicki L. III. Title.

HQ728 .B877 2003
306.81—dc21
                                                     2002021544

Printed in the United States of America

10 9 8 7 6 5 4 3 2   08 07 06 05 04

Photo Credits on page 210

Contents

Preface

Sometimes if an item is looked at too closely it can be disconcerting. At other times examining something with care can increase appreciation for its beauty. Strangely, close scrutiny of a painting or other work of art can produce both effects. Perhaps after examining a painting the viewer sees hidden images that are not as pleasant as the overall picture. Although disconcerting, it may add to the appreciation of the skill of the painter and the complexity of art.

A successful marriage is clearly a thing of beauty when looked at with a cursory glance. The images of marriage that wash over our minds when we think of this long-term relationship usually bring smiles. The image of two strangers who, although dramatically different, seem unavoidably drawn to each other; the image of a couple sharing every detail of their pasts with one another while walking by a cool mountain stream; the image of two ecstatic individuals sealing their relationship commitment before their community in a marriage ceremony; the image of two passionate lovers exploring love-making on a honeymoon; the image of a young husband massaging his wife's shoulders as she struggles to cope with the stress of a nascent career; the image of two new parents as they view the face of their firstborn child; the image of a middle-aged couple watching their teenagers beginning to fall in love for the first time; the image of two gentle elderly people assisting one another with the basic tasks of daily living.

Still, when examined in detail, many hidden images emerge from these views of marriage. Perhaps with the young couple there are several missed attempts at getting started down the courtship road because both are too preoccupied with school. Or maybe their families do not agree with their choice and much bickering occurs as they try to make the decision to marry. Each of the marriage images seems to be composed of numerous opportunities for pleasure and for pain.

It is our task in this book to look closely at courtship and marriage. Certainly a little of the luster might be worn off by this examination. Yet, hopefully, in the end, readers will have a greater appreciation for how wonderfully complex and beautiful marriage can be.

This book is intended to provide information so that partner selection can be done carefully, to help individuals and couples understand the contexts within which they are embedded so that they can develop systems of support for their relationship, and to present suggestions for nourishing the relationship regularly.

This book is a result of the integration of research and clinical practice. We conceived of the idea of a book that would walk readers through the experience of their own relationships, giving them the opportunity to use the Relationship Evaluation questionnaire (RELATE) to personalize the research and clinical vignettes that describe the pathways to marriage.

As educators and therapists, we see couples at all stages and conditions of marriage: beginning, middle, late, healthy, unhealthy, and dissolving. Often, the factors contributing to difficulties and breakups are similar to those of physical diseases: The warning signs are visible early, and with early detection and care can be treated and, if not cured, the effects at least can be minimized. Research from the RELATE Institute as well as other programs of research have made available a tremendous amount of information about the personal and social contexts of marriage. The goal of this book is to help translate the information from research into a tangible understanding of premarriage and early marriage.

This book is designed to fill a specific need in the existing literature by encouraging personal meaning through the understanding of premarital and early marital relationships. That is done by looking at the systems within which relationships are embedded, providing the research findings that are needed to fully understand the ways in which these systems affect relationships, and then providing a way to personalize that information through the use of the RELATE instrument. When the business of supporting marriages is left only in the hands of skilled professionals, the most effective support system for marriage is untapped. We have faith in couples' resourcefulness, and in the abilities of communities to come together to care for themselves and each other better than any single therapist can care for troubled marriages. The secret to strong marriages and families is in knowledge, commitment, and support. The recipe for developing these components is presented here, in *Pathways to Marriage: Premarital and Early Marital Relationships*.

About the Authors

Dean M. Busby received his Ph.D. in Marriage and Family Therapy in 1990 from Brigham Young University. He was an associate professor of Child and Family Studies at Syracuse University, where he taught a variety of courses on family relationships and family therapy for many years. Recently he has been the Department Chair for the Human Development and Families Studies Department at Texas Tech University, where he continues to teach about premarital and marital relationships. For the last 16 years he has been conducting research with couples in the premarital stage of their relationship to more clearly understand what aspects of new relationships influence long-term success in marriage. This research has been published and presented in a wide variety of settings, including professional conferences, journals, seminars, television programs, newspapers, and books. His research has won numerous awards from professional and university entities and has been funded by grants from university, business, and government agencies. This book is the result of his teaching, research, clinical, and enrichment work with couples and his colleagues. Dr. Busby currently resides in Lubbock, Texas, with his wife and three sons.

Vicki L. Loyer-Carlson received her Ph.D. in Human Development and Family Studies in 1989 from Oregon State University. She was an assistant professor of Family Studies at West Virginia University, where she chaired the Northeast Regional Committee on Youth at Risk and conducted research on family life quality. After completing an externship at the Family Therapy Practice Center in Washington D.C., she moved to Tucson, Arizona, where she founded the Family Wellness Center, Inc. She works in private practice as a marriage and family therapist, is a member of the RELATE Institute Executive Committee, and teaches family life education in a variety of settings. Her work has been featured in *Tucson Lifestyles* magazine; she has written several articles and books for professional and lay audiences; and she has conducted numerous teaching and training workshops across the United States. She is an adjunct faculty member in Family Studies at the University of Arizona and is a faculty member of the Arizona Institute of Family Therapy. Dr. Loyer-Carlson is a clinical member and approved supervisor of the American Association of Marriage and Family Therapy and a Certified Family Life Educator. She resides in Tucson with her husband and two daughters.

1

Introduction and Theoretical Overview

If you don't believe it, you won't understand it.

—St. Augustine, religious philosopher

If you don't understand it, you can't believe it.

—Dr. Wilford R. Gardner, scientist

In the modern world, science and religion, family and work, love and freedom, often appear to be in conflict. It seems as if people are forced to choose one at the expense of the other. However, most of the time, these principles are intersecting rather than separate spheres. Consider, for example, what scholars and parents have known for decades: Only when children feel loved and secure with parents do they have the freedom to explore the larger world without anxiety. When children are unsure of parental love or acceptance it is likely that they will be insecure and not have the freedom to independently investigate the world (Ainsworth & Bell, 1970; Rosenblum & Pauley, 1984; Waters, Vaughn, Posada, & Kondo-Ikemura, 1995). Clearly, love and freedom are not opposing forces; rather, they are dynamically interacting processes that reinforce one another.

Trouble appears when our thinking forces us to take an either/or stance. This is particularly true in relationships. As soon as a partner believes that his or her stance is the right one and the partner is wrong, compromise becomes difficult and conflict is likely. Concomitantly, if a person is in a partnership that consistently demands either staying together and sacrificing self or leaving and being lonely, distress is imminent. As professionals who work with families know all too well, the problem of either/or thinking is like a disease that is invasive and very difficult to

1

eradicate. Perhaps one of the reasons that this type of polarized thinking is so common and difficult to change is that social and cultural mores support thinking in an either/or way (see Figure 1.1).

Beyond either/or thinking is belief in the possibility of both/and thinking in relationships and in our partners. This is central to the maintenance of any relationship. How fragile are the webs of connection that hold us together! The trust and commitment that are central to relationships are based on beliefs. They may be beliefs based on experiences and impression, but they are still beliefs. When we carefully nurture our commitment it seems we can weather much of the strain, conflict, illness, and temporary distance in our relationships. Yet when commitment is weak, the slightest infraction, the smallest conflict, leads to instability and breakup. So as St. Augustine suggests, believing can lead us far in understanding our relationships and making them satisfying.

Still, we have all known those who believe more than seems possible in the goodness of a partner, the quality of a relationship, the eternal nature of love—and then, tragically, all is crushed in the winepress of divorce. In retrospect it often seems that the signs were clear; that trouble was afoot from the earliest moments. If the couple or one of the partners could have understood the need for change and addressed problems, so much pain would have been avoided. If, instead of just believing and hoping in the relationship, understanding and knowledge were available to the couple, the outcome might have been different. As Dr. Gardner

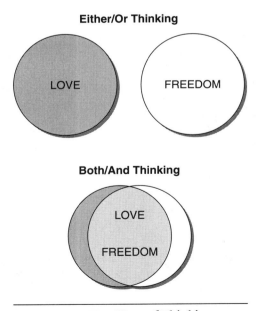

FIGURE 1.1   *Two Ways of Thinking*

admonishes us, we must work hard to understand relationships, what makes them work, the signs of trouble, and how other couples cope with problems. This understanding and knowledge can be a pathway to deeper beliefs in ourselves and our relationships.

In this book, we hope to increase your belief in relationships as pathways to happiness and to provide more understanding about relationships so that you have the knowledge necessary to improve your chance of success. We plan to do this by taking a unique approach: integrating applied knowledge, basic research, and a strong theoretical framework.

Applied Knowledge

If the topic of this book were biology or computer science, the primary purpose would be to provide knowledge that the student could use in a career or possibly use as a foundation for future courses. In some instances a student might obtain knowledge that could be applied immediately, but in many cases there might not be apparent avenues for the direct application of what is learned.

Dating, courtship, and marriage, however, are topics much different from computer science or biology. A person can elect to never learn much about biology or computer programming and find that life isn't dramatically different one way or the other. However, all people are strongly and directly influenced by courtship and marriage throughout their lives. Marriage is the foundational relationship of all of society. As some scholars have noted, marriage has a vast influence on practically every area of life. It influences physical and mental health, living arrangements, finances, happiness, sexuality, violence, gender roles, children, job performance, and much more (Waite & Gallagher, 2000). In addition, although you might learn computer programming and never use it other than in the class, almost all people marry, all people are the product of a relationship between a man and a woman, and everyone is a part of a plethora of relationships, so the principles learned about relationships can have far-reaching effects that ripple through lives and even generations of people. Therefore, this book will have a more personal, applied nature rather than being solely a presentation of facts or research regarding courtship and marriage.

In many courses in science, students will eventually need to apply their knowledge and expand their understanding by participating in labs. In a course on courtship and marriage, the lab is daily life—the relationships that surround each student. Therefore, while facts and figures will have their place, it is important that each reader learn more about relationships by experimenting in the lab of current relationships, thinking about the quality of these relationships, examining in depth patterns across relationships, and discussing with others what is or isn't working in these relationships. It will be impossible to adequately learn about the relationship called marriage without carefully exploring your thoughts, feelings, and behaviors in relationship with others.

Relationships as Mirrors to Self-Discovery

You have many types of relationships: some with people, some with animals, and some with larger systems such as work and school. Interestingly, the tone of your relationship style is consistent across types. In other words, you have one common relationship with the world. Relationships are not all identical—rather, you, the most critical component of your relationships, are the same in each relationship. This sameness creates common themes and struggles across contexts. If you are relatively shy and slow to warm up to people, this style will emerge in your relationships with your spouse, your colleagues, and your neighbors. With the extensive time you spend with your spouse, you will become comfortable more quickly than you will with your colleagues; yet the same struggles and satisfactions will emerge in both types of relationship because you bring the same personality, beliefs, background, and abilities to each relationship. In your relationship with your spouse your shyness may emerge when discussing intimacy, whereas in your relationship with a boss it may emerge when discussing the need for a raise. Either way, your shyness may impede your happiness because important issues are not discussed.

The main distinction between types of relationships is the intensity level. Those relationships that are more emotionally distant will not create as much intensity, discomfort, and enjoyment, but the primary tone will be the same, at least as far as you experience them. "Wait," you might say, "doesn't my partner have at least as much influence on the flavor of my relationships as I do?" Certainly, partners bring their unique style to the relationship, and this will significantly influence your experience.

Relationships provide one of the best ways of seeing yourself more clearly.

The point is that relationships can give you a chance to grow and learn personally. They are like a mirror held up in front of you at all times, making available the opportunity to see yourself and your influence in the world. If the relationship works and you are open to the growth that is being asked of you, you will see the reflection of yourself in your partner's reactions and experiences. If your partner is open to growth, then both of you will stay in love and move to a better place together. If either you or your partner is not open to the growth that is being asked of you, the relationship is likely to be dissatisfying and stagnant.

Most importantly, in the final analysis, you are the only person you can change to improve your relationships. If you select a career in which you will assist people with their interpersonal struggles, you will succeed largely based upon your ability to form relationships with those whom you help. If over time you push yourself to interact more with others and overcome your shyness, all your relationships will benefit. On the other hand, if you try to change those around you to improve your relationships, the result will be frustration.

This theoretical principle is simple but profound: It will shape the principles presented in this book. We hope to walk you through an actual assessment of yourself in a relationship with someone else. This will be accomplished by using a valid and reliable questionnaire (RELATE) that has been used with thousands of couples (Holman, Busby, Doxey, Klein, & Loyer-Carlson, 1997; Busby, Holman, & Taniguchi, 2001). With the understanding that comes to you about your relationship style and approach, you may gain a clearer sense of where you would like to change and grow so that your "one relationship" is more fulfilling.

Understanding and believing in yourself and relationships is an important beginning. Your single perspective and experience has limitations, however, and there are many ways to reach the same goal. Therefore, while we try to help you understand yourself and your partner more clearly, we will also provide additional information to expand your perspective and broaden your knowledge and skills.

To clarify, first we hope to help you understand yourself as you are in relationship with others. This understanding should provide a foundation for thinking about relationships. Second, we hope to help you understand relationships in general by exposing you to scientific findings about how relationships succeed and fail. This expanded information will help you grow beyond the limited experiences of your particular life and enhance your flexibility in handling the constant challenges created by intimate relationships.

Theoretical Framework for the Book

The RELATE questionnaire and this book are based on a comprehensive systemic framework. Relationships are developed and maintained within a series of subsystems, or "contexts." Although there are numerous contexts that are important, the most salient ones for premarital and marital relationships include the individual, familial, couple, and social contexts (see Figure 1.2; Larson & Holman, 1994; Holman & Associates, 2000).

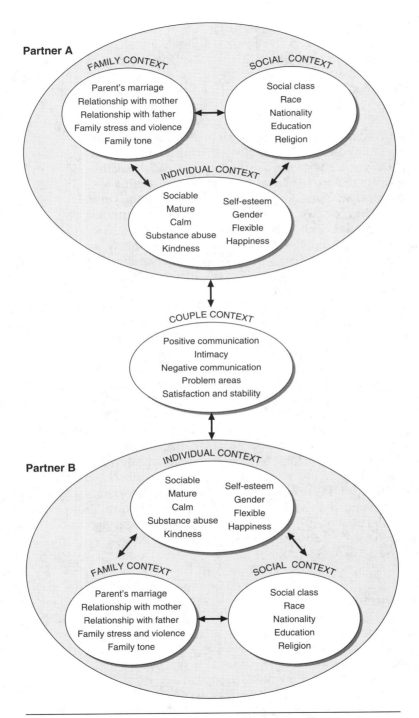

FIGURE 1.2 *The Interaction of Relationship Contexts*

The *individual context* is a combination of inherent individual characteristics (e.g., gender, age, physical appearance), styles of interacting and behaving (e.g., sociability, volatility, kindness, flexibility), and beliefs and attitudes (e.g., autonomy, spirituality, beliefs about gender and roles).

Some of the important aspects of the *familial context* include the style and quality of the parents' couple relationship, the quality of the relationship of each parent with the children, and the stressors and trauma a family must endure. These aspects of the family create a family tone that can be mapped on a continuum from safe/ predictable/rewarding to unsafe/chaotic/punishing. This family tone or process influences an individual's beliefs and behaviors in adult relationships.

The *couple context* is made up of patterns of relating to each other that can be measured in a variety of areas such as communication, conflict, sexuality, time together, and other shared activities. These relational patterns create a level of commitment and satisfaction for each partner.

The *social context* includes variables such as ethnicity, religion, socioeconomic status (SES), and geography. It also includes beliefs and values that are supported by social systems surrounding families and individuals.

The individual, familial, and social contexts are constantly influencing one another in a reciprocal manner (see Figure 1.2). Whenever two individuals form a relationship, their unique contexts interact with and influence one another. Each relationship is made up of multiple differences and similarities between the partners and contexts. Understanding the meanings these differences and similarities hold for each partner is crucial for relationship decisions and satisfaction.

The specific sections of this book, and the RELATE instrument, were developed by reviewing over 50 years of research that has delineated the important premarital predictors of later marital quality and stability (Larson & Holman, 1994). Table 1.1 reports the main findings from this review, presented within the contextual areas previously mentioned. As Table 1.1 shows, there are many attributes from each context that influence whether a relationship will succeed. Each relationship may have some of the characteristics that are likely to enhance relationship success and some of the characteristics that will decrease the chance of success. Hopefully, the chapters in this text will give you the information you need to decide which characteristics are the most important in any particular relationship.

The Organization of the Book

This book is divided into the following four main sections:

> Personal Context
> Family Context
> Social Context
> Couple Context

Each section is designed to help increase your knowledge and personal awareness by guiding you through a self, partner, and relationship evaluation in the context area under question. Beyond considering your own relationship, additional

TABLE 1.1   *Premarital and Marital Variables Predicting Marital Quality*

Context	Subcategory	Variable
Individual	Traits or Characteristics	Gender Age Physical Health
	Styles of Interacting or Behaving	Emotional Maturity Self-Esteem Depression (Happiness) Flexibility Calmness Sociability Kindness Substance Abuse
Family	Parents' Relationship	Parental Divorce Parental Marital Style (Validating, Avoidant, Volatile, Hostile) Parental Marital Satisfaction
	Parent/Child Relationship	Relationship with Mother Relationship with Father
	Family Environment	Family Status (step, adoptive, etc.) Family Stress Family Trauma and Addictions Family Tone and Influence Support from Parents and In-Laws
Social		Race Religion Occupation Education Income Support from Social Network
Couple	Interactional Patterns	Empathy Clear Sending Regard/Love Soothing Criticism Contempt Defensiveness Stonewalling Relational Style (Validating, Avoidant, Volatile, Hostile) Sexuality Boundaries Possessiveness Physical and Sexual Coercion

TABLE 1.1 *Continued*

Context	Subcategory	Variable
	Relational Traits or Behaviors	Length of the Relationship Status of the Relationship Cohabitation Pregnancy and Childbirth Problem Areas
	Homogamy/Consensus	Consensus on Values and Attitudes Perceptions of Partner Similarity on SES, Age, Religion, etc.
	Relational Outcomes	Satisfaction Stability

information will be presented that will help you see this context from a broader lens. This additional information will primarily be research on the chapter topics that can provide understanding of what has been learned through the scientific study of relationships.

Taking the RELATE Questionnaire

At this stage of your reading it would be best to take the RELATE instrument at the Web site http//relate.byu.edu. If you purchased the RELATE manual or if it was included with this text, there is a code or pin number in the front cover that you will need to use to complete your RELATE assessment. Your partner will also need this pin number. If you do not have a partner, it is advisable to ask someone who knows you well to take the instrument as your partner. It is very helpful to have someone take RELATE as your partner even if that person is a family member or friend, as this will allow you to learn how others perceive you. Knowing how others perceive you is one of the most important things you can learn to help you improve your relationships.

Data from RELATE Respondents

Throughout the text, statistics, figures, and summaries from a large national dataset will be presented to help you understand some of the important aspects of relationships. Unless otherwise noted, these figures will come from a subsample of the tens of thousands of respondents who have taken RELATE over the years. This subsample consisted of 805 couples that were stratified across race and religion so that the percentage of couples in the different categories would be as close as possible to national norms on these two variables. In addition, only couples who were

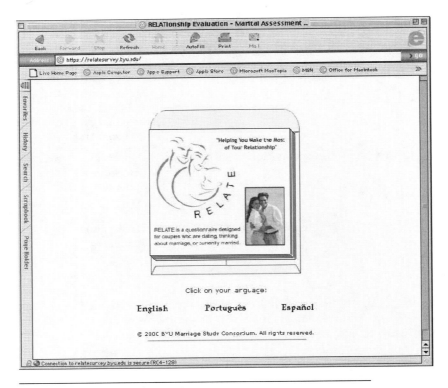

FIGURE 1.3   *RELATE Web Site*

premarital and who had been exclusively dating each other were selected from the larger sample. The final characteristics for this subsample included 10% African Americans, 10% Latinos, 4% Asians, 72% Caucasians, 1% Native Americans, and 3% biracial. In terms of religion, 55% were Protestant, 25% were Catholic, 8% did not have a religious affiliation, 7% belonged to "other religions," 3% were Jewish, and 2% were Latter-Day Saint (Mormon). Forty-five percent of the respondents were currently enrolled in college, 30% had a Bachelor's degree or higher, 24% of the respondents had either some college or a high school diploma, and 1% had less education than a high school diploma. The average age of the respondents was 25.21 years (SD 7.21). Seventy-seven percent of the couples were single and dating exclusively, 19% were cohabitating, and 4% had experienced a divorce with a previous partner. Twenty-eight percent of the couples were engaged at the time they completed RELATE.

2

Dating, Courtship, and Marriage Today

When men and women marry today, they are entering a union that looks very different from the one that their parents or grandparents entered.

—Popenoe & Whitehead

Before proceeding to a better understanding of your personal context, it is useful to consider the patterns of dating, courtship, and marriage today. Relationships in the twenty-first century are different than they were for people from previous generations. There was a time when a young man obtained permission from parents to court a young woman and then the courting occurred under very controlled circumstances. Now it is not uncommon for parents to find out that their daughter or son has a boyfriend or girlfriend long after they have become seriously involved. The timing of couples informing parents and the decision of whether or not to consult parents at all are only a few of the many issues that have changed for couples who are dating or marrying today.

Dating

The whole concept of dating is more ambiguous today than it has ever been, especially for college-age men and women. With the exception of special occasions such as proms or homecoming dances, many couples "hang out" with one another either consistently or off and on without ever really knowing if they are dating or whether they are an exclusive couple. On some college campuses coed dorms are common and students socialize day after day with members of the opposite sex in close living

11

quarters, making the concept of dating even less clear than it is during the high school years (Glenn & Marquardt, 2001). As high school students, many youth do not own a car, and often they don't have their own source of income other than parents, so dating activities have to be coordinated, if not approved, by parents. This makes high school a time during which it is more clear when a get-together is a formal date and when a young man and a young woman are a "couple."

With the dating process becoming more nebulous, research and surveys about dating are less common. Nevertheless, some research has been done on the dating experience, especially of high school youth. Approximately 90% of males and 88% of females report having had their first date before the age of 16 (Thorton, 1990). However, beyond the age at first date it is not known how often the "typical" person dates at different age ranges and how many different partners are dated during a specific time frame (Miller & Benson, 1999). Also, the occurrence and frequency of group "dates" are even less clear, because many people do not consider group activities dates, even if the majority of the time at the activity is spent with one person.

Interestingly, for some details regarding dating there is more research on the dating practices of divorced individuals than there is about never-married people. Divorced individuals usually start dating within the first year after their separation (McKenry & Price, 1991), even though divorced individuals usually aren't ready to fall in love again until two or three years after the divorce. Still, for a sizable minor-

Deciding how soon to be physically involved and what level of physical involvement to have with a partner are two of the most difficult decisions of the dating process.

ity, new relationships are formed quickly, as up to 30% of divorced individuals are married again within a year of the divorce (Colemen, Ganong, & Fine, 2000).

What characteristics make people more likely to be selected as dating partners? Little is known in this area other than that the obvious characteristics of propinquity (being in close physical proximity to one another, such as neighbors in a dorm or class), physical attractiveness, similarity in age, and similarity in religious denominations, race, and socoeconomic status (SES) influence who is selected as a dating partner. However, most of these characteristics are confounded with propinquity because people of the same SES, religion, race, and age groups tend to also congregate in similar locations for housing and tend to select the same colleges and jobs. One interesting study explored the relationship between stature (height) and dating (Sheppard & Strathman, 1989). These authors found that shorter women and taller men were more popular choices to ask on dates. Males tend to date women shorter than they are and consider shorter women more attractive, whereas although women tend to date taller men more often, they don't rate taller men as more attractive.

Clearly some people hardly ever date, some prefer to date many different people, while others are more prone to becoming exclusive with one partner, regardless of age. Because some of the primary purposes of dating at younger ages are to have fun, to learn how to interact with members of the opposite sex, and to learn one's personal preferences regarding partners, exclusive dating can be problematic and can increase the chance of marrying prior to the end of adolescence or marrying someone who may not be the best choice. A variety of studies have demonstrated that early marriage and early sexual involvement are serious problems in terms of the individual's ability to achieve a satisfying career, obtain relationship goals, and avoid deviant behavior (Seidman, Mosher, & Aral, 1989; Whitbeck, Conger, Simons, & Kao, 1993).

Sexual Involvement During Dating

As might be expected, the younger people are when they start dating and the more frequently they date, the more likely they are to engage in sexual intercourse at a young age. Of those who were dating when they were 14 years old or younger, close to 15% of the couples were engaging in sexual intercourse (Tang & Zuo, 2000). By the age of 15, 33% of all males have had sexual intercourse, while females had somewhat lower rates (Sonenstein, Pleck, & Ku, 1989). Nevertheless, dating behaviors and age are only a few of the many issues that influence sexual involvement.

There are biological and social factors that influence sexual involvement for both males and females. Early onset of pubertal development is associated with early initiation of sexual behaviors, and hormonal levels are associated with sexual involvement at all ages. However, the influence of hormones appears to have a stronger impact on males' sexual activities, whereas social factors such as peer group and family constitution are more relevant for females (Miller, Norton, Curtis, Hill, Schvaneveldt, & Young, 1997).

Consistent differences exist between the genders in regard to what is or is not appropriate in the sexual arena. For example, for males who are dating but not in love with their partner yet, almost 35% are participating in heavy petting and/or oral sex. For females in the same circumstance, about 15% are participating in heavy petting and/or oral sex (Roche, 1998). In addition, when males are dating someone, though not exclusively, and feel that they are in love, 43% believe it is acceptable to be involved in intercourse, whereas only 28% of the females in the same situation think intercourse is acceptable. During dating experiences, then, it is likely that the male will have had more sexual experiences prior to the current relationship, will want to become involved sexually earlier than the female, but will have a partner who prefers to become sexually involved only after there are feelings of love and commitment (Roche, 1998). This dynamic can create a variety of challenges for couples, one of the worst of which is having a female who feels coerced into participating in sexual behaviors. This problem of sexual abuse in dating relationships will be discussed in more detail in Chapter 16.

Some females and males purposely decide not to become sexually involved with partners before marriage. Although the actual numbers of people who abstain from sex is difficult to know, the reported percentage has been between 10 and 30 in some samples (Miller et al., 1997; Glenn & Marquardt, 2001). Couples report a variety a reasons for not becoming sexually involved. Some couples report that they are afraid of contracting a disease or afraid of parental disapproval; others report that they are abstaining from sex due to values to which they adhere of a religious or moral nature; a few report emotional reasons such as fear of embarrassment or pain (Blinn-Pike, 1999).

As one group of researchers implied, it is likely that the majority of males and females hold values and attitudes that are responsible and reasonable, even though many of them often become involved in sexual behaviors at a younger age and sooner than they would ideally prefer (Miller et al., 1997). The sexual dynamics in relationships and the unclear sense of the commitment level for couples are creating several unique challenges for modern couples, especially for women.

One group of researchers called the current state of relationships for women "Hanging Out, Hooking Up, and Hoping for Mr. Right" (Glenn & Marquardt, 2001). This title for a research project has reference to the fact that many couples get started by hanging out together in coed dorms, developing some degree of a relationship that is not clearly defined as exclusive or serious or anything more than a friendship. Often males and females find themselves hooking up, which usually refers to being sexually involved without a commitment to a relationship. They may hook up with several different partners over time or hook up with the same person several times in a row. In the midst of these experiences with different partners, most women are hoping to meet a future husband while in college but, not surprisingly, are not having success and are finding the college romantic scene disappointing. Older male students appear to be more likely to seek out first-year college women and encourage them to participate in the "hooking up" scene. Although some women find the new attention from all of these males appealing, others find themselves feeling exploited, disappointed, and confused.

Finding a partner is becoming more challenging as the rules about dating become less clear.

These researchers suggest important considerations for people dating today: (1) the absence of clear dating rituals eliminates markers that were once used as indicators of relationship seriousness; (2) the lack of direction and guidance by parents and college personnel, and the different goals of males and females in college, are confusing and producing less satisfying relationships; and (3) more sexual experiences with more partners are occurring, which increases risk but does not add to overall satisfaction in relationships. Most women in college would like a long-term commitment that could lead to marriage, but instead they are having serial relationships, some that are considered "close," and finding marriage to be as far away as ever (Glenn & Marquardt, 2001). It appears that dating is becoming more challenging today than it has ever been and the pathway from dating to courtship and engagement is not clear.

Courtship and Engagement

Cohabitation

Some couples believe that living together is the best pathway to marriage. In fact, 60% of couples who live together do get married (Frey, Abresch, & Yeasting, 2001). Other researchers have documented that now the majority of couples who marry cohabited at least some time prior to their marriage (Popenoe & Whitehead, 2000).

Although cohabitation may be a normative experience, the effects of cohabitation on the future success of marriage are quite clearly negative. Study after study continues to document that cohabitation before marriage increases the chance of divorce and dissatisfaction in marriage. In some studies, cohabitation has been shown to double the chance of divorce (McRae, 1999). The longer a couple cohabits, the more likely they are to be unenthusiastic about marriage and childrearing, even though most of them still eventually marry (Axinn & Barber, 1997).

At one level, the influence of cohabitation on marriage remains paradoxical. It makes some sense that testing out a relationship beforehand might be a good strategy to assure marital satisfaction. However, it seems clear that cohabitation is not a good substitute for other types of testing out the relationship, such as noncohabiting engagement or serious dating. Some professionals have suggested that cohabitation is problematic because it clarifies the lack of commitment in a relationship. Couples then progress through some of the hardest transitions in a romantic relationship, such as learning to get along and communicate with a partner day after day, without the necessary commitment to successfully negotiate this transition (Popenoe & Whitehead, 2000). What may be happening then is that, instead of developing a stronger relationship once the early transition is completed, as happens in many marriages, cohabiting couples know they are not committed to each other and therefore the regular difficulties endemic to learning to live together erode their satisfaction levels. Perhaps if people are testing something out by taking it home, they are more prone to notice flaws and problems with the product. If their expectation is that they can return the product without any obligation, yet there is some vague sense of a time limit to how long the test can last, the tendency to notice problems and be dissatisfied is even higher. If the product is another person who will sense that flaws are noticed and then react even more negatively, a downward spiral could easily ensue. Then if most people end up being "stuck" with the product anyway, it isn't difficult to imagine why cohabiting relationships are more likely to end in divorce. In contrast, if instead of testing out the product by taking it home and using it, a person carefully studies the product beforehand and then purchases it with the intention of never returning it, small flaws and problems are not as likely to lead to dissatisfaction or a negative relationship spiral. Some therapists have suggested that viewing marriage as a consumable good that must yield satisfaction prevents couples from being able to weather the storms in marriage (Doherty, 2002). Much more research needs to be conducted to fully understand the reasons that cohabitation often leads to poor relationship outcomes.

Engagement

At some point, most couples who marry become engaged. Only a few rush off and marry on a whim without an engagement. Yet it is difficult today to find accurate statistics on the length of engagements and other details about this stage of premarriage, even when considering the past 40 years of research! One magazine reported that the average engagement is 13 months (*Media Life*, 1999). Additional information on engagement can be gleaned by exploring results from previous couples who have used RELATE. Of those couples who were currently engaged when they completed RELATE, Table 2.1 illustrates how long they had been dating. The percentages in Table 2.1 suggest that almost 10% of the couples who were engaged had not been dating more than six months! Still, most couples who were engaged had been dating for much longer, with 72% of them having dated between one and five years. Another angle on the engagement issue is to explore how long couples who are currently engaged expect it to be before they get married. This information is illustrated in Table 2.2. Over 70% of the couples will have spent more than two years with each other prior to marriage. Clearly, most couples probably know each other quite well by the time they marry, assuming that they use these premarital years to communicate openly and share who they are.

Early Marriage

Almost 95% of Americans find a way to negotiate the challenges of dating and courtship to arrive at their wedding date (Lasswell & Lasswell, 1991). By the age of 25 for females and 27 for males, most people will have already married, or will be furiously planning for the rapidly approaching wedding (Popenoe & Whitehead, 2000). Although often looked at as one of the most exciting times for couples, the energy, effort, and finances to plan and complete an American wedding can be considerable. The announcements, dresses and tuxedos, transportation costs, marriage ceremony, receptions, music, rings, gifts, parties, and even hiring a "wedding professional" are no small affair for many couples. Some popular magazines suggest that it costs close to $20,000 for the typical couple and their families to make it through the wedding day (*Bride's Magazine,* 2001). Of course, these magazines would benefit from higher estimates, because they sell the products that contribute to such costs. Nevertheless, it is likely that the couple and their families will find themselves considerably poorer after the wedding day. The honeymoon can be an additional financial burden—the *Massachusetts Wedding Guide* (2001) estimates typical honeymoon costs to be between $3,000 and $4,500.

TABLE 2.1 *Percentage of Engaged Couples Who Have Been Dating Various Lengths of Time*

Length of Time Dating	Percentage of Engaged Couples
0 to 6 months	9%
6 to 12 months	12%
12 to 24 months	38%
36 to 60 months	36%
More than 60 months	5%

TABLE 2.2   Total Amount of Time between Starting to Date and Marriage

Amount of Time That Will Elapse	Percentage of Couples
Between 6 and 12 months	9%
Between 12 and 24 months	15%
Between 24 and 36 months	22%
Between 36 and 60 months	28%
More than 60 months	20%
Unsure	6%

After the Honeymoon

What can couples expect after the honeymoon? The chapters in this text will describe patterns and issues that couples will experience in the early years of their relationship as they adjust to the creation of a new family unit. It is encouraging to know that for the first time in almost two decades, the divorce rate in America has declined and now the majority of couples can expect to stay together (Popenoe & Whitehead, 2001). However, the United States still has one of the highest divorce rates in the world, and many couples can expect to have severe struggles to the point where they may end their marriage. Couples who do divorce will typically do so around the seventh year of their relationship (Newman & Newman, 1995).

On a more positive note, of those who stay married, the average length of time they will stay married before death is 45 years (Rice, 1995). In other words, couples who stay together until death will be able to see most of their grandchildren marry. It is interesting to contemplate how one's grandchildren will experience dating and marriage when the year 2050 rolls around.

What About Children?

After the marriage ceremony, on average, couples will have their first child before two years have passed (Rice, 1995). However, families are growing smaller, with the average number of children now at about 1.8 (Bengston, Rosenthal, & Burton, 1990). This means that most children will grow up without a sibling, or if they do have a sibling there will be only one. Children influence relationships in a variety of ways and can be a source of great enjoyment for a couple as well as a source of stress. The change in roles from partner to parent is a challenging one that will be left to another text on another stage of the life cycle.

Why Get Married?

Although it may seem like a strange question, there have been many couples who have asked themselves the question "Why do we need to get married?" Isn't marriage just a piece of paper? Can't we have a relationship that is just as fulfilling and meaningful without the ceremony? In a time of high divorce rates it is a natural tendency to feel tentative about such a big step.

The negativity and fear surrounding the potential for divorce has affected many people to such an extent that they are unsure whether marriage still holds benefits for individuals. What do you believe about marriage? As you read the following statements, decide whether they are true or false:

1. On average, a person who remains single will live as long as someone who marries.
2. Married people, because they are likely to have children and experience more stress, will generally be sick more often than those who don't marry.
3. A single person, over the course of a lifetime, will be better off financially than someone who marries.
4. Because people are more likely to be abused by someone they know than by a stranger, being married increases the chances of being physically abused for adults and children.
5. Getting a divorce is much better than staying in a relationship that is not fulfilling or satisfying.
6. Once a marriage becomes conflictual and dissatisfying, it isn't likely to improve.
7. Single people are not more likely to abuse alcohol than those who are married.
8. Cohabitation is usually a successful way of testing out the relationship before committing to marriage.
9. Married and unmarried people are just as likely to be happy.
10. When children have parents who are unhappy in their marriage it is better for them if their parents divorce than if they stay together.
11. Marriage generally is a positive experience for men, but for women it is often more of a burden.
12. Because the divorce rate is so high, many people do not plan or even want to get married.
13. Married people, because they often sacrifice ambition to spend time with their family, are less likely to be promoted and receive pay increases on the job.
14. Because sexual patterns can become routine after years of being with the same partner, married people tend to consider their single years more sexually fulfilling.

What did you answer to these 14 statements? All 14 statements are false! Look at those you thought were true and consider how the pessimism regarding marriage may have seeped into your attitude. Even in an unsure time when many marriages fail, most people still want and plan to marry (Popenoe & Whitehead, 2001). Marriage provides extensive benefits to both males and females. Couples may not be aware of how significant marriage can be for improving the quality of life (Waite & Gallagher, 2000).

Waite and Gallagher (2000) have summarized the many benefits of marriage in their book *The Case for Marriage: Why Married People Are Happier, Healthier, and Better Off Financially.* In this book, research findings are used to establish the fact that marriage is one of the few decisions in life that is likely to lead to better health, higher incomes, healthier children, less violence, and improved functioning in almost every facet of life.

From Waite and Gallagher's analysis, it seems that the extensive benefits to marriage are at least partially due to the following factors:

1. People who are married tend to engage in less risky behaviors, hence their life span, health, and conduct are improved.
2. Married partners feel more motivation to eat better, avoid alcohol or drugs, and get a good night's sleep, and to help their partners do the same.
3. The companionship provided in marriage improves mental and physical health and increases occupational performance and sexual satisfaction.
4. The commitment inherent in marriage helps adults and children live more stable, happy, and productive lives.
5. Although *extremely* conflictual marriages are detrimental to all family members, these relationships are rare and many marriages improve over time. Divorce is usually more injurious than sticking with a marriage that is less than ideal.
6. Marriage is more than just a piece of paper. It is a symbolic ritual that signals a change in status to the entire community and especially to the married partners, their families, and their future or existing children. Marriage connects people more fully to their communities and families than does cohabitation and results in less infidelity, separation, and sadness.

Perhaps many couples still innately sense these benefits in addition to the common desire to have a friend and companion with whom life can be shared. This may be why most people continue to want to marry and will eventually do so at some point in their development. Let us then move forward, letting go of the question of why people should marry. Instead let's consider the question of what attributes and experiences in the different contexts of life contribute to a better chance of being in a satisfying relationship.

3

Your Personal Style

I yam what I yam

—Popeye

Oh, that all of us might have as much clarity about who we are as Popeye! Perhaps there would be less despair and poor self-esteem if we took a lesson from this cartoon character. Yet, if having this much clarity about ourselves implies that our daily "episodes" are filled with the same villains, the same characters, the same solution (a can of spinach), and the same ending, in real life we might forgo the clarity of self for added variety.

Deciding who we are is one of the most important tasks of life, yet it is to some degree a moving target. Just as we begin to feel confident in our self-understanding, we might face some of the following changes: the loss of a job, the end of a relationship, a move to a new state, the loss of physical capabilities through injury or illness, newly developed maturity, the addition of new skills, or the experience of a relationship with someone who dramatically challenges our views. In these new circumstances, unknown parts of our personality emerge, some that surprise us. It is a daunting task to understand and know ourselves, primarily because so much of our knowledge of self is based on how we are in relationships, yet our relationships are dynamic living things.

Still, there are enduring qualities we possess that are identifiable to us and to our acquaintances. These qualities are usually what are referred to as our personality or character or style. Countless arguments have been published by scholars over the years as to whether our personality is innate, shaped by the environment, or a combination of the two. The argument is intriguing and could cover pages of this book, but both our genetics and usually our most significant foundational environment are given to us by our parents, hence the two are typically inseparable. What is most relevant for dating and marriage is understanding what your personal style is at this point in life and determining how this personal style helps or hinders your relational success.

A personality style is different from interests or talents, although there is a relationship between the two. Although a person may like art, music, and/or outdoor activities and sharing these interests with a partner can be important, what has a more lasting influence on the satisfaction of both partners is the style of behaving and interacting that each person brings to the relationship.

Flexibility: A Crucial Characteristic

Our changing nature and relationships illustrate a crucial component of personal style—flexibility or adaptability. This single principle has received a tremendous amount of empirical study from a variety of researchers (Buss, 1990; Buss & Barnes, 1986; Goodwin, 1990; Laner & Russell, 1998; Olson, 1989; Olson, Russell, & Sprenkle, 1989). The general finding of this research is that flexibility is a basic requirement and desired characteristic of successful human relationships.

Webster's dictionary defines flexibility as the "ability to bend without breaking; not stiff or rigid, pliant" (Guralnik, 1982, p. 533). This definition brings to mind a variety of physical metaphors that might symbolize flexibility, such as a tree. A tree that is rigid or nonpliant is at great risk for breaking under the stress of wind and stormy weather. A tree that is flexible can withstand astonishing forces and bend almost in half, but will return to its original shape once the winds die down. Paradoxically, then, flexibility is the characteristic that allows a tree to maintain its constant shape in an ever-changing environment, even though it is also the characteristic that allows the tree to bend and change shape temporarily.

In a similar vein, flexibility as a personality characteristic does not suggest someone who is without constancy or who is not clear about beliefs and relationship ideals. Rather, it suggests someone who can adapt or bend to the winds that blow in all human relationships, even to the edge of endurance if necessary. To thrive in the shifting world of relationships, flexibility must become, almost inflexibly, a constant attribute of partners. Perhaps on one day flexibility means delaying personal needs for those of a partner who is having a difficult struggle, while on another day it might mean asking that your partner consider your needs.

While each of us can hold clear and even absolute values regarding many aspects of life, the attribute of flexibility is the moisture of the tree, so to speak, that allows us to keep our constancy by adapting to the weather of the day. If one of our ideals is to consistently express love to those we are committed to, we must express that love flexibly depending on the circumstances of the moment. Sometimes expressing our love demands that we are willing to be vulnerable and open about our tenderness toward another, while in other circumstances we need to refrain from expressing some of our deepest feelings because our partner isn't in a place where these thoughts or feelings can be heard or appreciated. Both examples are acts of love although they are opposite actions. It is easy to imagine how a person who

Inflexibility in trees and relationships can lead to broken dreams.

expresses love the same way regardless of the circumstances would experience great difficulty in relationships.

Flexibility is one of the most important personality characteristics of individuals in influencing relationship satisfaction, according to the thousands of people who have taken RELATE. Most people see themselves and their partner as being quite flexible. Approximately 60% of females see themselves as either often or very often flexible, while 65% of males see themselves as often or very often flexible. Table 3.1 shows how males and females view self and partner on the RELATE flexibility scale. A score of 3 means the respondents rated flexibility as occurring sometimes, whereas a score of 4 means often and 5 means very often. The trends in Table 3.1 are interesting in that males see themselves as the most flexible, but their rating

TABLE 3.1 *Flexibility Means of Males and Females for Self and Partner*

Rating	Mean	Standard Deviation
Females' Rating of Self*	4.00	.54
Females' Rating of Partner*	3.91	.66
Males' Rating of Self*	4.03	.52
Males' Rating of Partner*	3.74	.61

*All means are significantly different from all other means except the female rating of self as compared with the male rating of self.

of their partner is the lowest flexibility score in the sample. Females are more likely to see their partner's flexibility as similar to their own.

Kindness: Sibling to Flexibility and Key to Relationship Success

It is difficult to imagine that anyone would be pleased with a partner who was unkind. Yet not all of us would merit the description, "That is a kind person." Synonyms for kindness, such as compassion, gentleness, consideration, and thoughtfulness, denote qualities that seem to be foundational to interpersonal success. For the most part, all of us know when we are the recipients of a kind act and all of us know when someone has been unkind to us. However, the characteristic or quality of kindness is something more than someone who does kind things or refrains from doing unkind acts. For someone to be considered a kind person there must be a consistency of gentle, considerate, and thoughtful acts over time.

Returning to the metaphor of the tree, whereas flexibility might be considered the ability of the tree to bend in the wind, kindness would be the life-giving sap that circulates throughout the tree and brings needed nutrients to the branches, leaves, and fruit. Without the sap, the tree would not have the ability to bend in the wind and would soon die, becoming rigid and brittle.

This fascinating connection between flexibility and kindness is more than just a metaphorical idea. In the data available for people who have taken RELATE, flexibility and kindness are more closely related to each other than any other personality scales. This suggests that when a person is evaluating whether a partner is kind or not, a considerable amount of the assessment has to do with how flexible that partner is. Although theoretically a person could be considered kind but not flexible, or flexible but not kind, in practical life these two characteristics are so closely related that it is not probable we would know someone who is flexible that we would not also consider kind. It is likely that what happens to us in relationships is that when someone seems rigid and inflexible it is difficult to be involved with such a person and we interpret this inflexibility as a lack of kindness, or selfishness. When we show consistent willingness to be flexible with others in our relationships it is certainly experienced as thoughtful, considerate, and kind.

It does appear that partners keep a mental tab or evaluation of each other's kind behaviors, as research demonstrates that certain ratios of kind to unkind behaviors are necessary to keep relationships healthy (Gottman, 1999). The typical ratio that must be maintained for partners to feel that the relationship is going well is five kind or positive behaviors to every unkind behavior. Of course, people fluctuate in their expressions of kindness, depending on a variety of factors such as fatigue, stress, and illness, but what is important is not so much that a certain day is filled with five kind behaviors to every one unkind behavior; rather, it is the general pattern that is experienced by the couple. If over the course of a relationship partners don't feel that they are being treated *most of the time* in a kind manner, the relationship is in trouble.

Kindness is the personality characteristic that has the strongest ability to predict relationship success. In fact, the influence of kindness on relationship satisfaction for females is four times stronger than the influence of any other personality characteristic and for males it is two times stronger than any other measure. Clearly, kindness is the noticeable presence of sap in the tree, the ingredient that cannot be missing if the relationship is to flourish. Kindness is so crucial that if a person wanted to evaluate only one personality characteristic of both partners to get the quickest sense of how satisfying a relationship is, it would be the female's perception of her partner's kindness. This one measure is much stronger than any other personality scale in determining relationship satisfaction. It is likely that many males underestimate the importance of kindness for their relationship success. Some males probably believe that other characteristics like maturity, reliability, attractiveness, and intelligence are as important as kindness.

Maturity: Cousin to Flexibility

Maturity is the third personality characteristic that has an important influence on relationship success. Common words used to describe a person with maturity are wise, responsible, reliable, and sensible. Immature people are often described as impulsive, childish, and self-indulgent.

It is not difficult to comprehend why a mature person would be preferred to an immature person. Sometimes immature people are rather interesting in short doses, as their irreverence and impulsivity help liven up social relationships and bring newness to experiences. However, this impulsivity and self-indulgence cannot usually be tolerated for long, as there is much to life that demands reliability and consistency. It is hard to keep a job, finish school, show up on time for dates, pay bills, stay faithful to a partner, and receive acceptance from family and friends if immaturity is prevalent. Still, it is possible to be too predictable or mature. Without some spontaneity and impulsivity we would all become as predictable as a Popeye cartoon and romance would be dead. This is why maturity is a close cousin to flexibility. Only when a person moderates maturity with a flexible approach to life can there be an appropriate balance between stability and newness in a relationship.

Maturity is perhaps most influential in determining whether a person will exhibit very distressing behaviors, such as hostility, violence, and substance abuse. The

impulsivity that is common in immature people leads to serious relationship difficulties when the impulses that are not controlled are very destructive, such as hitting a partner or abusing drugs. Some research has shown that higher levels of
impulsivity of men during the first few months of marriage have a negative influence on their marital satisfaction and the chance of staying married up to 50 years
later (Kelly & Conley, 1987). This suggests that immaturity is not something that
automatically improves with age. Immaturity may lead to destructive behaviors that
create long-term injury to a relationship.

The complex relationship between the concepts of maturity, flexibility, and
kindness and their influence on relationship satisfaction is illustrated by Figure 3.1.
This figure demonstrates that both hostility and kindness have a strong relationship
with satisfaction. Hostility decreases satisfaction and kindness increases satisfaction.
Flexibility also has a relationship with satisfaction but it is a moderate one. Flexibility has the strongest relationship with kindness. Maturity does not directly influence
satisfaction, although it does have a strong relationship to flexibility and hostility.
The important point that this figure illustrates is that personality characteristics are
strongly interrelated. Changes in one characteristic are likely to lead to changes in
other characteristics, as well as to changes in relationship satisfaction.

Extroversion and Organization

Two other characteristics that are measured by RELATE are extroversion (sociability) and organization. Extroversion is a concept that measures how outgoing and
expressive a person is. Shy or introverted are labels typically used to describe those
who are not extroverted. Organized is a scale that measures how orderly a person is.

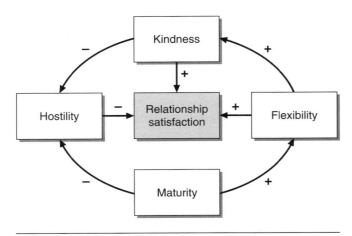

FIGURE 3.1   *Relationship Among Maturity, Flexibility,
Kindness, and Relationship Satisfaction*

Extroversion and organization are two principles that are strongly influenced by gender. Females desire a partner who is extroverted, but males don't seem to care about this characteristic. Males want a partner who is organized, but females don't seem to put this principle high on their priority list.

Ratings of self and partner on these two scales are not related. It appears to be quite possible for people to be in a relationship with a partner who is not at the same level of extroversion or organization as they are. The good news is that, although there are usually going to be larger differences on these two principles, it doesn't have a significant influence on how satisfied partners are in their relationship. Extroversion and organization are important principles to discuss, but only in the context of recognizing that females and males have different desires and perceptions in this area and that these variables are not likely to be anywhere near as important as other personality traits such as kindness or flexibility.

Extroversion and organization may be more important if the basics of kindness and flexibility are weak. If a relationship does not have enough kindness, partners begin to see each other in negative ways. Their overall ratings of one another drop in all areas and it is likely that if the partner is "too" introverted or disorganized, these areas may become a cause of contention and distress. On the other hand, when there is sufficient kindness and flexibility, partners probably overlook their differences in the areas of extroversion and organization.

Desired Characteristics of Mates

A variety of researchers have explored the desired characteristics that partners have for their future mates. The list of characteristics is often long, but similar traits consistently turn up as being the most important. In addition, these characteristics are surprisingly consistent across different cultures and even across relationship types, such as friend or spouse. Table 3.2 lists the top five characteristics desired in a spouse from three separate studies.

This table illustrates several principles that have not been presented yet in this chapter that may be important to consider in yourself and your partner. The principles of honesty and trust are salient issues at the core of any relationship. It is

TABLE 3.2   *Top Five Characteristics Desired in Spouses from Three Studies*

Buss & Barnes, 1986	*Buss, 1990*	*Laner & Russell, 1998*
Kind/Considerate	Mutual Attraction/Love	Communicative
Socially Exciting	Dependable Character	Open/Honest
Artistic/Intelligent	Emotional Maturity	Trusting
Easygoing/Adaptable	Pleasing Disposition	Sensitive/Warm
Conservative	Education/Intelligence	Social/Outgoing

impossible to think of a way to establish and maintain a satisfying relationship without high levels of honesty and the resulting trust that follows. Careful evaluation of personal and partner integrity is crucial before permanent relationship commitments are made. If couples are prone to hiding information or acting dishonestly in a relationship, warning bells should be going off in their heads. It would be crucial to find out what engenders this dishonesty. Sometimes people are dishonest because they are afraid of their partner's anger. Other times they are dishonest because they have habits that they are afraid others might discover or they are afraid that if others knew them they would leave. Some people have been taught that being "nice" is better than being honest, so relationships are built on false assumptions. Whatever the source of the dishonesty, it must be addressed for a relationship to succeed.

Another characteristic in Table 3.2 is intelligence. Intelligence is a controversial topic that has been both helpful and damaging to many people. Intelligence is also a multifaceted trait. A person can be highly intelligent in the area of math and yet not comprehend English or some other topic well at all. Some people are intelligent in the area of music, others in the area of social relationships, while others seem gifted in learning different languages. Some are intelligent in many areas and others in very few. Clearly, many people who are intelligent in one area are married and have good relationships with others who are intelligent in a very different area. What seems crucial is that each partner's intelligence interacts with the other's in such a way that the partners can enjoy one another intellectually. A relationship is not likely to be a very good if partners are not able to see each other as intelligent. If one person is perceived to be dense or slow, this feeling will be evident in interactions and attitudes and will erode self-esteem. Of course, the perception of someone as dense or slow may be an indication of a judgmental or haughty attitude in one partner or an indication of low self-esteem in another. In this case the issue is not really about intelligence at all, but it is still a strong indication of potential problems.

What About Change?

Is it possible to change your own or your partner's style of interacting? When looked at from a distance it seems that anyone could increase his or her flexibility, improve kindness, or become more mature with effort. Some people feel that change is quite simple. Initially they think they can easily be a different person, almost just by deciding to do so. Yet after trying to be different for a while it seems that old habits return, and they end up feeling like the same old person. On the other hand, most people have experienced a period of time when they did seem to make a rather dramatic change, and not just because of maturity or growing older. Perhaps they "came out of their shell" or through several experiences learned to be more confident. Whatever the case, it seems that our lives demonstrate to us that it is possible to change, and sometimes rather quickly, but that there are also enduring, sometimes frustrating, tendencies that we keep fighting for many years.

Perhaps it would be appropriate to return to the metaphor of a tree. Trees can and do change. Some grow thicker because of more prosperous weather and nutrients, whereas others grow taller and thinner to reach limited sunlight. Some trees must sink their roots very deeply to find meager moisture while other trees only need shallow root systems. Yet a birch tree cannot become an oak tree and a willow cannot become a pine. There is a limit to the adaptation and change that can occur.

Are people the same as trees? Most would think that people can change more readily than trees, mistaking mobility, intelligence, and reasoning for the ability to change. Some fascinating studies with twins cast some light on this principle of change. When identical twins are raised apart they develop very similar tastes for foods, preferences for certain kinds of artistic expression, and similar personalities. Amazingly, when they are raised together they often have very different preferences, personalities, and strengths. How do we explain this phenomenon? Some authors have determined that these studies speak loud and clear: Humans have the ability to choose (Schnarch, 1997). They are not limited to innate tendencies only, but can respond to the environment and to internal desires to be different until they have changed. Even so, these studies also suggest that there are innate tendencies that are relatively enduring.

Expectations of Change

The question of how much or how little people can or will change is intriguing but likely to remain unanswerable. What seems to be more important is having realistic expectations of change for self and partner. If you wanted an oak tree but could only find a maple tree, after planting it and watching it grow for a few years you may never be fully satisfied with your choice. Furthermore, you are not going to have any success with your tree if you try to change it from a maple to an oak by putting pressure on it, feeding it different chemicals, or pretending it is an oak.

The ideal is to be in a relationship in which you feel accepted for who you are and you accept your partner. This is especially true at the beginning of a relationship because, over time, all relationships will demand change of both people. Change is often difficult and painful, so if you start out in a relationship already thinking that your partner needs to change or feeling that your partner wants you to change, this should be a warning sign to you that serious trouble is likely ahead.

As logical and reasonable as this sounds, it is baffling how many people develop and stay in relationships in which they are hoping, emphasizing, and trying to get their partner to make significant changes. This is often the case even though many friends and family members may be saying, "Watch out, so-and-so has a problem with anger," or "Watch out, so-and-so seems to be pretty controlling," or "You may want to think about how much so-and-so is drinking." Even with this feedback from family and friends, people often might say to themselves, "But I love him or her, and I'm sure over time she or he will start drinking less." The ideas that love will change self and other quite dramatically and that serious problems will disappear because of love are far too common. Such unrealistic expectations can be quite destructive to relationships for the following reasons:

1. It is unfair to commit to a relationship with a partner whom you want to be significantly different. You are thus not committing to a relationship with that person, but to a relationship with a fantasy of who he or she might be.
2. Expecting partners to be different than they are is eroding to their self-esteem.
3. It is a common cliché that the only person you can change is yourself. There is great wisdom in this saying. For a relationship to work your focus needs to be on how you can become a better person rather than on how your partner needs to change. It is also unrealistic to expect that changes you make will automatically result in a partner who wants to change.
4. It is likely that your need to change your partner is only helping you avoid your need to change yourself to feel better about yourself so you can become involved with people who aren't struggling with so many serious problems.
5. In many ways relationships can make some changes more difficult, as habitual patterns become more rigid and partners continue to remind us of what we have done in the past, thereby reducing our belief in change.

RELATE has several questions that might help partners evaluate whether they have realistic expectations regarding change. The Change Expectation Scale is ideal for this purpose. Looking closely at whether you would like your partner to change and whether your partner wants you to change can give you a quick overall sense of how realistic you are in your relationship. If someone in the relationship wants significant change in their partner, it is very important to talk about this.

Congruence in Perceptions

Related to personality and change is the importance of learning how others perceive us. How do we know whether we are flexible, kind, or mature? There are inherent limitations to how well we can know ourselves by depending on our personal perceptions. Because we are perceiving who and how we are from inside, it is very difficult to know how we come across to others outside ourselves. Many of us have probably had the awful experience of seeing ourselves on videotape and being shocked at how we looked and acted in ways that were very different than we thought we were acting.

What is so helpful, though often horrifying, about relationships is that in our close encounters with others we are given the best mirrors we can have for accurately perceiving ourselves. The reactions of others to our behaviors are like videotaping ourselves. They provide us with an external view of who we are. This does not mean that our internal view is necessarily wrong; it is just different. However, if we find that our internal view is often greatly different from the way others perceive us, this is an important sign that adjustments are needed. If, for example, we feel strong feelings of love for a partner, but neglect to express those feelings, our partner will not experience us as loving. This suggests a need for change, to be more expressive so that there is a higher level of congruence between our internal views and our external behaviors.

RELATE is an excellent tool for assessing the congruence between how we see ourselves internally and how we are seen externally, at least by our partner. Since many of the questions are answered for self and partner, often there are four measures of each scale (see Figure 3.2). These four measures provide a variety of ways to measure congruence. If you do not have a partner, you can easily ask a family member or friend to rate you on the personality questions and get a sense of how consistent your self-ratings are with the ratings of someone who knows you well.

It is important to consider how similar your views of yourself are to those of your partner. What might it mean if you consider yourself more kind than your partner thinks you are? If you consistently view yourself more positively than your partner does, this is an issue to discuss and explore. It may be that you have an overly optimistic view of yourself. On the other hand, it may be that your partner is too negative. Rather than figure out who is right and who is wrong, it is more important to discuss these differences in perceptions and to consider what they are based on and what you are going to do about it. Perhaps when your partner rates kindness it is based on different behaviors than you are thinking about. Maybe you are expressing kindness, but not as often as your partner wants you to. Either way, these differences in perception are important in that they can lead to greater understanding, more congruence between how you view yourself and your partner views

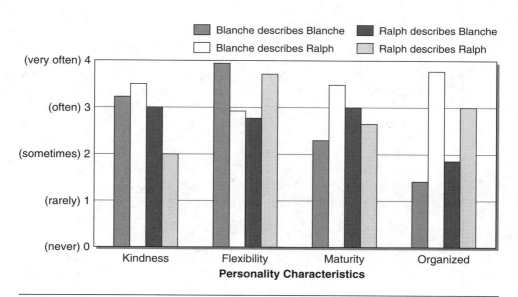

FIGURE 3.2   *Four Measures of Personality*

0 = Never, 1 = Rarely, 2 = Sometimes, 3 = Often, 4 = Very often

you, and more satisfaction. Sometimes, however, they will simply clarify that you and your partner are very different, and you will need to decide how important these differences are.

Similarity

Many people hold an ideal that it is important to have a partner who is similar to how they are. When people with these ideals are encouraged to describe in what ways a partner should be similar, it is often regarding similar interests, values, or goals. It is also not uncommon to find people who are attracted to others who are very different from them. Perhaps one person is rather quiet and reserved and is attracted to the outgoing, humorous side of someone else.

In the personality area, most of the principles discussed so far are necessary traits to make relationships work. In other words, very few would say they are attracted to their partner because that person is unkind or inflexible. This is why the amount of difference between partner ratings on the RELATE personality scales is not nearly as important as the overall rating a person has of their partner. Yet each person has different definitions for kindness and different expectations regarding how kindness will be demonstrated. There should be many differences between partners regarding individual characteristics. If both people were the same it would be like being in a relationship with yourself, which would not be anywhere near as interesting, exciting, or challenging as being in a relationship with someone different from you. Still, there are some differences that may make or break a relationship. Some people may insist that their partner have the same religion as they do or that their partner be organized. One of the purposes of the dating process is to find people who are similar in the areas that you need to be happy. Hopefully, completing an instrument such as RELATE or taking a class on marriage can help you understand in which areas it is crucial for you and your partner to be similar. Most people feel that there should be high similarity or consensus in values. Chapter 6 will contain more extensive information on the importance of consensus in values and beliefs.

4

Your Emotional Climate

The minute your mind starts turning down those dark corridors of doubt, judgment, and negativity, you need to draw on your reserves of love, and let emotion transform your thinking.

—Richard Carlson

The emotional climate of a relationship is similar to the temperature inside a building. Sometimes it feels hot, and sometimes it feels cold. When you are thinking about your own comfort you can adjust your environment any way necessary—turn up the heat, put on the air conditioner, open up a window. When the environment needs to be adjusted for two or more people, it is very important to have a common goal and to be aware of the potential for disagreements: No two people experience their environment exactly the same way. The same temperature may be experienced as too warm by some and as comfortable by others. Clearly, when there are extremes in temperature there is often consensus—for example, 100 degrees Fahrenheit is considered hot, and −20 degrees Fahrenheit is considered cold. At less extreme temperatures, however, hot or cold becomes simply a matter of opinion.

There are many ways of being "hot" in a relationship. Justin curses at other drivers. Taylor is grumpy most of the time. Dan is very seductive, and Marsha prides herself on her "hot" black pants. Relationships are warmed by subtle experiences: Ann cries at movies. (So does Bill, but he'd never admit it.) John wakes up early and happy, and he is thoughtful of his late-rising partner. Alice finds the good in everyone she meets. Then there are the colder moments. Susan pulls up her bed covers, grumbles at the morning sun, and dreads having to interact with others in her home. Bill ignores all requests from Jane. Martha is the queen of put-downs. There are even seasonal differences in relationship temperature: Susan wakes up early in the summer, and is happy constantly. With the dark and dreary winter, Susan is depressed and sleepy.

33

Emotion in a relationship is made up of physiological arousal and thoughts about that arousal (Berscheid, 1983): An individual's tendency to think about events one way rather than another underlies the emotional climate of an interaction. Partners in the relationship can be well matched in their preferred climates, like a gentle breeze on a balmy day, or can produce a horrendous mixture of extremes that creates a rapid tunnel of escalating fury.

Emotions, Moods, and Dispositions

Habitual ways of viewing and responding to events, as generally positive or generally negative, vary from person to person. People who have high self-esteem take a positive attitude toward themselves, see their basic worth even in the midst of difficulties, and do not tend to see themselves as failures. This kind of thinking contributes to a positive emotional climate. A person with high self-esteem is often better equipped to manage the stresses and strains of relationships than someone with low self-esteem. Those with low self-esteem can quickly become self-deprecating and stuck in a sense of hopelessness.

How do people describe their emotional states? With emotional labels they reflect both the domain and intensity of their experience (e.g., delighted or astounded, hurt or devastated). In this section we explore emotional climate in terms of *moods* and *dispositions.*

You may have heard it said that starry-eyed young lovers "think with their hearts." Actually, they think with a lot more than that! Add to their hearts their perceptual selves (smell, sound, and sight) to obtain information, their cognitive selves to process the meaning of the stimuli, their physical selves (heart rate, sweaty palms, and a flushing face and neck) to react to the information, and their behavioral selves to transmit responses appropriate to the message they want to convey. Emotions influence interactions because of how they are used in a relationship, not simply because they are present. Emotional styles, called dispositions, tend to be relatively enduring, which allows partners to anticipate the behavioral sequences of any given interaction. Anger, for example, elicited from someone you know well and who is likely to calm himself down is experienced differently than is anger from a stranger who could be equally likely to calm down or escalate.

Some partners have a calm disposition: They greet changes as opportunities, see the glass as half full, and give others the benefit of the doubt. On the RELATE questionnaire, they would rate themselves as more calm by indicating that they are less often fearful, tense, nervous, or worried. If a calm partner were to run up against something unexpected they could predictably take the surprise in stride. The risks incurred by interacting with someone who is typically calm are low, and the potential for pleasure in such interactions is reasonable, and so the relationship becomes a safe place for enjoyment and risk taking. The emotional climate in a relationship of this sort would be relatively warm.

Are there any negative aspects of interacting with calm partners? Certainly, if you are emotionally demonstrative and your partner remains calm to the point of showing little emotion, you may be frustrated. That same calmness that is so effective at one time may be perceived as uncaring at another time. It is not uncommon for the demonstrative partner to "turn up the heat" to get a reaction from the partner.

Interacting with others who tend to be anxious can also be challenging. When partners are anxious, they may listen for evidence of disrespect, curse the glass that is half empty, and be wary of any new information. Their bodies remain alert for signs of danger, and interacting with such a partner can be costly because their physiological arousal is often manifested in sadness, anger, and frustration rather than in happiness and satisfaction. On the other hand, these partners can be clearly impassioned and caring. They may notice discomforts early, take problems seriously, and remain vigilant until a solution is reached.

Emotional processes originate as solitary experiences. Your body and mind work together to warn you of impending demands for change. When your body is aroused, you collect as much information as necessary or possible to tell you what the arousal means. (See Figure 4.1.) Unfortunately for those people who are predisposed to feeling anxious or depressed, arousal often results in hypervigilance that cannot easily be redirected. Anxious people are quickly aware of the slightest sign of arousal and become so alert that they have a difficult time settling down. Arousal can be caused by one person doing something differently than the partner had expected, by something in the environment triggering a memory of a situation, or simply by the anticipation of an event or situation. Sometimes arousal is so automatic that the actual awareness of arousal may occur after the immediate danger has been averted (e.g., if a glass is knocked off of a shelf, you may grab for it to keep it from falling and then realize that your heartbeat has increased).

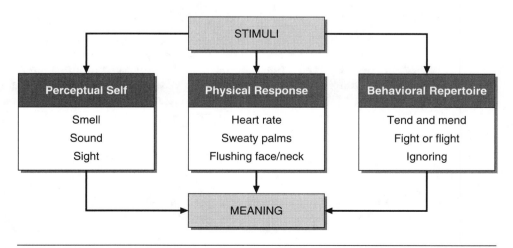

FIGURE 4.1 *Determining Emotional Meaning from Experiences*

It is sometimes difficult to identify a partner's emotion (i.e., are they feeling happy or content?), but the most intense emotions are obvious. In fact, some emotions are thought to have autonomic signatures (Gottman, 1999). For example, when one is afraid, her or his hands may be cold. When one is angry, hands may be hot. An increased heart rate occurs in love and in fear, and depending on the direction of the individual's attention it is ascribed positive or negative meaning. If you think about people as being vulnerable, this physiological arousal makes sense. If there is a potential for danger, physiological changes create heightened awareness. At its root, emotion is a reflex and exhibited even by newborn babies. When emotions are highly transient, they are called moods. Some partners are "moody"— known for changing their moods often. Other times partners are subject to dramatically wide mood swings, the extremes of which are seen in clinical settings (e.g., bipolar mood disorder).

Negative emotions in relationships are often activated by seemingly innocuous complaints (e.g., "Your car is parked too close to mine"), which lead to arousal and subsequently defensiveness (Berschied, 1983; Gottman, 1999). Complaints can stimulate a chemical reaction in the brain that sends a fight-or-flight message to the rest of the body. Men often experience *flooding,* a rapidly increasing arousal from a partner's complaint that influences the sequence of events to follow (Gottman, 1999; flooding will be discussed more thoroughly in Chapter 13). The more frequent response from women is *tend and mend*; as their arousal state becomes activated, they become intensely focused on repairing relationships and aiding those who are close to them. Imagine the challenge when one member is poised for "fight or flight" and the other is poised for "tend and mend."

Another option for complaint recipients is to soothe themselves with cognitive reframing (that is, thinking about the situation in a more helpful way) and to use self-talk to decrease their physiological reactions. The subsequent interactions, then, are logical responses to more positive beliefs. (See Figure 4.2.) In RELATE, respondents are asked to rate themselves and their partners on their tendencies to be overwhelmed and to be soothing. It is likely that respondents who are better at soothing themselves and their partners are also likely to be seen as more loving toward their partner. How do you achieve this more positive emotional experience? Dossey (1999) insists that individuals can decide to experience emotions, and make them become a reality. If they are unhappy they can force themselves to think, "I am happy" and begin behaving as if they were having the emotion of happiness, and their body would soon be "fooled" into being happy.

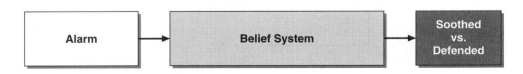

FIGURE 4.2   *The Role of Belief Systems in Filtering Alarms*

Your Emotions

Unlike animals of prey who are constantly aware of potential predators, the human animal uses intellect to predict safety. People become comfortable with sequences of behavior, or habits, and pay attention primarily when there is a change in that sequence. Without such habits it would be exhausting to accomplish all that needs to be completed in a day. Within these patterns, heightened arousal occurs mostly when there is a change to the sequence of behaviors that one has learned to expect. This is a crucial point: Because arousal is the result of unexpected events, people are much more aware of a partner's interferences than they are of their partner's assistance. This is called the *paradox of positive emotion* (Berschied, 1983).

How invisible are most behaviors? Imagine being home alone checking that the doors are locked for the night. When everything is fine you may walk from one room to the next without much thought about what you are observing. If, however, something unexpectedly moves, you will focus your attention on the movement. Whatever appeared to be moving causes a change to the expected sequence of behaviors and events, and at least for a moment causes you to focus. Physiological reactions are part of what connects us to our environment and helps us to keep ourselves safe (DeBecker, 1998): You notice what is good by comparing it against what is not good.

As relationships become predictable, there is a greater chance of causing frustration for each other than for providing excitement.

Relationships are often begun in the context of novelty, and with that novelty is ample opportunity for physiological arousal. Imagine that you have observed Matt and Brenda interacting. An attractive young man, Matt stands up when Brenda approaches the table at which he is sitting, smiles pleasantly, and appears genuinely interested in listening to her. Vicariously, the interaction feels nice. This emotional memory becomes part of how you know Matt and Brenda. Later when you meet Matt on campus, your emotional memory has stored warm feelings and you are more likely to experience liking for him. You are ready to reciprocate pleasant company, anticipating that Matt is appropriate and considerate even before knowing whether his pleasant behavior will be present with you.

Free-floating emotions involve physical discomfort that heightens your search for explanations. If you believe that Matt's behavior is appropriate and special, you may experience comfort or even excitement and heart palpitations at the thought of interacting with Matt. If, however, you are uncomfortable near Matt despite his apparently charming behavior, you may try to make sense of the emotional and behavioral incongruence and avoid interacting. It is not surprising that emotional disorders, such as depression, interfere with an individual's ability to form relationships with others. Sometimes the flat affect of a clinically depressed person, in a situation where the source of depression is not readily evident, is difficult for others to understand. Affect provides part of the situational information that is needed to know how to proceed in interactions. For instance, if you say something intended to be funny, and no one laughs, you may reassess your use of humor in the situation. If, however, you say something and it makes others laugh and smile, you have received feedback to keep going and say more funny things. Clinically depressed partners have an affect that is less responsive to good humor. It can be much more difficult to gauge the status of the interpersonal relationship because the feedback is cloudy, which can cause others to feel insecure and frustrated. Clinically depressed persons and their partners need to learn to identify flat affect as a condition of the disorder, and develop strategies of compensation. Medication and therapy, though not the entire solution, are often very helpful for those persons who experience depression.

Most behavioral sequences—those that are used to watch a performance, drive a car, or get ready for bed—are so habitual that it is possible to be relaxed and still perform all of the needed activities. Self-soothing skills that are consistent and effective are needed in relationships so that interruptions can be seen as part of life and become part of behavioral planning (Berschied, 1983). Partners with few self-soothing skills can benefit from simple relaxation techniques or cognitive reframing (deciding to think about a current situation in a new way).

Particularly for persons with emotional or behavioral disorders, learning to remain soothed in upsetting situations can be difficult. For example, although attention deficit hyperactivity disorder (ADHD) is often diagnosed in childhood, those children grow up to be adults, and those adults create emotional climates of tension and unpredictability. A characteristic of ADHD is a tremendous discomfort with interruptions in behavioral sequences, and difficulty self-soothing after arousal. Think about this true situation that was the focus of a therapy session:

Bob is an intelligent, wealthy businessman. He and his wife talked about their "miserable" trip to Disneyland. Early on the first day of their trip, Bob was watching a performance and leaned against a stage prop. When a staff member asked him to stop touching the props he became incensed. He did not want a teenager telling him what to do. He reported that he "toyed" with the staff member, and his wife reported that she felt he was ridiculing the staff member for saying anything to him. They both agreed that he remained in a foul mood for the rest of the day. Bob admitted that he tested the staff members whenever he could. He would do the opposite of whatever direction signs would instruct, he put his foot over lines intended for standing behind, criticized restaurant workers about their prices, and created a full day of testing limits. Each time he was asked to change his behavior he would become argumentative. His partner was embarrassed and angry. He was frustrated by the difficulty he had in managing his anger once he was embarrassed or upset.

Bob had very little ability to self-soothe, particularly immediately following a complaint, and his behavior tended to spiral downward in a series of negative interactions. The work that Bob focused on in therapy was how to use relaxation and positive self-talk to minimize the arousal he experienced. His wife learned to not take his outbursts personally, and to give him time to be quiet and withdrawn when he needed to adjust to frustrations (usually about five minutes). (See Figure 4.3.)

In summary, individuals have distinct ways of processing arousal, particularly in terms of their tendency to view things as generally positive or generally negative. For persons dealing with depression, anxiety, or adult attention deficit hyperactivity disorder, managing that arousal can be quite challenging.

The Origin of Emotions

When an emotion interrupts one's intended activities (e.g., "I'm too depressed to go out tonight"), individuals are typically able to pardon their own behaviors and make

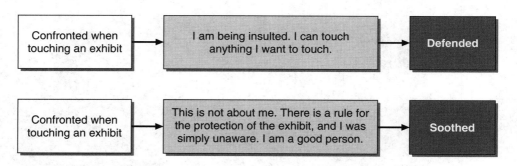

FIGURE 4.3 *Bob's Options for Processing His Dilemma*

adjustments for interruptions. When another person is involved, the tendency is to blame others for the interruptions. Humans are need-meeting organisms who operate to maximize their welfare and survival. Partners look at the amount of contribution they have made toward their relationship (cost) and the amount of return they have received on that investment (reward) and decide whether the relationship is good enough. Part of what is rewarding is shared positive emotions, while part of the costs are embedded in negative emotions. Unfortunately, at any one time an interruption of a behavioral sequence produces a cost for the recipient. Uninterrupted sequences, which should produce positive arousal, typically receive no attention because they match the original mission of behavioral sequences. This is the paradox of positive emotion (Berscheid, 1983). There is no such thing as a nice surprise. True surprises interrupt sequences of behavior and prevent people from anticipating adequate ways of taking care of themselves. *When the arousal in some way can be controlled it can be interpreted positively.* The euphoric feelings of romantic love are based on surprises, nested in a system of predictable, normative exchanges.

Amber was settling in for another quiet evening at home when a fellow to whom she has felt quite attracted called to invite her out for dinner. The physiological arousal from the unexpected interruption activated

The euphoric feelings of romantic love are based on surprises nested in a system of predictable exchanges.

anxiety ("What can I wear?"). Amber identified this arousal as excitement, which confirmed for her that she was attracted to him.

The search for the meaning of anxiety will direct itself to a reasonable explanation, and depending on the overall comfort level in the relationship, those labels will be positive, negative, or neutral. Consider what happens when a couple is past the initial stages of romance in the relationship:

> Mary was on the telephone trying to have an error corrected on her telephone bill. Bob came home from work loudly, and greeted her enthusiastically. Earlier in their relationship when he came in loudly she was so excited to see him that she would stop everything to greet him. Now, she found herself more reluctant to stop in the middle of her project. She identified this arousal as "mild irritation."

The belief that anxiety can be explained by something tangible underlies the search for meaning. Arousal is sometimes called "free-floating anxiety" because the heightened state remains until the person can find meaning to which it can be attached. That search is often fairly systematic until the free-floating anxiety can be transformed into something that makes sense in the context of one's life.

Obviously it is not possible to obtain all of the information needed about most situations, so assumptions are made about the behaviors of other people when part of the explanation is unclear or missing. Think now about Terra and Charlie:

> Charlie reluctantly agreed to help Terra wash the windows. It was important to Terra to get one big job done each Saturday, and this week it was windows. Charlie had learned in the past how seriously she took her projects, and she really needed his help. Terra assumed that Charlie was as interested in washing the windows as she was. Charlie assumed that Terra knew he was doing her a favor. Charlie watched the World Cup soccer tournament while they worked. In the last few seconds of the game, his team scored. He was so excited he almost forgot what he was doing and started to let go of the window. Terra was startled, and Charlie just laughed. She had not thought about his wanting to watch the game, and only when he almost dropped the window did she realize that Charlie had been doing something for her. She was so accustomed to having his help whenever she asked that she did not notice his thoughtful behavior.

According to John Gottman (1999), attributional patterns in relationships have great influence on satisfaction. If a situation is afforded positive or neutral intention, the emotions to follow will be based in more benevolent terms. The challenge in intimate relationships is that couples need to build up their reserve of positive affect, which serves as a protective factor when relationships are stressful.

The emotion from unexpected behavior, then, involves the initial arousal state, cognition about oneself, and also thought about the intention of the other.

Noticing only the negative sequences minimizes opportunities to establish positive "emotional bank accounts" with others. As relationships mature a conscious effort is needed to continue contributing to a bank account of positive sentiment.

Emotional Mixtures

Relationship stability is dependent on the level of dissonance that two sets of emotions create as compared with the amount of dissonance members of the couple can tolerate. Interpersonal behavioral sequences are more complicated because the arousal, cognition, and behavioral response of each participant contribute to a single emotional climate. (See Figure 4.4.) Sequences are largely independent of each other in early dating because partners are more concerned about their personal needs and enjoyment than about the experiences of the other. Consider the following activities:

> I am angry that I can't get my car into my parking space because there is a cart in the way. I can move the cart or choose another space.
>
> I do not have time to finish my work and I am frustrated. I need to rethink my tasks so that I can make the most of my next few hours.

The essence of any interpersonal relationship is that the behavior of one person is emitted in the other's presence, creating an experience for the other (Thibaut & Kelley, 1959; 1986). When relationships begin to develop some seriousness, the attempt to mesh sequences requires some accepting of the other's influence. With more serious relationships, couples make *transformations* for each other (Kelley, 1979). That is, the partners' experiences of liking and disliking begin to influence each one's own experience of liking and disliking. People in relationships want to be

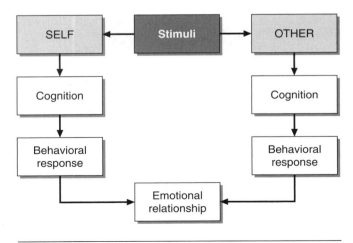

FIGURE 4.4 *Self and Other Contributions to Emotional Relationships*

happy, and want their partners to be happy. When a partner's experience is much different from how she or he thinks it should be, it is emotionally costly because the experience of one has meaning for the other. Imagine the previous independent sequences as interdependent sequences.

> Struggle for Influence. I am angry that I can't get my car into my parking space because there is a cart in the way. My partner keeps saying, "Now, don't get all upset," which makes me even angrier. I wish he wouldn't tell me how to feel. Now I am angry and feeling misunderstood.

> Resisting the Urge to Fix It. I do not have time to finish my work and I am frustrated. My partner doesn't want me to be frustrated and is trying to make jokes to make me laugh. I appreciate her concern, but I really need her to leave me alone and let me work. I find myself feeling irritated with my partner, even though she is trying to make me feel better. I feel frustrated and guilty.

With the dilemmas inherent in interdependent behavioral sequences, why would couples bother? Why not arrange relationships so that each person continues to take care of her or his own needs? Few people can sustain the emotional highs of a new romantic relationship for very long. These moments are the source of love songs and love stories, but they are relatively short-lived. Eventually, partners increase their sense of safety by developing trust. They learn to predict their partner's behaviors and begin to settle into sequences that require less awareness. The dependability decreases the physiological arousal experienced (Berschied, 1983). This accommodation, if interpreted as boredom, may create a clear challenge for those seeking long-term romantic love:

> Shannon and Tim are a young couple with a townhouse and two dogs. They each need to be at work by 8:00. They get up at 6:30 and Shannon gets in the shower right away. Tim puts on the coffee, Shannon makes the bed, and Tim takes the dogs out for a quick walk, picking up the newspaper on the way back in the house.

What happens when Shannon or Tim needs to leave on a business trip? Their behaviors are highly interdependent and each set of behaviors will be interrupted if one is not present, continually reminding them of the other's absence. When they are not together, the physiological arousal is probably labeled as "missing her (him)." Compare Shannon and Tim with Brad and Patty. They could never agree on who should do what in the morning. Both of them hate conflict, and they agreed to take care of themselves independently:

> Patty gets up at 5:30, makes her coffee, takes a shower, and dresses for the day. When she is out of the bathroom, Brad gets up. They leave notes about important things, and otherwise stay out of each other's way. Patty has breakfast, cleans up, and locks the doors when she leaves. Brad reads the sports page while he eats a banana, and after 15 minutes grabs his briefcase and leaves for the day.

What would happen if either needed to leave town? If the rest of the sequences are anything like the morning sequence, there is little reason for emotional response to the absence. There is little opportunity for Brad and Patty to contribute to each other's well-being in their current sequence. There are a lot of ways that Brad and Patty could negatively interrupt each other, but few ways to facilitate each other's goals. Since it is easier to notice negative events than positive events, it will be challenging to maintain an emotional connection.

Couples use their emotions in relationships in limitless ways. **Hot** couples use their emotions to bring energy into a relationship. One minute things will be very quiet, and the next minute the dyad appears with loud laughter, sharp critical responses, flashes of anger, or great passion. These couples are as likely to use their passion with bickering as with laughter. They are conflict-habituated (Cuber & Haroff, 1971) and they have a constant threat of explosion and minimal tolerance for others who do not agree to argue with them. **Warm** couples use their steady emotions to create balance. A mixture of dynamic interactions is intended to create change, express unmet needs, and demand attention, and it is interlaced with a pacing that allows for the quiet of a comfortable status quo. **Lukewarm** couples use their emotions to create a context of peace and quiet. They do not experience a lot of change in their interactions positively or negatively. The relationship is sedate. Some would consider it boring. But it is predictable with a clear absence of extreme emotion. Like a steady ship, these relationships stay on course, steer clear of bad weather, and have little room for upset. **Cold** couples use their emotional states to disconnect from each other. When there are bids for connection they communicate in a perfunctory fashion, primarily to exchange essential information. They share a number of the same friends and enjoy doing the same things, but they are more often next to each other than connected with each other.

Clearly, emotions are not inherently good or bad. Adding a second person to the emotional mixture can be helpful, like adding ice to boiling water to cool it down, or it can be toxic, like combining bleach and ammonia. Each partner ultimately must find a way to remain connected and involved in the life of the other, learning to work through the challenges of everyday life. The more similar two people are in values, interests, and background, the more likely that their interactions will be rewarding and the greater their opportunity for developing an intense, meaningful emotional climate.

Emotional First Aid

Research conducted by the RELATE Institute indicates a very consistent and clear pattern of influence when considering the emotional ratings of couples on their relationship satisfaction. First, the emotional climate of each person in the couple has a stronger influence on female satisfaction than it does on male satisfaction. Second, the ratings of female depression, by both the male and the female, have by far the strongest influence on relationship satisfaction for both males and females. The depression level of females, as perceived by self and partner, seems to be the most important emotional issue for couples. If she is less depressed, the male is happier in the relationship and she is happier in the relationship. Both partners will have higher self-esteem if they are not depressed, even if there is anxiety in the relationship. Consequently, future outcomes can be predicted from the emotional climate.

If there were an emotional first-aid kit, it would contain at least three things: (1) an armory of positive experiences; (2) empathy skills; and (3) self-soothing skills. The human need to minimize negative outcomes makes information about negative events much more available than information about positive events, resulting in the belief that relationships are more problematic than they are. Into the emotional first-aid kit should go the armory of positive emotions:

1. **History:** Notice instances of positive sequences each day, no matter how seemingly trivial. When they are written in a journal that is available to both partners it provides a foundation for positive sentiment. For example: "We worked together to make dinner and clean it up." "Bill went out of his way to open the garbage bin for Jan."
2. **Affirmations:** A list of positive partner affirmations in the back of the journal or one of the many books on positive affirmations can keep the couple focused on positives in the relationship that may otherwise go unnoticed.
3. **Friendship:** A daily check-in system between partners to connect as friends and loving humans helps expand the relationship beyond the chores of the relationship (Doherty, 2002).
4. **Future:** Sharing hopes and dreams gives partners an opportunity to share what is important to each of them.

Empathy is both understanding and accepting one's partner and conveying that understanding and acceptance back to the partner. It influences the emotional climate because discomfort can be addressed before it escalates. Dossey (1999) reported that taking on the perspective of another actually caused changes to people's immune system. When actors take on a particular role their bodies react as if the role were for real. Empathy makes a significant difference in people's ability to gain experiential understanding of another's arousal states (Dossey, 1999).

To add empathy to the emotional first-aid kit, there are three easy suggestions:

1. **Listen:** Listen to a partner for five minutes without giving any advice, using only minimal responses (simple noninterfering sounds such as hmmm, wow, and uh-huh) to encourage the partner to say more.
2. **Practice:** From only one paragraph of a dialogue in a novel or magazine, think about what the character is thinking and feeling. Practice responding to the character with understanding.
3. **Notice:** Notice the conversational style of people you most enjoy talking with.

The more intense emotions that people experience, the more likely they are to influence the emotions of the others with whom they interact. There is a tendency for people to become synchronized intrapersonally (mind and body) and interpersonally (people will sometimes become angry just by observing an angry person). It is possible to decide on a preferred emotional state and enact it in a way that helps others synchronize to you. When emotions are strong, flooding can occur, making it difficult to stay in a preferred emotional state. In the emotional first-aid kit, a seven-step process can help reduce flooding:

1. **Recognize flooding.** When flooding occurs, a door slams shut. Notice what your body feels like when you have had too much information to take in.
2. **Think calming thoughts.** Tell yourself that you are calm. Thoughts can override the body's emotional state, and telling yourself that you are calm can redirect your body's energy.
3. **Adjust your breathing.** During flooding, breathing may be rapid. Focus on your breathing and bring it to a comfortable pace (a resting rate).
4. **Repeat the word "relax" five times.** Repeating "relax" will work as a mantra, telling your body to synchronize with the idea of relaxing.
5. **Allow yourself to be relaxed.** You may need to give yourself explicit permission to relax even when external sources are trying to influence you into flooding.
6. **Resist the temptation to become synchronized with negative energy.** As you become more available to a different emotion it will be easy to synchronize with another person's negative emotional state.
7. **Provide safety to diffuse your partner's flooding.** Use empathy to hear your partner's concerns. Allow your partner to synchronize with your calmness. Take a break from the discussion until you and your partner are feeling more confident (within 24 hours).

Emotions are an important concept in romantic relationships. Although biologically, emotions are simply the product of physiological arousal to which meaning has been assigned, emotions also become part of how couples understand each other's behaviors. The tendency to overlook positive interactions and to notice and react to negative interactions is what is referred to as the fundamental paradox of positive emotion. Three points of emotional first aid were offered to create healthy emotional systems: Notice the positives, enhance empathic understanding in the relationship, and soothe the emotions of partners who have become overwhelmed.

5

Special Issues and Concerns

*To everything there is a season, and a time to every purpose under the heaven
. . . a time to embrace, and a time to refrain from embracing; . . . a time to keep,
and a time to cast away.*

—Ecclesiastes 3: 1–6

It takes dedication and commitment from two people to make a relationship work, and one person can end the relationship at any time. An individual's desire and ability to commit to a permanent relationship creates special considerations as the relationship moves toward marriage. As much as members of the couple may feel close to each other, they need to agree on the type of commitment they are able to give to the relationship and on the limits they bring to the relationship. Sometimes there are special concerns or issues that need to be discussed, but it may be difficult to know which questions to ask that could uncover special concerns.

The early signs of relationship challenges are sometimes available within the first few minutes of interaction with potential partners, but seeing those challenges ahead of time requires a willingness to do so. In this section we will focus on the timing of marriage, learning to love, danger signs, and working with special issues.

Issues of Timing

Most social groups hold fairly clear notions of "on time" and "off time" for major events, including becoming married (Riley, Foner, & Waring, 1988). This keeps social life fairly predictable, and consequently manageable. Few Americans would deny that marriage at 12 years of age is "off time," but there is a wide variety of opinion about whether marriage at age 20 or at age 26 is preferable. There are two primary issues of marital timing: (1) the impact of the social network on the individual's thinking, and (2) the presence of necessary breakup skills at any degree of relationship involvement.

The age of partners can be a general guide regarding emotional maturity, access to resources, and social support. When partners are too young they may not have learned skills that aid in decision making or problem resolution. Similarly, adequate preparation for the labor market and self-support occurs in early adulthood, and that preparation may be poorly achieved in early marriages. Early marriages are associated with earlier childbirth, greater numbers of children, less school achievement, and less financial security (Holman & Linford, 2001).

Your perception of marital timing, however, depends greatly on the people with whom you socialize. Imagine that all of your friends have had engagement parties in the past year or two, they're talking about where their honeymoons will be, and they are receiving both attention and gifts. It is understandable to want what other people around you have. Now imagine that none of your friends are planning marriages. How might their discussions and activities be different? Whether you are 23 years old or 28 years old, your concern about whether to marry is influenced by your social network. Those expectations vary some based on socioeconomic status, gender, and religious affiliation. Professional women tend to marry later than other women; women tend to marry earlier than men; and some cultures encourage earlier marriage than others. Overall, people have ideas about when something should occur, and they share those ideas with others in their social network.

These preset notions of timing can push people into making decisions that may not be right for them. There may be a grandparent, helpful friend, or sibling who insists on arranging dates for single friends or family, encouraging them to select a partner with whom they would be able to settle down. Adding to the pressure to conform to timing expectations are age mates who are "on time" in beginning their couple lives, including obligations to their spouses and babies that prevent them from participating with their single friends in the same way. All these can become part of the pull toward marriage. Whether the relationship is established because of a concern about timing, or because the relationship in itself is worthy of marriage can make a significant difference in the amount of work required to manage the relationship. It is sometimes difficult to distinguish between a "good relationship" and an "on time" one. When the push toward marriage is so strong, people may fall in love with their ideas about who the partner is without really knowing the partner very well.

There are some partners who are reluctant to commit to relationships regardless of other circumstances because they are interested in more casual dating. In a society that promotes selecting one's own partner it is simple to avoid deeper commitments: Keep the relationship casual, and end the relationship before it becomes too serious. Adding the influence of the social network, however, means that remaining uncommitted to a relationship can be difficult. It can also be difficult to stop a relationship from becoming serious. It is likely that partners will have different desires regarding how serious and exclusive a relationship should become. Negotiating a level of commitment that is compatible with both partners' desires is no small task.

When one person wants to slow down or end a relationship, the person who is being left will feel sad—or worse, rejected. Unfortunately, some couples end up moving on toward marriage without the necessary interpersonal commitment because they are not able to break up. Breaking up is a skill. The consequences of taking care of yourself, which may require stopping a relationship from becoming more serious than is appropriate for you, can result in some loss and sadness. Sadness is inevitable when relationships change, and some people do not have the skills or courage to productively manage that sadness. They allow the feelings that come with breakups to prevent them from ending relationships that should end.

In many instances couples may have a different preference for the speed at which a relationship progresses toward marriage simply because of different personalities and preferences. Some people make decisions more quickly than others, some worry more about what might happen, while others are more likely to make snap judgments and trust that things will work out in the end. There are also gender differences in comfort with commitment and the pace of relationships. Table 5.1 shows how males and females responded to the question "In your relationship, who is moving faster toward marriage?" from the RELATE questionnaire. The results suggest that almost half the couples felt that one person was moving more quickly toward marriage than the other and in most instances this person was the female. Also, in about 20% of the couples both partners felt that the move toward marriage was "fast." Couples, then, are very likely to have significant issues with the timing of marriage and find that it is challenging to get both people in agreement about when marriage should happen. There is also probably something to the stereotype of the reluctant male feeling hurried toward marriage by his partner and the social network.

Well-meaning members of a couple's social network may interfere with essential breakups. Family members may believe that the members of the couple should be married, and to prevent disappointing one's family and friends, relationships become more serious than they would otherwise. Collective thought that one

TABLE 5.1 *Responses on the RELATE Questionnaire of Females and Males to the Question "In your relationship, who is moving faster toward marriage?"* *

	Percentage of Respondents	
Marriage Statements	*Females*	*Males*
I want to get married much more than my partner	7%	3%
I want to get married a little more than my partner	17%	8%
My partner wants to get married a little more than me	12%	19%
My partner wants to get married much more than me	4%	10%
We both are moving quickly toward marriage	18%	19%
Neither of us is moving quickly toward marriage	35%	34%

*Seven percent of the couples did not feel that this question was applicable to them.

"should be married" may refer to being on time for marriage or to having located an endogamous partner (one whose physical or social characteristics are similar). The couple's parents may be satisfied that the members of the couple are well suited to each other because of the apparent similarities (e.g., the couple shares a similar economic background, shares religious beliefs, and agrees on child-rearing philosophies). Marriages also help to preserve the structure of certain friendship groups (e.g., one in which there are two or more couples who enjoy each other's company and enjoy a social life together) and the members of that group become invested in keeping the couple together. Couples may find that when they voice concerns or complaints about their relationship, others in the network absorb some of the disenchantment, causing it to be disregarded or undermined. Despite not being ready for a relationship, couples may be unsuccessful in going against the cultural tide that moves them toward more involvement rather than less. The words "cold feet" are often used to describe a fear of getting married and the notion that it will go away after the wedding. Valid concern about the relationship may be pushed off as fear of the wedding:

> The groom-to-be had been bothered through most of the engagement, saying that he wanted to be married some day, but not now. He did fall in love with his fiancée, and during one short period of time agreed that it would be nice to get married. His fiancée and her parents began planning the wedding as soon as he had "agreed." Because of a variety of concerns, she and her parents ended up planning the wedding so that it took place just before graduation. As the wedding drew closer the groom became very upset. He repeatedly told his friends and his family that he did not want to get married. His friends and his family did the best they could to assure him that all he had was "cold feet" and that he'd feel better after the wedding was over. The couple had been together through most of their college years; they were both about to graduate with their bachelor's degrees and head off on new career ventures. Their hometowns were fairly close to each other, so they did not have to worry about being pulled away from their homes. By the time the young man's complaints were heard seriously there was the added pressure of money that already had been invested in the wedding events. Rings had been purchased and dresses were fitted, and travel plans were made. Although his friends began to believe that he truly did not want to be married, there was a group effort to help him go through with the wedding. Interestingly, the groom forgot to pick up his tuxedo on Friday, and the shop was closed on Saturday, the wedding day. "Lucky" for them, the bride's parents were able to locate the owner of the shop, and the groom's tuxedo was made available to him. "Surely," they all thought, "he'll feel better after the wedding." He did feel better after the wedding but not for the reason they all expected. He was married on a Saturday, and he filed to have the marriage annulled on Monday. He really did not want to be married.

The combination of being "on time" and having one's social network invested in the couple can move the relationship toward marriage even when neither member of the couple wants to make a commitment to marriage. Sometimes when family pride becomes an issue, the couple may go through with what they both know to be a poor relationship to spare their parents the embarrassment of a cancelled wedding:

Bob and Elena were from the local university. They were beginning graduate school. They were ambitious, attractive, and were both very nice people. They seemed to have similar goals and values, and on the outside everything seemed to be right with the relationship. Both sets of parents were pleased about the upcoming wedding. Bob, the groom-to-be, had faced serious trauma two years before, and Elena, the bride-to-be, became his support system. He was grateful to her for helping him through; she was doubtful that he could manage without her. They attended premarital counseling to work through important, yet unresolved, dilemmas that were causing a great deal of distress between them. They requested a band-aid of sorts so they could get along well enough to get through the wedding without arguing so much. They had postponed the wedding one time, her choice, but the plans for the wedding were not stopped at that time. The parents agreed among themselves that because the halt to the wedding was probably temporary, and the halls were difficult to schedule, they would keep the reservations in place and hope the problems were straightened out soon. The engagement was back on, and immediately their wedding was scheduled. At the minister's advice they sought out premarital counseling one month before their wedding.

They agreed that their relationship was not much fun, and they agreed that they should have waited until they were finished with school to become engaged. They both thought that they would like to stay single for a while longer even though it was awkward to be with her friends who were almost all married. It was embarrassing sometimes for her to go to family functions and be asked about her love life. The wedding had already been postponed one time, and although the differences were serious and causing a great deal of stress between the two of them, there was no possibility of postponing the wedding. She became extremely tense at the suggestion that they rethink their decision to marry at this time. "That would never work. My dad would be so mad." Her family held a very high status in a small community. Her father was accustomed to being respected and having a perfect family. A broken engagement would be shameful to their family and it could never happen. Her mother assured her that she could work things out after marriage. She was clear that she could not make her parents unhappy. They wanted to give her a big wedding and she wanted to have it. Bob did not typically tell his parents much about what was happening. They were proud of him and he knew they would support his decisions. This couple was on a social escalator, arriving at the altar before they were ready, and they did not know how to jump off.

There are special concerns in preparing for marriage, particularly when the reasons for marriage have more to do with the social network than the relationship between the partners. When people find themselves on time for marriage there is frequently an urgency to become married. During that time it is possible to overlook important differences in the relationship or hope that those discovered will go away. Unfortunately, difficulties before marriage continue to exist after marriage, and sometimes become even more problematic as time passes. It is difficult to address some of the social network factors creating an escalator toward marriage, particularly when the desires of parents and other significant people in one's life are so important. When faced with the uncomfortable choice of ending a relationship and disappointing others, or ending the marriage by divorce, most people would agree that it is best to break up before marriage. It is the eternal optimism that keeps couples from acknowledging the potential problems in creating a marriage where serious difficulties are present.

Problems that are seen before marriage do not go away after marriage, and truly do not go away after the birth of the first child (when sleep deprivation and financial concerns peak!). Acknowledging problems, also, does not necessarily mean that a breakup must occur. When problems can be acknowledged and strategies for managing the dilemmas developed, they do not have to grow into marital poison. If the dilemmas cannot be managed, breakup is a viable option. As difficult and embarrassing as broken engagements can be, they are not nearly as traumatic, or costly, as unhappy marriages or divorce.

Learning to Love

Often people talk about "turning a new page," meaning that they want to start fresh. In interpersonal relationships, starting fresh is not like turning a blank page. Relationships have histories. The human brain uses prior information to make sense of current information. Humans are always influenced by what came before because they have the unique capacity for verbal (remembering what is said) and sensory (remembering feelings or other perceptual information) memory. All experiences influence what one expects to have happen next. While all experiences have the ability to imprint new information, no one can fully erase what has been learned in the past.

Trust

Early in infancy babies learn whether their cry can elicit the cooperation of persons caring for them. It is here that children understand their personal power and their value. They learn whether they can trust others, and how best to take care of themselves. Attachment issues can range from fairly minor dilemmas (for example, Amy has difficulty saying goodbye and is worried that Bill will look at other women) to more serious problems (for example, abused and abandoned children may be careful to trust only themselves and to distance themselves from others to avoid pain). The following is an example of how tragic loss from the past can affect a marriage:

> Matt was only 5 years old when his mother was killed by his father. He remembered her protecting him, putting him behind her back, and watching his father strike with the final blow. She fell to the ground, still holding Matt's hand. His father grabbed him and ran from the house. He was in a drunken rage when he killed her, and realized what he had done when he sobered up. He called the police and waited for them to arrive. Matt remembered waiting on the front steps with his father and he remembered the teddy bear the social worker gave him. He remembered being afraid of keeping the bear because his father might not want him to have it. He was sent to live with his grandparents, and remembered thinking that it was odd that no one ever talked about that night again. When he was 16 years old he was court ordered to therapy for substance abuse.
>
> Matt never saw or heard from his father, and he assumed that he was in jail. Matt put that night behind him and decided to never let anyone love him the way his mother loved him. He had made his father angry, and his mother died protecting him. Matt laughed at himself because until that day he believed Superman would protect them.
>
> Over the years Matt dealt with his mother's murder in his own way. He came to marital therapy with his wife, Jenny, who cries every time he tells the story of his childhood. She protects him every way possible. She has trouble being angry with him because "he had such a lousy childhood" but she is very hurt by him, as well. Matt became upset when Jenny told him she would like to have a baby, and he objected. She entered therapy describing him as "stuck," and wanted him to deal with his past so he could move on.

As trust increases in a relationship, so does the risk taking (self-disclosure) and the understanding (empathy). For some partners this increased intimacy is scary, and the way they may manage the discomfort is to keep the relationship at a shallow level of trust. This may be an issue of lack of skills (in which case the missing skills can be taught), or a level of discomfort with the trust cycle. The experience of being trusting and having that trust misused is often a problem for future relationships. Through experience, some partners learn that they are the only people they can trust. They structure their lives so that they are not depending on anyone to be kind to them; they make sure that they are not vulnerable at any time. When self-protection is threatened, those who have experienced danger in their close relationships react with a "fight-or-flight" response to regain distance and control. Matt's ability to connect with Jenny was seriously compromised by the intense fear reaction that he felt as he experienced his love for her. The memories of loving his mother made intimacy much more difficult for him than it might be for someone without such trauma. In therapy he was able to address these issues and he and his wife began their family.

Trust includes being willing to follow through on promises, as well as being open to other people's trusting behaviors. Trust includes risk taking and regulating levels of vulnerability. Regulating vulnerabilities is difficult, particularly for those who have been victimized. Sometimes these problems take the form of being too trusting. Controlling partner behaviors are initially viewed as being doting, full of nurturing and thoughtful behaviors. Not surprisingly, such vulnerability can be misused. Trust and power are closely associated and sometimes trust is manipulated to control others. For example, Mike trusted Emily and decided to share a secret about something embarrassing. In the heat of an argument, Emily used that information to strengthen her argument against him. Misusing that information was misusing trust: Trust can be manipulated to control others. Control of a partner requires a great deal of vigilance and the ability to influence a partner. Controlling partners can quickly accelerate from attentive to obsessive because the mechanism that they are using to maintain control (power) only works as long as the partner is willing to participate. Possessiveness is measured in RELATE, focusing on the desire to keep a partner interacting and confiding solely within the context of the relationship. Very high levels of possessiveness are danger signs in romantic relationships. Inappropriate levels of gift giving and idealization often culminate in the use of coercive power to keep the relationship intact.

> Max bought Gretchen every present imaginable. He never said "I love you," because words are cheap. All he asked for, in return for the gifts, dinners, and attention he so liberally showered on her, was for her to report to him every couple hours to tell him where she was. He even bought her a cellular telephone so she could make the calls. When she went more than three hours without calling, Max tried to call her. When he found her cellular telephone was turned off, he began searching the city for her. By the time he found Gretchen he was so upset that he grabbed her and screamed at her. They both agreed that it was her fault for upsetting him. They reported that he trusted her and she let him down. He labeled her behavior "disrespectful" and told her that he could not trust her anymore. Now he prefers to go with her wherever she is going.

Trust that is inequitably distributed (e.g., she trusts him, but he continually requires proof of her truthfulness) or too quickly established (e.g., on the first date she tells him some of her most difficult past experiences) is a sign of danger. Trust begins when behavior is consistent and predictable, and moves gradually to an ability to depend on another person. Faith develops over a long period of time, as partners are increasingly more dependable. Often gut-level information tells a partner that the adoration is a sign of possessive behavior, but that information is ignored in favor of having faith that the partner is being loving. Obsessive jealousy and possessiveness are danger signs in relationships that are often overlooked. A cycle of partner abuse is beginning between Max and Gretchen (more about relationship violence will be covered in Chapter 16).

Expectations

Expectations influence relationship events, investments, and satisfaction. Imagine that while you were growing up your mother baked cookies for your father every Wednesday. Although the family learned to expect the cookies, Dad always made a big fuss out of them and you, as a child, knew that these cookies were special. Your brother's wife thought that this was a great tradition, and adopted it in her family as well. As you began a new relationship you were surprised to realize that you were expecting your partner to begin baking you cookies as a sign of her love for you. Your partner, unfortunately, had a different set of expectations.

Personal and relational history is, actually, similar to a computer's memory. I might think that I've dealt with a file of information for as long as it was relevant, and then deleted it. However, many times it is clear that information is often not entirely gone from a computer. Unexpectedly sometimes, expectations become ignited in a current relationship based on learning from prior relationships. Sometimes you want that old information to come back. Other times, however, you really want that old information gone, and instead it gets in the way. Previously learned relationship rules, even when not intentionally brought into a relationship, can be triggered by something in the environment.

In the new relationship, there may be other examples of expectations that you and your partner do not share, that are important to one or the other of you. Sometimes couples enter into relationships believing that if they wait long enough, or complain loudly enough, their partner will change for them. A good question for all partners to ask themselves is whether they are happy with who their partner is, or if they are trying to change their partner.

Expectations play key roles in deciding whether or not a relationship is salvageable. One evening I listened to a woman advise a bride-to-be, "You don't have to stay married if you don't like it. Try it out for a while; if it works, great, if not, there's always divorce." The other women who were listening laughed, and agreed with the wisdom of this woman's statement. They expected marriages to be difficult, and divorce to be common. Expectations about marital unhappiness and the inevitability of divorce affect the amount of energy that one is willing to put into maintaining a relationship. Those approaching a marriage comforted by the thought "I can always get divorced" may want to rethink their choice to marry. Marriages can be extremely challenging in the best of relationships, but divorce is equally difficult. People with long-term, stable marriages often say that their relationship success is based on neither of them giving up on marriage even when things were not going well. Your expectations about the permanence of marriage will influence your ability to get through the difficult times.

The ability to expect a relationship to last is not as natural as one might hope. People learn as babies to love and to trust, and some of those babies learn that loving and trusting is unwise. Throughout life, people with attachment fears have difficulty in intimate relationships, and nowhere is the intimacy demand greater than within a marital relationship. Expectations in marriage are learned and are met, in part, because the expectation exists. Those expectations can be beneficial (for example, I expect my husband to care how my day went, so I tell him about my day while we talk at dinner time) or hurtful (for example, I expect that my wife doesn't care about my day, so I won't bother telling her). Expectations become self-fulfilling prophesies that influence the behavioral sequences in relationships, and consequently the satisfaction experienced in the relationship. Positive expectations can help produce better relationships.

Danger Signs and Other Challenges

The length of a relationship is an interesting gauge of potential marital difficulties. An extremely short courtship is indicative of a readiness for marriage and openness to finding an available partner. There is a concern, however, that marriages that take place too early can be at risk for difficulties. In the very earliest stage of dating, falling in love with love is common. The information that is available about the partners is limited, for the most part, to that which can be observed or readily shared in daily interaction. These *manifest* qualifiers allow new partners to make assumptions about each other's values and characteristics that may not be accurate. In a culture in which marital partners are expected to fulfill a number of psychological and social needs, it is risky to make long-term decisions based on little more than a partner's manifest qualifiers.

An urgency to become married can be a result of a number of life situations, sometimes amounting to "jumping from the frying pan into the fire." Marrying to escape an unhappy home life or a parent's tight control sometimes causes trouble because over time the marriage also begins to feel restrictive. Particularly when one's family is very strict and marriage is the only way out of the house, marriages can happen quickly:

> Crystal, 26, and Manny, 28, had been working through their second adolescence. Both agreed that they had gotten married too early. She was 19 years old and living at home with a very strict father. She still had a 10:00 PM curfew and wasn't allowed to go anywhere overnight with friends unless a chaperone was also going. Although she had a great deal of love for her family, she felt like she needed to move away from home as soon as possible so that she could live her own life. Becoming married seemed like the best way to move away with her parents' approval. Manny asked Crystal's father for her hand in marriage, and months later they had an elaborate wedding. On their honeymoon Crystal became pregnant and Manito was born within the year. Now, seven years later,

they were arguing a lot and feared that their marriage was ending. Crystal believed that she missed out on the fun her friends had during college. She said that she still loved Manny, but that she didn't know who she was. "I went right from my father's house to Manny's. My Dad made my decisions then, and Manny does now." Crystal found the need to re-negotiate their marriage so that it was a better fit for the woman she had become.

Couples may also use marriage to avoid the pain of a relationship breaking up, rebounding quickly to a new partner rather than healing the loss from a previous relationship. When circumstances outside of the relationship create urgency for marriage, it may be too risky to really learn about each other. Prior to marriage, partners may develop mental images of each other that may or may not be accurate. After marriage, they may find themselves arguing about how much one or the other has changed since their courtship. Couples who becomes serious too quickly are at risk of encountering difficulties incurred from initially seeing only the parts of their partner that fit with their own image of the perfect partner.

The process of moving for a job or for college may also speed up the commitment process because of the difficulty inherent in long-distance relationships. Relocating alone or sustaining a long-distance relationship is difficult. It requires concentrated effort for partners to communicate regularly and remain part of each other's lives despite the distance. In each of these situations, in which an early commitment to marriage is indicated, a comprehensive look at personal characteristics and values before marriage is highly recommended. Using the RELATE questionnaire can fill in some of those missing pieces that couples may not have time to discover in their relationship.

On the other end of the spectrum are the very long-lasting courtship relationships (more than four years) that may raise concerns about the actual trajectory of the courtship experience. Some courtships are long simply because of circumstances outside of the couple's control (e.g., one member had to move away for two years), and those are not particularly problematic. Other couples, however, have very turbulent relationships involving frequent breakups and seriously hurt feelings. The process of these relationships becomes important, then, in terms of the degree to which the relationship is actually stable. Questions that are salient for these relationships include (1) what happens in the relationship as it becomes more intimate; (2) how does the couple break up; and (3) who initiates the reunion. Very long relationships could be the product of the couple being more compatible as friends than as sweethearts. The *latent* qualifiers define those aspects of the partner's self that require more time to emerge. As the couple is together long enough to know each other well, and have the opportunity to negotiate interactions, they see more of the real partner and less of the idealized partner. They have time to move away from interactions that are socially scripted (e.g., first dates, first holiday celebrations, first carnivals) and into interactions that are more personally revealing.

Premarital relationship length, then, has a curvilinear relationship to relationship stability. Relationships that are too short may be unstable because of the difficulty of really knowing a partner in a very short period of time. At the other end, however, relationships that are too long may be characterized by frequent breakups or partners who can't commit. Long premarital relationships also may reveal a reluctant social network in which many people outside the couple are interfering with committing to marriage. More about disapproval from friends and family will be covered in Chapter 16.

Caregiving Responsibilities

Children can put a great deal of stress on even a healthy marriage, and when children are present before marriage, or a premarital pregnancy occurs, the couple is faced with negotiating the new marital relationship and the new parenting relationship at the same time. This creates a special concern for marriage. The task in the first year of marriage is to become interdependent with the new spouse, and independent from friends and family. The concept of "honeymoon" stems from beliefs that the new couple should have a "month of honey" where they are left alone to form their new relationship without the interference of friends or family. This is not, however, always possible. When a pregnancy precedes marriage, couples often need to meet children's needs before the couple bond is well established. The time that the couple needs to obsessively focus on themselves and their relationship patterns and rules is unavailable. They must remain part of a larger family to share the joy of children and to receive childcare help from others. Predictable dilemmas in the new marriage are tended to as one of many issues the couple deals with, rather

When children precede the marriage a "month of honey" is often not possible.

than as the primary issues. When caregiving extends to other ill or disabled members of the family, the couple's loyalties may be in distinctly different places. Even more complicated are situations in which children from former relationships are brought into the marriage. Then, not only are children brought into the marriage, but also the child's other parent is brought in. The child and stepparent may have a difficult time negotiating their relationship, as is often the case for ex-partners who must often establish a way of working together.

Sometimes, however, the risk of children is that the marriage is a by-product of an attachment between the stepparent and child, rather than between the woman and the man.

> Clara and Davis were having trouble getting along now that their daughters had grown and moved out of the house. The wife requested to meet alone with the therapist because there was something that she couldn't bring herself to tell her husband. Somberly, she described her decision to be married. "His girls were 8 and 10 when Davis and I met, and they needed a mother. I became so attached to them. We had a lot of fun together. On their days off school, Davis would go to work and the girls and I would plan our day. It was great: shopping, manicures, you name it. Then, they grew up and they don't really need me the same way anymore. I realized that Davis and I haven't really worked on our marriage. We both loved Sara and Kim, and that's what we built our relationship on."

When a partner has been previously married, and in particular when that partner brings children into the marriage, a number of challenges are also brought to the marriage: step-parenting relationships, loyalty issues between children and their biological parents, ex-spouses, new spouses, and financial arrangements stemming from these previous commitments. This can be particularly difficult for never-married persons whose partners are in their second marriages. These marriages rarely have the luxury of operating as if it were a first relationship, yet some of the challenges can be overcome with flexibility and persistent effort.

Illness and Disability

Illnesses and disability affect marriages differently depending on whether they are visible (e.g., missing limbs) or invisible (e.g., deafness), and whether they are acute (e.g., heart attack) or chronic (e.g., asthma). While some illnesses and disabilities are known at the time a couple begins dating (e.g., the need for a wheelchair), others become apparent as the relationship progresses (e.g., clinical depression). Serious mental illness, such as schizophrenia, often emerges in the late teens and early twenties, while other types of mental illness are diagnosed in childhood (such as attention deficit hyperactivity disorder—ADHD).

Some disabilities affect marriages more than others do. Some affect communication (hearing), others affect the ability to obtain and sustain employment (e.g., chronic pain), and others affect the ability to participate in favorite social experiences (e.g., the inability to dance). Because some illnesses and disabilities are genetically passed on, it is important for partners to discuss these issues and make decisions about having children and consider genetic testing for some of the more serious genetic disorders:

> Bill has known about his problem since early childhood. Born with a rare disorder, Bill's spine is degenerating, and soon he will be unable to walk. He has had several surgeries, and is in constant pain. He is now 25 years old, and he reported that he did not waste time going to college. He went right to work as a mechanic, saved his money and bought a house. He wanted to be sure that he had a place to live and a family before he became disabled. He accomplished most of his goals before he was forced to go on disability. His wife was his high-school sweetheart, and they fought frequently. He was surprised at how explosive their arguments became and he was ashamed of the way that he treated her. He supposed that they weren't ready for marriage.

It is possible that Bill and his wife weren't ready for marriage, and it is also very likely that any couple with so many losses would have a difficult time managing the stress without the support of their family and community. A disabling illness for a 25-year-old primary wage earner is a serious crisis, and without help, marriages in crisis can be quite brittle (Boss, 1988).

Substance Use

Substance-related disorders are illnesses that are often difficult to understand. It is confusing for some people to move from a college or mate selection environment in which there may be fewer sanctions against drinking alcohol (e.g., happy hours, bars, and dancing) or using recreational drugs, to a marital relationship where dependability and responsibilities require sobriety. In homes where substances are abused, the environment is more chaotic, and often more violent. The lowered inhibitions of the substance abusing member cause her or his behavior to be more toxic to the family environment, and family members find themselves with little control over the potential legal difficulties brought on by alcohol or drug abuse (e.g., driving under the influence, domestic violence, etc.).

The most important questions to ask premaritally are how much alcohol or drug use is comfortable for each member of the couple, and whether the members can control their use. A simple litmus test to take in order to check whether substance abuse is out of control is to go for three weeks without any use. If even small slip-ups occur, such as "just one drink," it is likely that the addiction is serious and needs professional attention. See Chapter 16 for more information about marriage and substance use.

Working with Special Issues

It is not uncommon to hear people lament that they will be happy after this or that is accomplished. This is the *"We'll be happy afterwards" myth* . . . and nearly anything can come after that beginning: After we get married, after we finish school, after we find a house, after we pay for the house. When people continue to wait until after a major event to be the happy family that they want to become, they rarely achieve that happiness. Their marital process is developed around waiting for something beyond themselves. Particularly when special concerns make marriages a bit more challenging, it is tempting to put off working on the marriage until tomorrow. Marital happiness can be a priority during the difficult transitions, or marriage can be a disappointment because there is always something to deal with next. This, of course, leads to one of the major excuses in marriage: There's not enough time for each other.

Couples always find enough time to argue, and it takes as long to argue as it does to anticipate some of the issues that may come up. When the relationship is a top priority, there is enough time to work on it. For a marriage to be satisfying it needs to be a top priority to the couple. All couples have special issues, but not all couples have the same needs or resources for handling special problems. Connecting couples to resources in their communities often helps alleviate some of the mismatches of their needs and resources. These community resources can be family members, religious or other social groups, neighbors, educational programs, or therapeutic professionals.

6

Values, Behavior, and the Family

Everything we do, every decision we make and course of action we take, is based on our consciously or unconsciously held beliefs, attitudes and values.

—Simon, Howe, & Kirschenbaum

We need to examine our core values and beliefs (what really matters to us in a partner) so that we know where we can compromise and where we can't.

—Lerner

If you were granted just three wishes, what would they be? If you had one extra day this week, how would you use it? If you were handed a sizeable check, how would you spend it? And if you knew that you would die tomorrow, how would you want to be remembered? The answers to these questions give insight to your values. There is a strong relationship between the way you spend your time and your money and your hopes and your dreams.

Self-Awareness

There are many formal systems of values that provide guidelines for behavior, such as different systems of religion, various forms of government, and several styles of marriage. Simply, some value systems work better for some people than for others. There are also some people who disavow all formal systems of values. Despite such disavowal, values are continuously operating, even when their greatest contribution is to object to other systems. Behavior (or the absence of behavior) is chosen because it makes sense to do so given a specific value system within a specific situation for which responses are possible. A person's values, then, become known through committed or omitted behaviors. Everyday decisions such as whether to purchase Starbucks coffee, Circle K coffee, or any coffee at all, are influenced by value systems.

So what about when you do something and think, "That wasn't really me." Is that possible? Sometimes our behaviors lag behind our values. In other words, it is one of our main purposes in life to bring our values and behaviors into sync. Sometimes we are weak and although we value honesty we slip up and lie; at other times we have habits that must be unlearned. Regardless of the cause of our duplicity, it is probably very common for most of us to act in contrast to our values, although hopefully with time, maturity, and growth this becomes less common. The challenge is when there is a limit to your self-awareness, such that you are unaware that your values and your behaviors are incongruent. For example, the value of honesty operates differently in different people's lives. One person may say, "I do not believe in lying except when I need a good excuse for not completing an assignment on time." Whereas another person would say, "I cannot lie about not completing my assignment, so I will suffer the consequences." Values are passed on from parents to children, and in social groups from experienced members of the group to the newer members. A basic function of parenting is to socialize new members of society, which means to pass on values and the accompanying appropriate behavioral skills. When there is incongruence between family values and behaviors, children learn from their parents' actions more than from their words:

> Mary was 14 years old and truant from school. The school counselors requested home visits for the family to help the mother learn parenting skills to gain more compliance from Mary about going to school. During the first home visit the mother, Jennifer, said that she did all she could to get her daughter to school. The therapist taught Jennifer behavioral management strategies that had been used successfully by parents in similar situations. The next day, Mary again was not in school. When the therapist called, Jennifer explained that she knew Mary needed to go to school because that was the law. She was looking forward to Mary's 16th birthday so that Mary could legally quit. Jennifer found school to be boring and difficult and felt bad for Mary that she had to endure that pain for two more years.

Jennifer's values, although initially appearing to be similar to the therapist's, were not. The therapist was working with Mary to get her to attend school so that she could have an opportunity to learn. Jennifer was working with the therapist because she was concerned that Mary was breaking the law and took comfort in only needing to tolerate the issue of school for a couple more years. Consequently, Mary did not value school and did not attend unless absolutely forced to do so. Compare this to other children who may not enjoy school but have not even entertained the option of staying home because of the clarity of the parents' values and enforcement of school obligations.

Small children blindly follow the rules of parents and accept their value systems. Value systems tell them what to be proud of, what to be ashamed of, and what to hide. As adolescents, some of the parental values are called into question, but because of the dependence that children have on their parents, most often the basic parental values continue to operate (either smoothly or vis-à-vis conflict). Adults tend to adopt many of the values of their families of origin (actual, enacted values) and may make some modifications to fit their unique personalities. Someplace between learning parents' value systems and breaking away from parents' influence is the development of a unique sense of what it means to be an adult.

> Bob's parents raised him to be responsible and show up for work every day. The exception to having to work was illness: he could call in sick if he absolutely had to, but he was rarely sick. Bob noticed that when his father needed to work on Saturday, his parents would stay in on Friday night, and his father would go to bed early so that he was well rested. Now that he's in college, Bob doesn't stay in the night before he works, but he does get up and go to work whenever he's scheduled, no matter how tired he is. He kept his family's work attendance ethic, while putting aside the value of being well rested. Perhaps over time he will also revert to the principle of getting more rest.

The importance of individual values in adult relationships lies not in whether one value is right and another wrong, but in their clarity of meaning. Successful relationships depend on sharing with your partner values that fit your understanding of yourself and having that understanding be congruent with your behaviors. A woman may believe that she values a free-spirited life, yet consistently make conservative choices in her use of money, time, personal grooming habits, and even in her approach to her work. A free-spirited partner may be attractive to her initially, but probably not when his free-spiritedness spreads beyond playful free time. If she truly valued free-spiritedness, as she believes that she does, she would not typically choose conservative behaviors for herself. Looking at your behavioral choices alone, how would you describe your values? Do you see yourself as traditional? Or is it important to you for a husband and wife to equally share in wage earning and in child rearing?

Sometimes people go to great lengths to define their behavior as fitting a preferred value system, even when that means putting a twist in the rules that go along with the belief system. A religious leader who steals from a church may say that she does not believe in stealing, and may actually believe that her values prohibit stealing. When she does steal, however, she is rationalizing her behavior by changing her value system: "I do not believe in stealing. When you take money from people who are like family you are sharing rather than stealing." Others who are a part of her organization may not agree with her rationalization and will simply treat her as an individual who manipulated their trust to steal from them.

Self-awareness involves knowing how the choices that you make fit within your value system and understanding the places where your uniqueness distinguishes you from others with the same apparent values. Your unique values influence what you ask for and what you end up with in relationships. Sometimes true values remain unarticulated, and even outside the awareness of the individual. Bill may be unaware that it matters to him to have a clean house, and he may never talk about how nice his room looks when it is clean, until he moves away to college and his parents are not there to clean up after him. Then, with trial and error he learns that one of the things that he wants in life is a neat and clean living space.

Before deciding on the values that you must have in a partner, take an inventory of the values that you yourself live by. Allow your self-awareness to expand to what you do and do not want, what you feel entitled to, and what you are willing to settle for (Lerner, 2001). Sometimes partners say that they value spontaneity, when they only value it in a climate of security and predictability. Take a few minutes to think about the 10 questions in the following self-awareness inventory.

1. What I want in life:
2. What I do not want in life:
3. What I am entitled to in relation to other people:
4. What I am willing to settle for in relation to other people:
5. Most frequent conflicts I find myself involved in:
6. Places I am most comfortable:
7. Clothing I most typically choose:
8. People who I enjoy the most:
9. Greatest disappointments:
10. Greatest pleasures:

The responses to these questions have implications about an individual's value system. It should be possible after answering these questions to categorize the values into at least five values that are most important. These values are often reflected in how people spend their free time, how they spend their money, and the events that have caused them anger, embarrassment, or thrill.

The relationship inventory RELATE looks at values in eight areas that may affect satisfaction in marriage. Those areas are the importance of marriage (M), gender-based roles (G), employment or labor force participation (E), money and material things ($), togetherness or autonomy (T), children or family planning (C), religiosity (R), and marital sexuality (S). Someone who responded "What I want most in life is a house on the beach" would be indicating a value of money and material things. When couples argue in early marriage, the arguments often focus on money (what it is for and how it should be spent) and the household division of labor (how much each partner should contribute to the daily household cleanliness and functioning). Labor force participation involves the decisions to have dual careers or to have one partner as a primary caregiver of children, and decisions about whose job is most important and why. This often distinguishes traditional family values from nontraditional values, particularly when children are present. RELATE questions reflect situations in which the decision is simply between the two adults (whether the wife or husband earns more money) and those situations in which children are involved (the wife working and the husband caring for the children).

Autonomy involves the value of spending time alone and how much of that time can be unaccounted for, while gender-based roles distinguish the types of rules that apply to women versus men in the household. Religiosity considers spirituality and organized religions, and the extent to which any form of religious belief system influences the partner's life.

The decision about what money is for and how it should be spent underlies a couple's search for their first home.

Some of these values may be issues premaritally (e.g., how money is spent), but others only become apparent after marriage (e.g., gender roles) or after the birth of a child (e.g., religious orientation). When there is an opportunity to see the value in action before marriage, it is often as a response to a conflict of interest (something that is a little bit different from what the other would expect) or open conflict (an actual discussion or argument about a different approach to an issue; Kelley, 1979).

Table 6.1 contains the means of males and females who have taken RELATE on the different value scales. A high score on these scales indicates a person holds a more traditional value. A score of 1 means the respondents disagree strongly with that value; a 3 means respondents are not sure about the value; and a score of 5 means respondents strongly agree with the value. It may be helpful to see how you compare to the averages in this table, as this might suggest where your values are unique from those of most people.

Even more importantly, it is crucial that you look carefully at how your responses compare with those of your partner. If there are substantial differences, discussion needs to occur to see if there is enough common ground to work out problems in the future.

Conflict

Someone who values frugality and would not shop without coupons may impulsively buy an expensive, disposable holiday decoration. Another person who is

TABLE 6.1   *Male and Female Average Scores on the Value Scales of RELATE*

Scale*	Females**	Males
Importance of Marriage	3.4	3.4
Gender-Based Roles	2.3	2.4
Employment for Females/Males	3.6	3.6
Money or Materialism	3.6	3.7
Togetherness or Autonomy	2.4	2.5
Children or Family Planning	3.8	3.6
Religiosity	3.7	3.4
Marital Sexuality	3.3	3.4

*1 = Strongly Disagree, 3 = Neutral, 5 = Strongly Agree
**Female and male averages were significantly different for all scales except the importance of marriage and employment.

angry about gossip may tell her friend in detail about the gossip the other person was spreading. The teacher who values autonomy may hover over her students to be sure that they are completing their assignments correctly.

During times of difficulty values are more easily clarified. Through conflict, issues of importance become apparent, and opportunities are available to learn about others with whom your values are not shared (Johnson, 2000). When challenged, the frugal shopper may clarify his value that he saves his money where he can so that he can spend it with reckless abandon when he sees something he likes. His savings, as he thinks of them, are specifically intended for his free-spending purse. A person may distinguish sharing a story from gossip based on one's intentions behind the sharing. If the story is intended to hurt or disadvantage another it is gossip ("Did you hear the scoop? John and Rita broke up!"), but it is not if it is shared with good intentions (e.g., "John and Rita may need our help because they have broken up and that is very difficult"). The teacher who believes in autonomy may specify that she is authoritative in the classroom, and within the choices she provides, students are permitted to make their own decisions. Each value looks slightly different in process than it does in definition, and it is partially the role of conflict to clarify that meaning.

On September 10, 2001, few people owned an American flag in many neighborhoods. Except for the few older men who had actually served in the military during a war, Flag Day went virtually unobserved. What was much more common were the cute flags displayed during Halloween or springtime of cartoon characters or flowers.

On September 11, 2001, the American people were in crisis. The World Trade Center in New York and the Pentagon in Washington, D.C. were the sites of terrorist attacks on U.S. soil, and thousands of civilian workers and travelers were killed. Some people became more patriotic than others, but overall the values of people as Americans came to front and center. Editorialists from around the world commented on the response of the American people: bonding together; contributing money, food, and blood to help the victims; and widespread participation in singing patriotic songs and displaying the American flag. All of the stores sold out of flags so quickly that some local newspapers printed a one-page flag that could be torn out and displayed in car windows, something that was widely used.

The Declaration of Independence and the Constitution resurfaced in newspapers, talk shows, and grade school lessons as illustrations of the country's mission statements to its citizens. In a touching article about the American response, one foreign writer concluded that the only thing that could account for the sincerity of the response and the ability to be so consumed with patriotism, without a hint of melodrama, was the freedom for which America and its citizens stand. The elected officials stopped arguing with each other, children were taught about past wars, and American veterans of war, police, and firefighters were revered. Through conflict American values were stated and, in some cases, redefined.

Thankfully, we do not often have such tragic opportunities to clarify what is important to us. Typically, taking an inventory of top priorities usually facilitates awareness of values and an evaluation of how often behavior is consistent with articulated values. Self-help books at local bookstores are available to help readers clarify their value systems and to offer suggestions of systems that have worked for others. These books are used in discussion groups and shared among friends for the purpose of eliciting new ways of thinking about old concepts. Some of the more popular value systems today include the Ten Commandments (Exodus), which underscore Judeo-Christian values; the Four Agreements (Ruiz, 1997), which present Toltec values; and the Don't Sweat guide series (Carlson, 2001), which presents a psychologist's values. Although these books are distinctly different, they all underscore one single similar value: respect for self and others. These books help readers clarify what they care about and what they are committed to, and help readers understand who other people are and what their values are. As you look back over the past month of your life, what is the most frequent conflict in which you have been actively engaged? Which value does that conflict represent, and with whom do you differ? Is your difference in whether the value is viable in your situation, or in differing interpretations of that value?

Compatible Values

There are no one-size-fits-all values, and there are differing emphases in values depending on the specific situation. Take a minute to think about what values you want to see in a partner in three different situations. If you received an all-expenses-paid, weekend trip to the Hawaiian island of your choice, whom would you go with, and why? Allow yourself to imagine that there is a perfect person whom you could choose that would fit all of your preferences in this given situation. Now, imagine that you have been chosen to begin a journey that will take you at least 20–30 years to complete. It is a challenging course, and you are allowed to bring just one other person. Whom would you go with, and why? Again, allow yourself to imagine that there is a perfect person you could choose who would fit all of your preferences in this given situation.

A marital journey has ample opportunities to resemble The Trip (the quick trip to Hawaii) and The Journey (the decades-long journey). The only difference, in most cases, is that the partner chosen in the marital journey needs to have all of the characteristics that were chosen in both situations.

In their book on premarital counseling, Stahmann and Hiebert (1997) suggest a similar exercise in which the origins of values are explored. They suggest making a list of "Who influences my values and how much" by writing down the issues, identifying specific other people in the individual's life, and what the expectations of the others are. They also recommend couples sharing their lists and making a new list of the values and expectations salient in their relationship.

Although the implementation of values may change over time, root values developed from childhood can be fairly enduring. Some couples will find that they are more in agreement than others, particularly if they are quite similar in religiosity, socioeconomic status, region of the country, and ethnicity. Still, there are many times in marriage when couples need to find room for tolerance of each other's individual values, and to find ways to respect the values of the other.

Tolerating Differences

David Johnson (2000) asserts that an important step in building effective relationships with diverse people is to adopt a set of pluralistic values. This is not only true in general social relationships, but in intimate social relationships as well. There is a tendency for family members to expect a type of group thinking in which values and attitudes are shared. In romantic relationships it is sometimes overlooked that women and men are socialized to be part of two distinctly different cultures. In those cultures very different values are adopted. The values and behaviors that are characteristic of women involve connectedness, nurturing, and emotionality (Walters, Carter, Papp, & Silverstein, 1988). The values and characteristics of men tend to involve differentiation and objectivity. These differences in values socialization tend to be reflected in reoccurring arguments that couples experience in their marital life.

One person's values end up affecting other people in the family because of the interdependence that develops during relationships. Because interdependence is developed over time, the differences may not become relevant until some time into the marital journey. For example, it may not be a problem to have one person valuing connectedness and one valuing differentiation until parenting issues arise. Then, if there is also a value of equitable distributions of emotional labor, the couple will continue to wrestle with how connected is connected enough, and how far one is permitted to go to fulfill his value of differentiation. It is in the merging of value systems that couples need to take a close look at their expectations and values in each of the known areas that may affect satisfaction in marriage (religiosity, importance of marriage, gender-based roles, labor force participation, money and material things, autonomy, marital sexuality, and family planning), not only for the short journey but also for the long journey. In those reflections, an honest appraisal of which of your values must be completely shared and which are available for agreeing to disagree is needed for a peaceful coexistence to be possible.

7

Your Parents' Marriage

. . . whenever I see my mother and father together, I know they're residing in a state where I want to live with Camille, a state of such blessed mellowness that they make the Dalai Lama seem like a Type A personality.

—Bill Cosby

How nice it would be if we all had parents with marriages that we wanted to emulate. There would probably be no better way to learn the path to a successful relationship than to have our parents walk that path in front of us and show us the pitfalls and triumphs. Nevertheless, if divorce rates continue to be as high as they are now, soon just having biological parents who are still married will be an exception to the rule, let alone the very rare case of parents who are married and satisfied. In fact, while almost half of all marriages end in divorce, close to 30% of children are growing up in mother-only households (Chadwick & Heaton, 1992). More and more of us will need to negotiate the rapids of marriage without the guide we need from our parents' marriage. All is not lost, however; humans seem to be able to learn from bad examples just as they can learn from good examples. Even if an adult had parents who were never married or together, there will still be many examples of other couple relationships that will influence beliefs, attitudes, and behaviors. The purpose of this chapter is to explore both the specific characteristics of your parents' marriage and the scripts, ideas, and expectations you have regarding marriage that will influence your intimate relationships.

What Is the Big Deal About My Parents' Marriage?

If many people have parents who are not even married anymore and others never had parents who were married at all, why focus on this topic? The primary answer to this question is that family scholars continue to find that the intimate relationship(s) of your primary caregivers, whether they were your parents or not, is likely to have a lasting influence on your approach to relationships and in some respects your approach to life. One scholar put it this way, "Ask adults whose parents were unhappily married to describe their childhood memories, and chances are you'll hear tales of sadness, confusion, false hope, and bitterness . . . you might learn about the pain of watching the two most important people in that young person's life hurt each other day in and day out" (Gottman & Declaire, 1997, p. 138). Here is another relevant quote from two eminent family scholars:

> Contrary to the popular notion that the media is chiefly responsible for young people's attitudes about mating and marriage, available evidence strongly suggests that young people get many of their ideas and models of marriage from parents and the parental generation. The noncollege men and women in our study consistently mentioned family influences as the source of both hopes and fears about future marriage. Yet, according to the participants in our study, many parents have had almost nothing good to say about marriage, and often say nothing at all. Much of this negativism may be due to the parental generation's own marital problems and failures. (Popenoe & Whitehead, 2000, p. 20)

Although both quotes are negative, it isn't difficult to imagine that many people feel like Bill Cosby does about his parents. The important point is that people

Poorly handled parental conflict will often have lasting negative effects on children.

approaching marriage have attitudes regarding intimate relationships that have been strongly influenced by parents.

The primary "weather pattern" in the home environment is established by the quality of the parents' marriage. If this marriage is satisfying and respectful, children learn that intimate relationships are places where love is felt, support is given through difficult times, and encouragement to grow is provided. If this marriage is conflictual or dissatisfying, children may learn that intimate relationships are places of pain, depression, and hopelessness.

Respondents who have taken RELATE bear out the importance of the parents' marriage on attitudes about relationships and self-esteem. For example, the parents' marriage has, by far, the strongest influence on whether or not a person sees relationships as experiences that are likely to be positive and rewarding. The parents' marriage influences self-esteem for men and women and even influences what kind of partner is selected. In other words, those who come from homes where parents had a positive relationship are more likely to select partners with higher self-esteem and partners who came from families with good parental marriages.

Almost every important marker of a healthy life is influenced by the quality of the parents' relationship. The ability of a child to make friends, the ability to succeed at work and school, the ability to resist violence and promiscuity, and even the ability to resist infectious diseases are all affected by the conflict between parents during the growing-up years (Gottman & Katz, 1989; Mackellar & Yanagishita, 1995). We cannot escape the inevitable conclusion that humans are always learning from their experiences, and pathways are set in the brain from the earliest moments of life regarding how relationships work—or how they don't. In the end, studying our parents' marriage, or our caregivers' relationships, is a way of studying ourselves.

Conflict and Emotions

As will be discussed in more detail in Chapter 12, there are four primary types of couples when it comes to handling conflict; Volatile, Avoidant, Validating, and Hostile (Gottman, 1994). A brief description of the meaning of these four types is given in Table 7.1 from the RELATE instrument (Holman et al., 1997).

Although some parents' marriages will not fit squarely into one of these four types of couples, most will when it is remembered that these types apply only to the "significant" experiences of conflict in a relationship. Even though the daily discussions your parents had might be more characteristic of a validating relationship, when conflict arose and arguments ensued, if they were hostile that would be the category they fit in. You should carefully consider what type of marriage fits your parents' approach to conflict. Every couple has times when they handle conflict in unique ways, but the issue is how conflict is *usually* handled.

Conflict is not just a characteristic of dysfunctional relationships, it is a part of all relationships. Beyond their parents' marriage, children experience daily conflict in their peer and sibling relationships. This normal conflict that is a part of negotiating relationships is not the kind that has lasting negative effects on children.

TABLE 7.1 *Gottman's Four Types of Conflict as Written in RELATE*

VOLATILE couples generally have arguments that are fought on a grand scale, often trying to persuade each other to their points of view. Although they argue hotly, they have an even better time making up, and are still usually able to resolve their differences. In fact, their conflicts are just a small part of a warm and loving relationship, since they have a lot of affection, laughing, and zest for life.

AVOIDANT couples tend to be "conflict minimizers." They would rather make light of their differences than spend time and energy arguing to resolve them. They think it is better to "agree to disagree" since open conflict and anger does not seem to get them anywhere. These couples resolve issues by letting time take its course, or minimizing them. They often think that the good companionship and sharing in their marriage is so important that they can overlook disagreements.

VALIDATING couples generally show each other, even in the midst of disagreements, that they value each other and recognize the worth of their opinions and emotions, even if they do not agree with that opinion. They usually display self-control, being able to remain calm while they listen to the other, and then good-naturedly try to persuade the other or negotiate a compromise. They often value and share similar interests, activities, and their sense of being a couple over individual goals and desires.

HOSTILE couples argue often and hotly, using insults, put-downs, and sarcasm in their discussions. During conflict they often do not look at each other or listen to what is being said, and often one or the other of them may be detached and emotionally uninvolved. Criticism, contempt for each other (such as sarcastic remarks), defensiveness, and ignoring one another may be typical of these couples' conflict styles. The relationships for these couples often are more negative than positive.

However, parental conflict that is characterized by contempt and hostility seems to create the worst side effects for children. When parents are contemptuous and hostile toward one another, this creates a loud background noise in the home that steals a child's attention, peace, and security, leaving the child with less energy to focus on school work, friendships, and interests (Cummings, 1987; Heatherington, 1992). Other researchers have shown that growing up in a home where parents were hostile and contemptuous can lead to many different types of adult problems such as emotional distress, immaturity, poor educational attainment, higher rates of divorce, and shorter life spans (Friedman, Tucker, Schwartz, Tomlinson-Keasey, & Martin, 1995; Zill, Morrison, & Coiro, 1993).

Parents who had volatile, avoidant, or validating relationships can all have enduring, satisfying marriages. These three styles of handling conflict can reflect both personal and cultural preferences. Even though the validating style is typically presented as the ideal, there are many couples in volatile and avoidant relationships that are perfectly satisfied with their relationship.

Table 7.2 shows the percentage of people who reported having parents that fit in each of the four couple types. Thankfully, the largest number of people had parents who were validating. Yet many did have parents in the hostile category and

TABLE 7.2 *The Percentage of Parents in the Four Types of Couple Relationships*

Conflict Style	Males	Females
Volatile	10%	10%
Avoidant	19%	15%
Validating	31%	25%
Hostile	14%	21%
Mixed Type	18%	20%
No Parents' Marriage	8%	9%

others were not able to easily decide which category their parents fit into. It is certainly true that some parents change over the years from a less extreme category such as avoidant or volatile into a hostile couple.

More than anything else, it is important to consider the model your parents provided regarding how conflict should be managed. It may be that one parent preferred avoidance, while another preferred a more volatile form of expressing conflict. You were influenced by your parents' style in some way. Sometimes this influence does not become clear until you engage in adult relationships of enough duration and intensity that conflict begins to emerge. If you haven't been in a relationship that lasted longer than a few months or were in one that wasn't very intense, it may be that you haven't yet determined your preferences regarding conflict management.

Again, considering how your parents expressed themselves during conflict is important, as well as considering how you react to your parents' style. It may be that your parents avoided most conflict and this was fine for them. You, though, may have been driven crazy by their refusal to just "talk things out." This may be a helpful reaction for you that keeps you from bottling up frustrations and it may be a problematic reaction for you if you become involved with someone who needs some time alone to figure out their feelings. You may interpret this time alone as avoidance and it may trigger intense feelings in you that are out of proportion to the problem because the last thing you want is to have a relationship with someone like your parents. If you understand your parents' style and your reaction to it, the relationship dynamics you have regarding conflict will be clearer and the possibility will be higher of finding a style that is workable for you and your partner, rather than falling into reactive patterns from your past.

Your vulnerability to replicating or reacting to your parents' style will be lessened if one or both parents helped you understand and express your emotions in appropriate ways. This emotional coaching will be discussed in more detail in the next chapter, but it is important to note here that even children who came from homes where parents had a high degree of hostility can avoid this conflict style, especially if at least one parent was a good emotional coach (Gottman & Declaire,

1997). This is true because the successful management of conflict is primarily about knowing what to do with strong feelings. By definition, conflict involves strong emotions, and many people, even in homes where parents were not hostile, do not learn how to express or process these emotions in a way that is helpful. Many people are taught that emotions are dangerous and should be repressed. Others are taught that certain emotions are allowable but some, like anger, are not. In some families people are taught that only a certain gender should express emotions, and others are taught that expressing feelings freely without censoring is the way to relate with others.

Parents who helped children to identify their feelings and to learn to appreciate that strong feelings are necessary and important for relationships, and who taught children to express feelings in ways that are not destructive to self or other, gave their children a resiliency that will help them overcome the hostility, divorce, or other negative experiences from their parents' marriage (Gottman and Declaire, 1997). Even if your parents didn't coach you well regarding emotions, it is, of course, never too late to learn how to express emotions better and your adult relationships will be one of the primary places where this learning can take place. Knowing you need more work in the area of managing conflict and emotions is an important starting point, because it allows you to consider alternative ways of acting and hopefully makes you more willing to learn from others.

Power and Control

How were power and control handled in your parents' marriage? Often this isn't immediately clear, as the "rules" regarding power and control are rarely explicit. Sometimes the clearest way to understand the way power and control were used in your family is to consider how decisions were made. Which of your parents or caregivers usually brought up the fact that a decision needed to be made? Who seemed to have the final word? Was there compromise? Did the decision-making process seem fair and just?

Another symbol of power in the family is money. Who earned the money in your family? Who managed it? Who made most of the major purchases?

Before drawing conclusions prematurely, though, it is important to remember that in many marriages spouses freely decide to divide responsibilities according to strengths and preferences. In some families the wife manages the money, in others the husband does, and in still others both manage the money together. Who handles the money isn't as important as how that decision was made and how happy both parents were with the arrangement. If one parent didn't want anything to do with the finances but could have been involved if desired, it doesn't mean she or he didn't have power or control regarding money.

This issue of power and control in a relationship is one that is not likely to emerge until marriage for most couples, even if their parents had struggles with it. This occurs because the most significant struggles regarding decisions and who is in charge don't emerge until finances are fully shared, job decisions have to be made, children are in the picture, and other shared responsibilities need to be decided. This is evidenced by the fact that most couples prior to marriage do not report having problems with relationship equality or with who is in charge, whereas after marriage there is a significantly higher likelihood that couples will experience problems in these areas. This difference between married and unmarried couples exists regardless of the length of the relationship. Even though many married couples have been together less time than the nonmarried couples who have been dating for many years, married couples still have significantly more problems than nonmarried couples with power and control. Approximately 30% of the married couples are not satisfied with the equality in their relationship and report that who is in charge is a common problem. Only about 13% of unmarried couples are struggling with these concerns.

One source of these problems regarding power and control can be traced to the parents' marriage and values that were passed on to children regarding who is in charge and how decisions are made. In the Values section on the RELATE inventory, which was discussed in Chapter 6 and will be discussed in more detail in Chapter 11, couples are expressing mixed messages regarding the roles and responsibilities of men and women and are not sure about who should be in charge. Although most report that the partners should have equal say in the relationship, when it comes to who should make more money, who should spend more time with the children, who should stay home if there are young children in the home, and whether roles should be specialized between men and women, there is considerable confusion. Although you are likely to have some similar basic values with your partner regarding the ideal that both people should have equal power and control in the relationship, when it comes down to the difficult decisions that demonstrate how power and control are exercised, the reality may be different from the ideal. As importantly, since couples tend to assume that they agree on these issues and many of the decisions that symbolize power don't emerge until after marriage, couples are often left to make decisions about difficult issues based on scripts that were given to them by their parents.

In this area of power and control it may be useful to project into the future regarding important decisions that will need to be made, such as the following:

- How did I learn to think about job transfers, and what impact will that experience have on my relationship when one of us gets a job far away?
- How did my parents' ways of managing finances affect the way that I think about how we will manage finances?
- How did my parents' child-rearing practices influence my opinion about who should take care of small children and take time off from a career?
- How did my parents' income arrangements influence my thoughts about who should shoulder the heaviest financial burden?
- What have I learned to expect as inevitable when my partner and I cannot agree on important decisions?
- Thinking about how my parents managed discipline, do I believe that one person should/should not be more of a disciplinarian to the children?

- The household division of labor in my parents' marriage led to my thinking about who should be in charge of washing clothes, taking care of the cars, repairing the house, cleaning the dishes, in what way?

It may also be helpful to consider how these decisions were made by each set of parents. This may help each person uncover scripts from the family of origin that will influence feelings, even if values have changed. For example, it is not uncommon for couples to decide that at a particular time the woman's career opportunity takes precedence over the man's. However, because the man or woman might have grown up in a system where the man was supposed to be the primary breadwinner, there might be unspoken guilt on the part of the woman and frustration on the part of the man.

Trust and Commitment

Was there trust in your parents' marriage? What was their level of commitment? Do you trust members of the opposite sex? How do you feel about committing yourself whole-heartedly to someone else? About 15% of RELATE respondents do not think relationships are safe, rewarding, or likely to end up positively. Other researchers have found that more and more people are becoming pessimistic about relationships and about the potential for relationships to last a lifetime (Popenoe & Whitehead, 2000). Whereas some may argue that this pessimism is realistic and healthy, others express fear that approaching such a significant experience in life with a pessimistic attitude can't enable individuals to manage the regular problems in the life of a marriage.

Is it possible to approach marriage with an optimistic attitude even though we all know divorce is common? National statistics are not as important as carefully considering your personal feelings about commitment and trust. When you think of your own marriage, even if it is far in the future, do you expect that it will last a lifetime? Your expectations are different from your hopes. Even though many are becoming pessimistic, most people still hope for a long-term, fulfilling relationship (Popenoe & Whitehead, 2000). Hope is important but expectations are, too. Expectations are built on both past and present experiences as well as on knowledge about yourself. Even though your parents may have passed on to you a distrust in marriage or in members of the opposite sex, if your personal experience with friends and romantic partners indicates that you do have the ability to make a relationship work, your expectations for success will grow.

One of the most unsettling aspects of marriage is that there are no guarantees: Although you may expect that a relationship will last and you exert considerable effort to make it do so, your partner may still decide to leave. If the mere idea that your partner may leave you despite all of the work that you have put into making a relationship work makes you reluctant to commit to relationships, this basic issue of trust will undermine the relationship.

Part of trusting in relationships is trusting in yourself and in the axiom that strong positive efforts will generally result in satisfying relationships. This is not to suggest that your effort will force someone else to stay with you. It is simply a statement of the reality that good effort brings good results in most instances. The fact that you did poorly on one test, even though you studied hard, should not result in the general attitude that you shouldn't study any more and that you aren't likely to do well after concentrated effort. Sometimes other people do things we wish they wouldn't. Sometimes teachers write poor tests, and sometimes partners leave us or mistreat us so much that we have to leave them.

Perhaps the saddest realization for people who distrust relationships and who avoid commitment is that this stance results in precisely the outcome that is so feared. What we all seem to want to avoid is having relationships that are painful and damaging, and that end in awful conflicts. We are afraid of putting tremendous effort into something so important that only ends in divorce. We are afraid of ending up alone and miserable. However, isn't the end result the same if we avoid commitment and do not trust ourselves or others? Don't we end up alone and miserable anyway? It seems that the only alternative is to risk, to exert strong effort, and to trust that most people will find a partner with whom they can be happy and satisfied. Luckily, research on successful couples shows that consistent positive effort and commitment do result in satisfying relationships that can last a lifetime.

Although it is important to evaluate your own level of trust and commitment in long-term relationships, it is also crucial to evaluate this in your partner. One way of doing this is discussing your partner's parents' marriage and trying to understand whether the effects of this marriage have resulted in a pessimistic stance toward relationships.

Relational Scripts

Our relationships and responsibilities demand immediate decisions and actions every day. We make hundreds of choices in a day and perform countless actions. It is not possible or practical to make each of these choices with careful thought. Many actions we perform automatically, like a script we are acting out that we learned at some previous time. This is true of many of the behaviors we exhibit in our intimate relationships. These scripts can be consistent with the ways our parents acted, or may be in direct opposition to how our parents' marriage was. Regardless of the motivation for our scripts, we act them out over and over again, sometimes despite sensing that they are not helping us.

Sometimes it is helpful to explore the ways our parents acted in their repetitive sequences to help us understand our own scripts. What were some of those scripts that your parents acted out? How did your parents interact with each other on most days? What was the general tone of their relationship? How much do you want your relationship to be like theirs? About 40% of the RELATE respondents want their relationship to be like their parents', 15% aren't sure, and 45% clearly do not want their relationship to be like their parents. Most people do not want marriages like that of their parents. Although this does not necessarily mean their parents' marriage was poor, it at least means that most people want to find ways to escape the scripts their parents passed on to them regarding relationships. However, many couples do want to emulate their parents' marriage, or at least several aspects of it.

The good news is that the influence of the parents' relationship on your marriage is consistent but not strong. Couples repeatedly show their resiliency and ability to develop a different relationship from that of their parents. Couples also show the ability to assimilate the positive qualities of their parents' marriage while rejecting the negative qualities.

Discussion with Parents Regarding Their Marriage

One way to both understand and overcome relationship scripts that were passed on by parents is to discuss your parents' relationship with them. Adults often find great insight and understanding after discussing with parents their relationship and their views on marriage. Children often have distorted or incomplete memories of their parents' marriage, but the incompleteness of these memories doesn't prevent attitudes from forming. Sometimes children remember certain events as occurring often, when they may actually have occurred only once or twice, and sometimes children do not remember everyday experiences that occurred frequently that were fulfilling and enjoyable for their parents. Usually parents try to shield their children from many of the details of their relationships, adding to the distortion.

Some parents are initially reluctant to disclose details about their relationship, but with persistence they will often share with their adult children experiences that will enrich the lives of all family members. Sometimes it is helpful to explain that you are taking a class on courtship and marriage and your parents' marriage is one of the topics that is being studied. However, if your parents are extremely reluctant to discuss their marriage with you it is probably better to allow them their privacy and trust that with time more information will be forthcoming.

If parents are approachable, talking with them about their relationship can be fulfilling for them, too. Many people do not stop and carefully consider their own relationships and doing so can help them understand their lives better. There is something liberating about seeing growth in our parents. It is helpful to understand how they developed in their relationships over time and to hear about the mistakes they have made. Often knowing more clearly where we came from can help us map out where we are going.

8

Your Relationship with Each Parent

The most frequent source of discord between parents and children is parental insistence that their child perceive matters as they do and respond accordingly—despite St. Paul's warnings that a child can think and understand only as a child and not as adults do.

—Bruno Bettelheim

Mothers and fathers are like primary colors: They are the basic intimate relationship with which all other relationships are mixed. Of the respondents who have completed RELATE, 64% reported living with both biological parents the entire time they were growing up, while only 7% never lived with both biological parents. Although there are a number of people who can fulfill a parenting role, every person has only one biological mother and one biological father. Your experience with each of your biological parents provides the referent with which all other parenting relationships are compared. As you consider your relationship with each parent, think about who you are biologically related to, and who actually nurtured and guided you in your life.

Biological origins and social experience are involved in human development, and there has long been a controversy about which, nature or nurture, makes the most difference. All development is a combination of potential (nature) and opportunity (nurture). In looking at the influence of your relationship with each parent on your adult relationships, you may be able to assimilate the parenting experience by thinking of the same people when you consider your social parents and biological parents. However, some readers will find themselves thinking of a number of different persons and influences that parented them and contributed to their self-perception, depending on the time in their life that is being examined. Here, we'll look at your relationship with each of your parents as you learned about yourself as a human, experienced your worth in relation to other humans, developed social expectations of adults of your gender, and learned how to interact with members of the opposite sex.

Your Biological Self: Who You Are Today

One of the most obvious contributions of biology is physical appearance. Members of families tend to resemble each other. They also have a notion of who they are in the world: the best farmers, the greatest intellects, the best rebels, and so on, and pass on that identity to their members. Based on biology, futures are mapped out and children have the first opportunity to either live up to, or disappoint, the family tradition into which they are born.

Identification

Parents and children can become embarrassed by each other's behavior in a way that friends and strangers do not experience. This is because family members *identify* with each other. They share features such as "noble" noses, bright red hair, tall slender bodies, or short stocky frames. Such shared physical features are often accompanied by family lore, pride, or shame, and the bearer of the trait is often associated with other members of the family who have the same characteristic. What one wears, how one speaks, and one's temperament can all evoke pride or embarrassment, particularly between parents and teens. Do the men in your family pride themselves on their balding heads? Do you have a bumper sticker that says, "Only a few heads are perfect, the rest are covered with hair," or are the men in your family hiding their receding hairlines? Are the women in your family expected to be philanthropists, surgeons, homemakers, or hourly workers? How would your extended family react if you did something unexpected?

We tend to like others whom we experience as being similar to ourselves in appearance, mannerisms, and values. We also tend to be wary of that which is different, or that we cannot understand. Physical similarity to one's parents facilitates bonding (a biologically based mechanism) and attachment (a socially developed mechanism) to assure the survival of the species. The emotional attachment is reinforced by similarity of appearance and mannerisms.

Loyalties

"Blood is thicker than water" is a dictum often used to describe the loyalty within families. This dictum comes with an expectation that families are reasonably self-sufficient, protective units. When the biological and social parents are the same, there is boundary clarity. For better or worse, these parents and children are related. In anger parents may call their child "lazy" and yet be furious to hear someone outside of the family say the same thing. A difficult teenager wrote an angry letter about a school administrator and was required to attend therapy. He was a personable young boy, but typically behaved disrespectfully and was disinterested in what his parents had to say. It was surprising that the reason he cited for writing the letter was the administrator's rudeness toward his parents.

Parenting is tricky, involving a process of being available and letting go at the same time. There is a benefit to learning to achieve this balance. Parents who are able to skillfully balance their child's needs for both independence and guidance were able to keep a closer relationship with their children into adulthood than were other parents. Boundary clarity makes this balancing act easier for everyone.

A dilemma occurs when nonbiological parents are responsible for raising a child. Boss (1988) has discussed a notion of boundary ambiguity in which it is unclear who is in and who is out of a family. Even when a child has never met her or his biological parents (e.g., a child adopted at birth or whose parent was never part of the child's life), the parents are psychologically present in the child's life. Some have referred to these physically absent parents as "ghosts" to which the present parent is constantly compared. Unfortunately, this can interfere with nonbiological relationships because the ghosts can remain flawless in one's imagination, while the present parent will make mistakes. Particularly if the absent parent is alive somewhere, there is a distance that some biological children enforce to protect themselves in case their biological parent were ever to reappear.

The parent-child relationship is the most inherently rewarding, yet potentially distressing, relationship possible. The rules of the relationship are constantly negotiated as each goes through life with new trials and tribulations. The relationship moves from the infant's total dependence on the adult to a potential dependence of the aging adult on the adult child. When the relationship is developed with love and sensitivity to each other's needs, and a trust is developed that transcends the stresses and strains of normal development, the relationship is rewarding and safe. When even one member of the dyad abuses her or his position of emotional or physical power, the relationship can be very painful, and typically participants establish walls for protection that interfere with intimacy in future intimate relationships.

Attachment and Personal Worth

What mental image develops for you when you hear, "That's a kid that only a mother could love." Can you see a slightly dirty-looking eight-year-old little boy, with a slingshot behind his back and a mischievous smile? Parents are supposed to love and care for their children. Mothers are supposedly selfless and revel in the discoveries of their children. Fathers are loving and wise, willing and able to share their perspectives on all potential dilemmas. Not surprisingly, adults who grew up being abused or abandoned frequently ask why their own mothers could not love them. Why their father did not think they were worth protecting. In your relationship with your first love objects, your mother and your father, you learn about love and hate, letting go, and staying present. Fundamentally, you learn about how the world is for you and what kind of behavior you can expect from those whom you depend on and love.

Love and Hate

First love. Intense. Unrequited. This tends to be true in romance and in infancy. In the relationship with a parent, all of a baby's needs are met: food, clothing, shelter, comfort, love, and safety. Without a caregiver, an infant would have no chance for survival. Babies do not "love" their parents, they depend on their parents. To fulfill any wants, babies also must look to their parents. The cry of anger from a frustrated newborn is unmistakable to anyone who has had children. Even toward the parent who has completely frustrated them, babies must learn to smile and babble and engage their caregiver to maintain the relationship in order to receive what they need for survival. It is not surprising that when babies are old enough to realize that their primary caregivers are separate people from themselves, they go through a long period of separation anxiety in which being separated from the caregiver is initially upsetting. Mature, self-assured parents know that these intense infant emotional expressions are about the baby's needs rather than being a statement about the parent. Some parents, however, see these early attempts to meet needs as manipulation and begin retaliating for a baby's unfairness. Babies, most of whom will grow to be husbands or wives, learn early on whether they can get what they want upon request, or if they must take care of themselves. They learn what it means to disappoint others, and whether they are in great danger of retaliation when someone is disappointed in them. They also learn whether they can ever be good enough for those they love and upon whom they depend.

Attachment difficulties from childhood stem from not being able to trust primary caretakers to stay in your life and help to meet your needs. These difficulties persist into adulthood and can be replayed in other intimate relationships such as your marriage and your own parenting. Some adults are good at initiating relationships with others, but have a hard time staying present during difficult times. Rather than maintain the relationship, they may choose to walk away from the intimacy and take care of themselves.

In thinking about your relationship with your parents, ask yourself what happened when the going got tough. Were you and your parents like birds in flight? Some birds fly in formation, taking turns being a leader, and staying close together whatever the weather. Or was your relationship with your parents more like fair weather friends, surrounding you when things were good and you were easy to love, but dispersed if you needed anything? Research has found that the difference between resilient people and people who are not able to recover from childhood problems is that the former had at least one responsible adult in their lives who really cared about them (McHale, 1993; Roosa, 1993). Who taught you about love and that you were worth standing up for, even when things were very difficult? Ideally, it is in your relationship with your parents that this was first experienced.

Of the persons who took RELATE, 62% reported some sort of family stressors. However, 71% with stress characterized their families as positive. Although most families reported a stressor, almost all of them, 93%, reported high levels of positive interaction. Most of the families, then, were able to provide the safe and peaceful environment necessary to provide a strong foundation for adulthood. Not surprisingly, it is the relationship with parents that helps to mediate the effects of any of the stressors on the overall family relationship. Parents are the emotional leaders of the family.

Breaking Away

Evaluating whether a relationship is right for you is important. Very early into a relationship (within two weeks), participants usually know whether it is satisfying enough to maintain (Berg, 1984). Breaking away from a relationship that is not right, however, requires a sound sense of what is appropriate for you and a belief that there is an appropriate relationship available to you outside of the current relationship (Sabatelli, 1987). It also requires confidence that you can end something that is not good for you. Some people do not know how to break up. Either for fear that there will be no other person willing to love them, or for lack of skill in simply letting go when it is appropriate, some relationships continue that never should have begun. It is likely that some of the struggles that people have with breaking up are at least partially related to how they became independent from parents.

How did you separate yourself from your parents and become an adult? What choices did you make that they would have done differently? How did you maintain the quality of your relationship while breaking away in areas in which you needed to be independent? Eighty-five percent of the RELATE respondents reported that their parents encouraged them to be independent and to make their own decisions. There are a number of instances in which children and young adults need to break away from their parents as they are maturing, and it is the parents who need to monitor the tempo of differentiation and connection, allowing differentiation when it is appropriate, while staying connected enough to keep growing up safe. When parents are not able to allow separation, or they encourage it prematurely, problems can develop for their children.

Connectedness

There is a difference between connecting to and suffocating a partner. Babies learn to have less separation anxiety through the experience that their primary love object is dependable and will predictably return for them and care for them. In lives where that predictability was not present in childhood, it is sometimes difficult to maintain healthy connectedness and autonomy. The patterns that parents use to show their love and teach their children to reciprocate love and caring are brought into adult romantic relationships. Connecting is a learned skill that depends on safety and the development of trust in a relationship. When either safety or trust is unavailable, the process of connection can be laden with fear and hurt. The emotional distance with which partners feel comfortable is a reflection of their ability to distinguish trust and separation. How did your parents connect with you? Did they guide you from a distance, or did they try to run your life? Of the people who took RELATE, 19% report that their parents tried to run their lives. In such situations, current relationships can be affected either by identification or reaction. On the one hand, you may identify with your parents and embrace their connecting style (e.g., you may feel compelled to run the life of someone you know, which sometimes translates into being "bossy" or "possessive"). On the other hand, you may react against your parents' dominance by becoming reluctant to do anything that isn't exactly what you want to do, particularly if your partner wants you to do it. As you think about growing up with your parents, do you feel comfortable with the decisions that your parents allowed you to make? Were your parents able to stay connected with you without "butting in"?

True connectedness is the result of mutual give and take, in which the needs of each person are considered. Did your family connect physically (you all were together all of the time) and emotionally (when you were apart you thought of each other, connected with phone calls or letters, etc.)? Were you comfortable with the ways in which your parents connected with each other and with you? The connection with your family probably has an influence on the decisions that you make every day in your current close relationships. Thirty-two percent of the RELATE respondents said that there were matters from their family experience that negatively affected their ability to form close relationships. It is probable that even those 68% who didn't report a negative influence from their family will discover that there are many ways that their relationship with each parent influences their adult relationships with others.

Gender

So far we have been talking about your relationship with your parents as a single entity, focusing on learning about the nurturance and intimacy that characterize the parent-child relationship. Your relationships with your parents are more than that, however. Your relationship with your same-sex parent is quite influential in the ways in which you see yourself as a person of gender, and your relationship with your opposite-sex parent is a practice ground for associating with members of the opposite sex. Living with your parents provides a firsthand look at how women and men think and behave. Did you grow up to be "a chip off the old block"? Will you try to "marry a girl just like the girl that married dear old Dad"?

Your Same-Sex Parent: Your Social Mentor

There is no manual provided with the rules and regulations of how to be a woman or how to be a man. A primary function of families is to socialize the younger members, and part of that socialization is to teach them how to present themselves (e.g., whether to wear ties or dresses) and how to interact with others (e.g., for whom do they open doors, and how much sensitivity they are allowed to exhibit). Although this instruction can be formal (reading a book on etiquette), it is often purely observational. Girls may watch their mothers apply makeup, talk with their fathers, interact with others in the community, and develop an understanding about what women do and do not do in their particular culture. Boys watch the men in their lives, watch them shave their faces, imitate the way they walk, the deepness of their

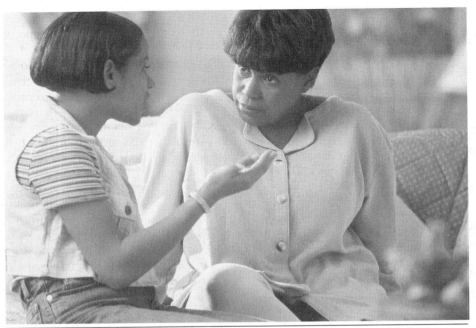

The more time parents and children share together the more time they have for sharing values and beliefs with each other.

voices, and how they behave toward others, and learn what men do and do not do in their particular culture. Certainly there are exceptions to everything. Some girls watch their highly feminine mothers and reject the social construction of gender. Some boys watch the patriarchy of their fathers and decide that they will not perpetuate the inequitable use of power. Children with a close relationship with their parents, however, typically adopt similar values in a number of areas, even if they differentiate themselves with some specific behaviors.

A young adult sat at a formal gathering with his parents. The parents were conservatively dressed. Their son's clothing was appropriate for the occasion, but his hairstyle and color were unique, and he proudly exhibited body piercing and tattoos. He learned the social expectations of men's appearance and behavior (he and his father wore ties, held open doors, sat back quietly while his mother engaged in animated conversations with others around her), yet distinguished himself in other ways. He and his father walked alike, and although the son was much taller than the father, they closely resembled each other. Folk wisdom has asserted that if you want to know what spouses will look and act like after marriage, take a good look at their same-sex parents. The biological inheritance from the same-sex parent and a lifetime of observation and modeling make it likely that they will share a number of characteristics. Without conscious awareness, a child will likely perform behaviors similar to those of her or his parents.

Among the respondents who have taken RELATE, 85% of women reported participating in enjoyable activities with their mothers, and 57% reported being able to share their feelings with their mothers. Seventy-eight percent of men reported participating in enjoyable activities with their fathers, and 39% reported being able to share their feelings with their fathers. These parent-child dyads that shared time and activities together also had more time for sharing values and more opportunities to resolve dilemmas. The more opportunity children and parents have had to disappoint each other, and to rebound from that disappointment with a stronger relationship, the more opportunity they have to be stronger in their belief of what it means to be connected and what it means to be a woman or a man in society.

Opposite-Sex Parent: Lessons in Courtship

Mothers are boys' first love objects and they must break away from their mother and identify with their father, lest their father become angry about their love for their mother. Girls, in love with their father, must identify with their mother in order to not anger their mother over their love for their father. Freud presented these ideas as the Oedipus and Electra complexes. Although psychoanalytic ideas such as this have been the source of discussion and debate for years, the point for this chapter is that most boys do fall in love with their mothers and most girls fall in love with their fathers. Although many reject Freud's idea that this is a "sexual" kind of love, for a period of time during development this love can seem like a type of "romantic" practice for children. On the healthy side, society encourages these role trials with social events such as "father-daughter dinner dances," allowing fathers and daughters to dress up and go on a "date." When unhealthy, these roles are played out in identifying with parental weaknesses such as violent or addictive behaviors.

Among the respondents who have taken RELATE, 76% of women reported participating in enjoyable activities with their fathers and 32% reported being able to share their feelings with their fathers. Eighty-three percent of men reported participating in enjoyable activities with their mothers, and 58% reported being able to share their feelings with their mother. Overall, children are more able to share their feelings with their mothers than they are with their fathers.

Parents and children also demonstrate close physical affection as a way of being close. Of the RELATE respondents, 68% of males said their fathers showed appropriate physical affection to them and 72% of females said their fathers showed appropriate physical affection to them. The percentages were slightly higher for children's experiences with their mothers: 88% of the males and 87% of the females reported that their mothers showed appropriate physical affection toward them.

Although physical affection and other displays of caring are able to create closeness in parent-child relationships, it is likely that the greater comfort with and expression of feelings that mothers and their children have is teaching males and females to not expect as much sharing of feelings from males.

These opposite-sex parent-child dyads who shared time and activities together also had more time for sharing values, opportunities to resolve dilemmas, and

Spending leisure time with Dad gives this daughter an opportunity to learn more about members of the opposite sex.

opportunities to hear how members of the opposite sex respond. It is helpful if this information provides more experience in terms of what you do want in a partner than simply what you do not want in a partner.

Where there is more liking for the opposite-sex parent, there may be better ability to learn to trust the opposite sex, and an opportunity to learn in more depth the effect of one's behavior on a partner. Children do watch the effect of one parent's behavior on the satisfaction of the other parent, particularly the negative effects. Sixty-five percent of women reported that their fathers were happy in their marriages, and 63% of the men reported that their mothers were happy in their marriages. Over 30% of women and men, then, noticed that their opposite-sex parent was unhappy in his or her relationship, and this parenting relationship could provide information that would help children avoid the relational difficulties of their parents.

Fathering

A section on fathering is not often included in a chapter on parental relationships because mothers have historically been the primary socializing parent. Parenthood and motherhood are often understood as synonymous. Typically, mothers connect with their children from birth and assume a great deal of emotional and physical responsibility for their children irrespective of the social context of the relationship. Men, however, tend to have fewer opportunities for learning to nurture, listen to, and connect with their children. Structurally, the American culture is still better suited to maternity leaves than paternity leaves, and when there is a choice to have only one wage earner it is typically the mother who cares for the children full time. Mothers continue to be seen as the more comfortable parent, although something as simple as fathers participating in the prenatal doctor's visits can influence men's participation with their children (Gottman & Declaire, 1997).

Max and Dayna were a dual-earner couple, enjoying their new marriage, when Dayna became pregnant. The two of them went to all of the prenatal appointments together and learned together how to be parents. Max's own father deserted him when he was very young, but he had a stepfather who raised him. Max saw how important mothers were to children, and really did not feel that fathers were particularly critical. Max was prepared for Dayna to be the primary parent, and was sure that he didn't know what to do with a child.

After Billy's birth, Dayna became very depressed. After a few weeks she was not able to care for Billy, and was treated as a psychiatric inpatient so that she could be safe while her depression was stabilized with medication. Max was left to care for Billy. Neither he nor Dayna had family nearby, so Max learned to nurture Billy. In a short period of time he began to feel more comfortable understanding Billy's cries and comforting him. When Dayna returned home, Max transitioned back to work and Dayna once again took over the parenting responsibilities.

Max found that he had loved his time with Billy and enjoyed being with him. He was saddened that his work took him away from home for so long and so often, and he thought about how much he and Billy would miss if he continued his current schedule. Although he knew that he was making a career decision, he chose to take fewer out-of-town opportunities and spend more time with his child.

Clearly, most fathers are not refusing to have a relationship with their children, but are simply unaware of the difference between living with and connecting with a child. This may account for the larger number of respondents who report that they are comfortable talking with their mothers than who report comfort with their fathers. As you think about your father, was he able to stay involved in a conversation with you, or did he lecture to you? When you were upset or hurt, was he able to allow you to talk about your dilemma, understanding your experience, or did he try to solve it for you? Did this differ from the ways in which your mother interacted with you?

Understanding and accepting the experience of another, and conveying that understanding and acceptance back to that person, is the fundamental process of empathy. What is sometimes difficult for people who feel uncomfortable with emotion is that when one listens correctly, and creates an environment of acceptance, others can share strong emotions. The sharing of strong emotions is uncomfortable for some people, particularly if they have been socialized to "fix" things and find that they cannot. Fathers, often, have learned that their role is to earn income and to solve problems. Although society is changing and more people are feeling comfortable taking on egalitarian roles, some socialization has been slow to change, including gender roles in families.

When children have an opportunity to have an ongoing, nurturing, and connecting relationship with their fathers, they have opportunities that are not available when they are interacting primarily with their mothers. Gottman and Declaire (1997) reported that caregiving fathers played differently with children than did mothers, giving the children a wider range of emotional experiences and more active play: The level of excitement is higher and the games involve more inventive rules. These children develop more skills that allow them to reap the benefits of androgynous children: They are more popular with their peers and are more skilled at interacting with a wider range of other people.

Emotional Coaching

In addition to activities, fathers and mothers need to use empathic skills to sustain a connected set of interactions that allow them to share with their children ways of understanding and dealing with the range of feelings that humans experience. The steps to empathically connecting with a child are quite simple, are easily learned (Dossey, 1999), and are at the heart of emotional coaching (Gottman & Declaire, 1997). Emotional coaching includes three components: understanding the emotion of the child, identifying and addressing the needs of the child's emotional experience, and providing a forum for the child to resolve a dilemma. Emotional coaching is also used to help the child understand the interactions between the adults in her or his life. Adults have conflict management styles that can sometimes be difficult for children to understand, and emotional coaching helps them to put the disagreements into context. Five key steps for emotional coaching are presented in *Raising an Emotionally Intelligent Child: The Heart of Parenting* (Gottman & Declaire, 1997). To build empathy into their relationships with their children, parents need to:

1. Be aware of the child's emotions
2. Recognize the emotion as an opportunity for intimacy and teaching
3. Listen empathetically and validate the child's feelings
4. Help the child verbally label emotions
5. Set limits while helping the child problem-solve

These steps are effective for fathers and mothers, but Gottman and Declaire add some suggestions that are particular to men's needs. Structural antinatalism—that is, social structures that create barriers to effective parenting—makes it difficult for men to put limits on their work decisions, and to stay involved in their children's lives after divorce. Although mothers have more opportunities to learn to connect and to actually connect with their children, the father's influence in the child's life, when he maintains a connected and involved relationship, can have a tremendous influence. The most common theme that businessmen articulated about their families after 25 years of being executives was like this statement from the president of Davis, Ball, & Colombatto:

> Twenty-five years ago I didn't know the meaning of the word "balance". . . I know (now) that balance means saying YES to leaving the office early to watch your son's Little League game, and without your cellular phone. It means arriving late to the office because you wanted to drive your daughter to class; or not coming in at all so you can do something that can't be done on the weekend and is important to you. (Edler, 1995, p. 97)

Your father may have been present for you, empathic and bonding, and have shared with you a way of seeing the world as an adult male would understand it. Or maybe your father tried to connect with you, but was only able to manage a loving greeting, a few minutes of listening, and then you bonded side by side watching television. Hopefully you were one of the lucky ones, and your father was aware and able enough to connect with you, heart to heart, about the things that really mattered to you at the moment: missing bugs that you had carefully captured and put in a can, frustrations with teachers and friends, and decisions about whether to go to parties where there was no parental supervision. Fathers can make a difference in their children's lives, but they cannot make a difference if they are not there.

9

The Stress and Trauma in Your Family

> Everything at the Oblonskys' was topsy-turvy. Oblonsky's wife had found out
> that he had been having an affair . . . and told him she could no longer stay
> under the same roof with him. This was the third day things had been this way,
> and . . . the family and the whole household were painfully aware of it.
> Everyone in the house felt that there was no sense in their living together, and
> that people who had casually dropped into any Inn would have more connection
> with each other than they, the Oblonsky family and household. . . . The children
> were running around the house as though lost.
>
> —Leo Tolstoy

As is clear from the great Russian author's description in *Anna Karenina*, traumatic events influence all members of the family. An event such as an affair and the chaos and anger that succeed its discovery can create intense stress in children, family, and friends. An affair, an accident, a death, a serious illness, abuse, natural disasters, frequent moving, an arrest, and other extreme events in life leave an imprint upon the soul. Although people commonly overcome these traumatic experiences, the difficulties are never forgotten and life is forever different.

Too often, psychologists and other helping professionals preach the benefits of a stress-free life and encourage their clients to pursue such a course, almost building up the expectation that life can be smooth and trouble free. However, as clients soon discover, life cannot be controlled so easily, and trauma comes to one and all. Perhaps all of this stress-free emphasis builds up the expectation that life shouldn't include difficulties and troubles and that if it does there must be something wrong with us.

This chapter is not meant to be another voice in the already crowded market of how to live stress-free. It is meant to explore the influence of trauma and stress in the family of origin on the attitudes and relationships of children when they become adults. Although the primary theme will be that these family experiences do influence children throughout their lives, the secondary theme is just as important: Stress and trauma are inevitable and oftentimes it is the overcoming of these traumatic experiences that creates the sensitivity, gentleness, and compassion needed to make relationships work.

Although each life is full of one stress or another, over time capacities can be increased and endurance is strengthened by appropriately responding to this stress. The human body, for example, is a wonderful organism that adapts to the circumstances in which it is placed. When stressed on a regular frequency muscles respond, grow stronger and firmer, and the body can end up with increased capacity to lift, run, jump, and endure. Interestingly, the growth and improvement of muscles involves some degree of pain and difficulty. In fact, the reality is that muscle strengthening is really a process of tearing and rebuilding muscles. The tearing and rebuilding is not so extreme that permanent damage occurs but it is nonetheless a process of injury and repair.

However, should a person be thrust into a physically demanding experience beyond her or his capacity, permanent injury is likely and muscles may be forever changed so that they are always less capable. This occurs because the degree of tearing is too great and the muscles cannot repair themselves unless reattached through surgery. Sometime injuries occur because of extreme damage, such as when bones are broken or crushed, or nerves are severed. Such injuries may not occur because of a physically demanding experience, but because something unexpected or accidental does direct harm of an extreme nature to the body.

There are certain limits to what can be endured and certain extreme circumstances will produce serious, often permanent, injury. These extreme experiences are often called "traumatic." Although some people recover almost completely from trauma, others become devastated and are never whole again; so it is with emotional and psychological well-being. The differences in how people recover seem to be related to innate capacities, support systems, the nature of the trauma, and choices that are made regarding how to respond to the trauma.

Not all trauma is the same. Much depends on whether the trauma comes from inside or outside the family and on the amount of control the recipients of trauma perceive. The different types of trauma that will be discussed in this chapter can be divided between experiences that might be called *volitional,* in that they occur because of family members' choices, such as affairs, divorce, abuse, and arrests, and those that can be labeled *nonvolitional* because they are not the result of choices, such as losing a job because of a plant closure, someone dying from an accident, natural disasters, or an assault by a criminal. Although these two categories are not entirely separate (leaving your doors unlocked may make you more vulnerable to robbery), in general they are distinct and different in one important way: who is responsible for the trauma. Although you might have a little responsibility for a burglary of your home if you don't lock your doors, the primary and most important responsibility rests with the burglar. Because family members are responsible for such traumas as divorce and abuse, these experiences can leave the victims unsure about the safety of family relationships, and can change attitudes about the value of marriage, parents, and even life in general. The trauma that occurs because of an act of nature or an assault from someone outside the family leaves people less secure in the predictability of the world in general and can lead to distrust of outsiders, but family members are not usually blamed for these experiences and the effects are often very different.

Trauma Resulting from Volitional Acts

When family members, especially parents, make certain choices there are clear negative effects that are experienced as traumatic or highly stressful by others. Some of these choices, such as divorce and alcohol abuse, are so common now that millions of people are victimized each year. This has led some people to question whether something so common as divorce is really as traumatic as others say. This argument is specious and missing the point. Even if everyone in a nation experiences certain events, such as warfare, it doesn't change the effects of the experiences; it should only change the number of people who are understanding and compassionate to those who suffer. The research on even these "common" types of trauma continues to demonstrate that long-term difficulties are experienced by family members.

Divorce, Separation, Extreme Marital Conflict, Affairs

Never have so many people grown up in homes where both biological parents were not together. Approximately 25% of the adults between the ages of 18 and 44 had parents who divorced. Only about 26% of households represent married parents with children. (Wallerstein, Lewis, & Blackslee, 2000). Even if the separation or divorce occurred when the child was very young, there is a significant and ongoing loss that surrounds the child. This experience of loss is the defining characteristic of all trauma. Whatever form it takes, trauma means deep and difficult loss. Who can gauge the loss of the child who experiences emotional pain each time "father" is mentioned? Who can determine the real effects on a child who associates "marriage" with memories of the two most important people she knows screaming at each other and saying awful things to one another? These losses must be acknowledged, and overcome one way or another.

Divorce and other forms of marital distress have been extensively studied and documented (Amato, 2001; Amato & Keith, 1991; Reifman, Villa, Amans, Rethinam, & Telesca, 2001). Although there is much written on how to get through a divorce with as little damage as possible, the idea that divorce can occur without serious negative consequences to family members is a fallacy. Trauma affects people and changes their experiences in courtship and marriage. Yet, many if not most people find ways to overcome these traumatic experiences and lead happy, fulfilling lives. The difficulties caused by trauma can be minimized through discussions between partners and family members, and through attempts at resolution and

The effects of divorce can include short-term distress for the couple and children as well as long-term adjustment problems.

growth. Denial of the trauma or its effects extends and exacerbates the possible negative outcomes.

Some of the most common effects of divorce on children include the following (Amato & Keith, 1991; Reifman et al., 2001; Wallerstein et al., 2000):

- Lower school achievement
- A higher risk of being abused or neglected
- Higher levels of immature behavior
- Higher levels of depression and anxiety
- Lower self-esteem
- Poorer social adjustment
- Less satisfying relationships with each parent
- Lack of good role models for marriage
- Higher levels of substance abuse
- Less hope that marriage might last
- Higher likelihood of living in poverty

These negative effects are also the same for children who grew up in homes where there was high conflict and violence between parents (Amato, Loomis, & Booth, 1995). This finding has led some people to conjecture that it is worse for a child if parents stay together when they are not getting along than it is if they divorce. Some research does indicate that children do improve if their parents divorce when conflict is high or violence is occurring between parents (Amato et al., 1995; Horn, 2000). Yet when parents are unsatisfied in their relationship but are not in extremely hostile relationships, children do better if parents stay together. Importantly, only 30% of the couples that divorce have hostile or violent relationships (Horn, 2000). This means that in most cases parents could improve their relationships or just stay together and children would be better off. Wallerstein et al. (2000) have asserted that divorce for children becomes a theme for their book of life, whereas divorce for adults is merely a chapter in their life book. Regardless, as adults we are stuck with the decisions our parents made and must figure out what to do about them.

The results from people who have taken RELATE provide some hope that the effects of divorce can be overcome. Those respondents who had divorced parents had poorer relationships with their fathers and did not place as much importance on marriage as those with parents who stayed together. However, levels of self-esteem, maturity, substance abuse, depression, and couple stability were not different between the two groups. Most of the respondents and their relationships were young, however, so the long-term effects, both positive and negative, may emerge later in life, as some suggest (Wallerstein et al., 2000).

Sometimes those who came from divorced families have a forward-looking perspective and desire to just forget about the past and move on. This attitude is not problematic as long as the children of divorced couples do not use it as an excuse to avoid addressing unresolved feelings and difficulties with family members. Resolving anger or disappointment toward one or both parents who divorced can help adults improve their romantic relationships. Each of us seems to understand and know that retaining frustration or anger toward someone interferes with other relationships. Negative emotions take up energy and reduce stamina over time and they make us more sensitive to the actions of others that are similar to the actions that caused us pain in our families. This reduced stamina and increased reactivity is not an insignificant problem that can just be forgotten by focusing on the future. As the unresolved feelings are discussed and progress is made, there is usually a sense of freedom and growth. Also, the improvement in family relationships can help these relationships become a source of support rather than a drain on energy.

Physical Abuse

Using physical pain as a form of punishment continues to be a common technique that parents use toward their children. The use of hitting—"spanking"—by parents is one of the more controversial topics in modern family life. When does hitting become physically abusive? Some would say any hitting, whether called spanking or discipline, is an abuse of power, while others would say that there is nothing wrong with spanking if used properly. So what is abuse and what isn't?

Abuse is whenever someone misuses authority or power to vent frustrations, anger, or strong feelings on someone else in a way that is injurious. With this broad definition we are all abusive, even though we do not all belong in jail. Haven't we all inflicted pain on others who didn't deserve it? Isn't this abusive? It is important to recognize that power is commonly misused by all of us. Making improvements in the use of our authority or power is something to keep as a lifetime goal.

However, usually "physical abuse" is used to label hitting or other acts that cause injuries to the child, or that occur frequently, or are so harsh that the child is demeaned and humiliated. In the RELATE questionnaire, the more extreme forms of abuse, such as slapping, pushing, kicking, hitting with a fist, or hitting with an object, are used to designate physical violence. This is not an exhaustive list, as there are many forms of violence that are traumatic, but it includes the most common forms of harsher physical violence in families.

Table 9.1 illustrates that physical abuse is occurring in the majority of the families of those who have taken RELATE. Nevertheless, most of the physical abuse is happening only rarely or sometimes. In addition, males and females are reporting similar levels of violence in their homes.

Table 9.2 demonstrates that in more than 30% of the families, there is violence between the parents, a particularly destructive form of violence in terms of how it affects children and how it affects the quality of the home environment. Surprisingly, almost 40% of the people who took RELATE report that they were violent toward another family member. The family members who were most likely to be violent were fathers, including stepfathers, followed closely by brothers. Sisters were the least likely to be violent.

What does all of this mean? It suggests that most people are experiencing violence in their lives while growing up and many who are not personally victimized by violence are at least witnessing it. What are the effects of this violence? Certainly some of this violence includes rare fights between siblings. This fighting between siblings, if it occurs rarely and is not extreme, probably has few lasting negative effects on family members. Part of growing up and maturing includes learning to control emotions and actions that could cause injury to others. Families are the places people must learn these lessons and sometimes mistakes are made. However, physical abuse is another matter. When a child is physically abused or is a witness to physical abuse between other family members, the effects can be devastating and long lasting.

Competing Needs. There are two major needs within each child—the need to belong and the need to be unique (Busby & Smith, 2000). If development works

TABLE 9.1 *Percentages of Males and Females Who Reported Physical Violence in Their Homes*

Level of Violence	Males	Females
There was **never** physical violence in the home	48%	47%
There was **rarely** physical violence in the home	31%	31%
There was **sometimes** physical violence in the home	14%	15%
There was **often** physical violence in the home	5%	5%
There was **very often** physical violence in the home	2%	2%

TABLE 9.2 *Percentages of Males and Females Who Reported Different Types of Violence in the Home*

Violence Statements	Males	Females
Someone in the family was violent	53%	52%
Your father was violent toward your mother	28%	28%
Your mother was violent toward your father	24%	20%
You were violent in your family	42%	35%

properly and the home environment is nurturing and safe, the child is able to find her uniqueness through belonging. A connection is built in the early years that lets her know she is loved for who she is, not what she does. She learns through this connection that she is a combination of her father and mother, with whom she identifies deeply. Yet she also realizes as she exercises her will that she is more than a simple combination of her parents—she is unique. However, the struggle to belong and to be unique creates tension, anxiety, or frustration. As the child struggles with these competing desires, sometimes she acts out and feels like there is a monster inside her. Consider the typical temper tantrum of the young child in a grocery store. She wants a candy but her parent says no. The child is connected to her parent, but at the moment the need to be unique is stronger and the tension builds. The child persists with her will, her uniqueness, and the parent persists with a "no." Then a tantrum develops, with the child trying to win over the parent. If the parent is mature and wise she or he will model for the child a way of not losing control. This allows the child to learn to control her violent impulses because every day she sees parents who are usually under control. She learns that the natural progression is to begin to discipline herself, to act in ways that are not injurious to others.

When abuse occurs within the family this whole process goes awry. The child cannot connect because it is not safe. She cannot fully identify with her parents because she has feelings of hate and protection toward them. Instead of having the luxury of worshipping her parents when she is young, in her innocence, and slowly coming to the realization that they are imperfect humans, she must deal with the reality that her parents are part monster before she has learned to control the monster within herself. When the child feels the tension that comes from wanting to belong and wanting to be unique, she cannot express it at all because anger and frustration have led to so much damage in her family. When she tries to express her anger it is not tolerated or she is severely punished. A vicious cycle develops in which the child cannot connect because it is not safe. Hence, she cannot understand how she is unique because she has never connected. She pursues connection and uniqueness nonetheless, but each time seems to be further away, less sure of who she is and more sure that she is not loved.

Choices for Physically Abused Children.   Often children who are traumatized are left to do one of three things. First, as their need to connect is thwarted it becomes greater and greater and they become clingy, usually to the parent who is most often a victim. As these children grow older they sometimes try to be the perfect child so that there is never any reason for parents to get upset. The second option is that children can begin to act out, which in the end is identifying with the perpetrator. They cope with the world through fighting and trying to control anything and everyone through aggression or other manipulative behaviors. The third option is to withdraw into depression, anxiety, or even to literally run away. In some instances children may adopt all three approaches, alternating between withdrawal, aggression, and hypercompliance at different stages of their life.

Messages Learned from Physical Abuse in Families.   The most destructive message that is sent in violent families about anger is to blame others for outbursts. "You make me so angry"; "I wouldn't explode if you didn't keep making stupid mistakes"; "I only lose control when you pester me for hours on end"; "I wish you would just behave and then we wouldn't have so much conflict around here." These and other remarks regularly reinforce the idea that other people make us angry and we are justified in our explosiveness. The beginning step to overcoming the effects of violence is learning to take responsibility for your anger and your violence. Nobody can make you violent; it is always a matter of choice. This step of taking responsibility may be one that has to be retaken many times before it results in change. When violent and controlling behaviors have become a common approach to relationship problems, it is usually necessary to get assistance from professionals to stay on the difficult path of change and healing.

Sexual Abuse

This form of trauma can be particularly devastating to victims. It is not only a physical trauma but it is an invasion of the very private, personal, and sacred parts of an individual for the gratification of someone else. Added to all the destructive effects of physical abuse are the struggles with sexuality and intimacy that are likely to occur when a child is introduced into sexual behaviors by another. Rather than experiencing sexual intimacy as a beautiful part of adult relationships that can be learned in a safe, trusting, and committed relationship, sexuality can become a feared, hated, and confusing experience. To make matters worse, sometimes perpetrators of sexual abuse present their behaviors to the victims as a way to show love and affection. The result may be that children have a difficult time recognizing that they are victims and affection may be viewed as something aversive.

In Table 9.3 some patterns of sexual abuse are apparent. The most common perpetrator of sexual abuse is a relative other than a parent or sibling. The second most common perpetrator is likely to be a father or stepfather, and then a brother. Females are twice as likely as males to report sexual abuse in their homes. However, of the people who have taken RELATE, women were much more likely to be sexually abused by dating partners or friends than by family members. Sexual abuse in the dating relationship will be discussed in Chapter 16.

One of the keys to healing from sexual abuse is the presence of a supportive relationship, usually with a family member (Busby & Preece, 2000). The effects of a

TABLE 9.3   *Percentages of Males and Females Who Reported Different Types of Sexual Abuse in Their Homes*

Sexual Abuse Statement	Males	Females
A family member was sexually abusive to the respondent	5%	9%
Someone outside the family was sexually abusive to the respondent	5%	17%
Other family members were sexually abused but not the respondent	4%	9%
The respondent was sexually abusive to another family member	4%	2%

strong supportive relationship with a family member are so powerful as to almost entirely remove the effects of abuse on the self-esteem of the victims (Busby & Preece, 2000). These findings are hopeful and speak to both the innate capacity of humans to recover and the healing powers of supportive relationships.

Psychological/Emotional Abuse

The trauma experienced by some people is not so easy to define as physical or sexual abuse. Many people have home environments in which they frequently feel disrespected, humiliated, and abused, even though they may never be hit or sexually violated. Again, perhaps the most destructive component of such treatment is that it comes at the hands of those who should be the child's greatest advocates, protectors, and supporters. A negative result of such treatment is that it might leave a person feeling that relationships are not safe and supportive, but are instead destructive or painful. The possible negative consequences are great for individuals, couples, families, and communities when numerous people are leaving their families with such attitudes toward relationships.

From the analyses of RELATE responses, approximately 20% of females and 17% of males feel that relationships are not safe, rewarding, or a source of support. If these results are in any way representative of national norms, millions of individuals are very skeptical about relationships and expect them to be primarily negative experiences. In the end, the only solution to such attitudes is having better experiences in relationships. New relationships that are rewarding and supportive will provide the only true evidence for individuals that all relationships need not be destructive and painful.

Drug Addiction

Twenty-eight percent of the male RELATE respondents and 33% of female respondents are reporting that at least one member of their immediate family struggled with addiction to alcohol or other drugs. Individuals respond in a variety of ways to the addictions of family members. Some try to rescue and support addicted members until they are forced to realize they cannot change the addict; others get angry and don't want anything to do with the addict; while some remain relatively oblivious to the problem. Addictions are powerfully negative forces in families and usually are accompanied by other problems such as violence, affairs, and neglect.

Repairing family relationships that have been injured by substance abuse is challenging. If the family member is still using the substance it is impossible to repair the relationship, because the addict's primary commitment will be to the drug rather than to people. Sometimes it takes many years before an addict's life falls apart to the point of causing behavior change. Unfortunately, most addicts will solicit help from family members whenever they are in dire straits, only to return to their addiction time and time again. When dealing with a family member who is addicted, a no-tolerance stance, clear setting of boundaries, and a refusal to cover for the addict are necessary steps to take to avoid getting pulled into the addictive cycle with the addict. Often it is helpful to attend Al-Anon or other support meetings for family members of addicts. These meetings can be a great asset in helping family members keep aware of the patterns that addicts have that can trap family members. Al-Anon meetings are also helpful in keeping the responsibility for the addiction with the user rather than the family members. Support groups are helpful in talking through the intense feelings that accompany the violations, abandonment, and abuse that are part of the addictive cycle.

Some research suggests that addictions to drugs have a genetic origin. If this is true, children who had family members who were addicted may want to avoid drugs altogether even if they are legal and accessible, such as alcohol.

Trauma Resulting from Nonvolitional Acts

Numerous difficulties can afflict families as a result of nonvolitional acts. Problems that might be traumatic to family members include unemployment, frequent moves, poverty, chronic illness and impairments, assault, robbery, and death. Although it is beyond the scope of this chapter to cover all these traumas, it is important to consider common responses that families might adopt to cope with trauma and how these coping responses might be helpful or harmful to children.

Trauma has a way of exacerbating existing weaknesses in family relationships and within individuals. This means that if a person tends to be too critical, after a traumatic experience criticism is likely to become even worse. If a relationship is plagued by unclear communication, communication will usually erode even further after trauma is experienced.

These weaknesses of individuals and relationships may be viewed in the same way as a weak knee or a fragile hip would be seen. If family members can quickly recognize that the additional stress is causing preexisting weaknesses to become worse, steps can be taken to minimize the pain. Just as a person would learn to wear a knee brace when involved in a physical activity that is more risky, families can take extra precautions to avoid injury. Usually when involuntary traumas have occurred, if family members are willing to be more careful in how they treat each other, be more forgiving, seek support from friends and extended family, and avoid drawing incorrect conclusions about relationships during times of trouble, the difficulties can be weathered and relationships will actually grow stronger. However, this positive outcome is not always achieved, and sometimes family relationships seem to unravel after a traumatic event. Nevertheless, when the trauma is not a result of volitional acts, relationship repair may be easier to accomplish than if the trauma was a result of willful, injurious acts.

Death

Eleven percent of RELATE respondents experienced the loss of a parent. When this 11% is added to the percent of those who have lost a sibling or another close relative, it is likely that death is the most common nonvolitional traumatic event in the lives of individuals.

Losing a loved one can shake a person's foundation. All that seemed stable and good in life can become sour. The immune systems of surviving family members may become weaker and depression may result for a period of time. Sometimes family relationships that continue are neglected because the grief is so consuming that emotional resources are low.

Death is the most common type of extreme stress that family members go through.

A key to recovering from death is the availability of a supportive system within which the grief can be expressed. The support system may be friends, family, or community relationships. As loss and loneliness are such central feelings after the death of a family member, sharing these feelings with another is the best antidote. Additionally, sharing intense, difficult feelings in a trusting relationship is one of the primary mechanisms for building intimacy and love. Hence it is often the case that if family and friends can provide this vital support, the loss is slowly overcome by deeper, more meaningful relationships with others.

Although people can carry on after a loved one's death, it is devastating enough to create a guardedness or fear of being hurt in some people. Another response to death may be bitterness toward God or others. These less functional responses to death may be temporary attitudes or they may become a permanent approach to life.

Evaluating the Effects of Trauma

It is essential for people who have experienced any type of trauma to evaluate the effects of this trauma on the self and on relationships. Few people will experience trauma without some negative effects that will require extended periods of time and effort to resolve. It may be helpful to construct a stress and trauma genogram to illustrate the trauma you have gone through and consider the effects on you and your relationships. It is sometimes useful to designate which of the issues are still unresolved and which seem to be resolved. An example of a stress and trauma genogram is illustrated in Figure 9.1. The italic text indicates unresolved issues. To resolve an issue it may be necessary to have conversations with family members that are tense and difficult. Sometimes, such as with Rose's refusal to deal with her divorce in Figure 9.1, issues will never be resolved. This is an issue that is only likely to affect Alice in an indirect way and it may be that pushing for resolution will cause more problems than it solves. However, it does seem that it might be useful for Alice to resolve her issues with her brother Thomas. She may be able to successfully do this by having another family member assist them during their conversations.

When determining whether to resolve unfinished issues in family relationships, it may be helpful to consider the following questions.

1. Am I likely to be interacting with the family member for many more years?
2. Do I find myself reacting to other people who remind me of the family member?
3. Is the issue I'm still struggling with something that may affect my reactions to current partners or future partners?
4. Could the person in my family who has the unresolved issue be a source of support and help to me if the issue were resolved?
5. Do I find myself regularly thinking about the unresolved issue?
6. Do I find myself reacting strongly to similar issues in a way that seems out of proportion to the problem?

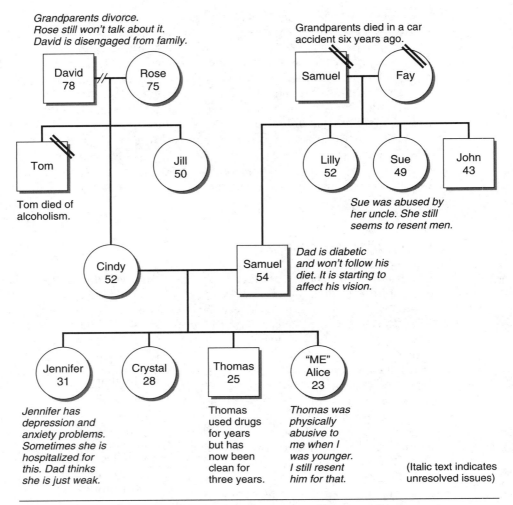

Grandparents divorce.
Rose still won't talk about it.
David is disengaged from family.

Grandparents died in a car
accident six years ago.

David
78

Rose
75

Samuel

Fay

Tom

Jill
50

Lilly
52

Sue
49

John
43

Tom died of
alcoholism.

Sue was abused by
her uncle. She still
seems to resent men.

Cindy
52

Samuel
54

Dad is diabetic
and won't follow his
diet. It is starting to
affect his vision.

Jennifer
31

Crystal
28

Thomas
25

"ME"
Alice
23

Jennifer has
depression and
anxiety problems.
Sometimes she is
hospitalized for
this. Dad thinks
she is just weak.

Thomas
used drugs
for years
but has
now been
clean for
three years.

Thomas was
physically
abusive to
me when I
was younger.
I still resent
him for that.

(Italic text indicates
unresolved issues)

FIGURE 9.1   *Example of a Three-Generation Stress and Trauma Genogram*

If you answered yes to any of these questions it may be worth the extra effort to try to resolve the issue. In instances of abuse or addictions, a professional therapist may be able to facilitate resolution of the problem, especially if the therapist has special training in working with trauma.

10

Gender, Race, Ethnicity, and Geography

> *. . . family structures are not simply personal arrangements among family members. They are manifestations of the values of the cultural group to which the family belongs.*
>
> —Harry Aponte

Is it the thrill of differences or the comfort of similarity that creates a successful marriage? Choosing a lifelong partner can be challenging. Sociologists in the 1960s and 1970s thought similarity of race and ethnicity led to relationship stability. Sociological literature focused on issues of **homogamy,** marriage between spouses of similar sociodemographic characteristics, and **heterogamy,** marriage between spouses of different sociodemographic characteristics. Many couples were homogamous, particularly in terms of residential background, age, race, education, and socioeconomic status (Levinger & Rands, 1985). Udry (1966) proposed that homogamous marriages were the products of (1) social organizations that enable persons to meet others like themselves, (2) social prescriptions that encouraged homogamy and discouraged heterogamy, and (3) similarities among homogamous persons in attitudes, mannerisms, and vocabulary that contributed to easy interaction. The situation seems to be similar for relationships today. Of the respondents who have taken RELATE, 80% are very homogamous, 14% are moderately homogamous, and only 6% are heterogamous.

Homogamy alone, however, is insufficient as an explanation of what creates stability. Researchers found that although a number of people who married were homogamous, there were also a number of people who were homogamous who divorced. Hill, Rubin, and Peplau (1976) suggested that couples who were somewhat alike in age, educational plans, intelligence, and physical attractiveness were more likely to stay together than those couples who were not similar in these areas. Stable dating couples tended to match on social attitudes and values, but not necessarily on religious denomination, sex-role traditionalism, religiosity, or desired family size. Marriage fulfills both social and personal needs, and its success depends to a large extent on whether it supports and is supported by the needs of a larger cultural group within which it is nested. Race, ethnicity, and geography were associated with relationship stability but their influence was based in the attitudinal similarity that came with common experiences. Homogamous couples shared patterned and predictable ways of thinking, feeling, and behaving as products of their environmental training. In the long run it was, in fact, the similarity or dissimilarity in attitudes and behaviors that were found to distinguish those who stayed together from those who divorced (Hill, Rubin, & Peplau, 1976). Among those respondents who have taken RELATE, 31% report very similar values, and 64% some similar values. Only 5% have few similar values with their partners.

Examining the social context, then, merely provides a glimpse of the issues that couples may need to negotiate in marriages. The degree to which those challenges will be successfully navigated is largely dependent on the interpersonal process that couples use in their relationships (Kelley, 1979). All heterosexual couples bring at least one major cultural issue into their relationships: gender role socialization. The differences in genetics and training that are commonplace in even the most equalitarian households means that the thinking, feeling, and behaving of women and men provide fertile ground for cultural dissimilarity. Fortunately, the ways in which couples use their dissimilarities is more influential in their satisfaction than simply having dissimilarities:

> Klaus and Maria were married for seven years and were stuck in a hostile pattern of interaction that made for a destructive marriage. They had each recently immigrated to the United States: Klaus was a new citizen, and Maria had not yet applied for citizenship. The issues that they fought over most frequently dealt with cultural expectations for patterns of behavior: the role of in-laws, use of money, power, and privilege. The therapist encouraged the couple to explore their own cultures and talk with each other about the expectations that they brought into the marriage. This infuriated Klaus. He asserted that it was ridiculous to imply that they even try to understand each other because they were who they were, and their differences were between them, not their ethnicity. They had been married for more years than most of their friends who were Americans, and Klaus explained with pride that his marriage was just like any other American marriage. Klaus was right: His marriage was just like any other American marriage in which the couple disrespected each other, lacked the insight into their partner's interpretation of particular behaviors, and were willing to relentlessly insult each other during arguments. In fact, their process of defensiveness and stonewalling was impenetrable. What they could become good at, with intervention and an openness to change, was recognizing the subtle nuances of their partners' expectations in everyday behaviors. A simple lack of understanding kept them from being able to successfully connect with each other. Without the ability to understand the partner's ways of thinking, feeling,

and behaving, the couple could only take information out of context and put it into a model for which it was poorly fit. They had no apparent method of enjoying each other's differences because they did not know how to understand the behavior of the other.

Members of subcultures tend to have needs that are distinctive and not known by members of the larger culture. Everyone must know the rules of the larger culture to succeed, but members of the larger culture do not need to know the nuances of minority cultures (Walters, Carter, Papp, & Silverstein, 1988). If the language of the culture is English, and you speak English, there is no reason to need another language. If, however, you speak Polish and the dominant culture speaks English, you will need to learn English in addition to Polish. Those who are the least powerful are dependent on the satisfaction of the more powerful partners, and therefore are vigilant of the moods and attitudes of those who are more powerful. Rules in the larger culture tend to be geared for an American prototype: an English-speaking, Caucasian, Protestant male. People who fit these characteristics are also seen to have more potential power than, for example, a non-English speaking female of color. Rules of interaction differ according to personal characteristics and social context: for the young and old, for women and men, and for traditional and egalitarian couples.

A challenge of marriage and its interaction with the social context is that the rules are shaped and negotiated as the couple moves from the early stages (e.g., pre-parenthood) through the middle years (parenthood and launching) to the years of retirement (older adults with no children). At each stage gender roles evolve, rules and rituals from one's ethnicity become more or less important, and geographic residence may change. As you think about the marriages among your family and friends, what do you notice about what is expected from married couples? In some cases, social groups determine the couple's residence: Some cultures insist on **matrilocal** residence (living near the woman's family), some insist on **patrilocal** (living near the man's family), and other's allow for **neolocal** (the couple selects a residence away from both sets of parents). Sometimes the functions of the married couples are to perform certain acts of assistance, such as being an additional set of parents to the children of close friends and family members by taking care of children. In other cases, married couples are completely independent of others and are expected to take care of themselves and their families without seeking to give and receive help from the social network. Marriage can be viewed sometimes as the initiation into true adulthood, and in other cases it is seen as little more than a piece of paper forcing the members into an uncomfortable set of rules. As you think about the married couples you know, which expectations for residence, assistance, or adult status are relevant to you?

Social Purpose of Marriage

The social purpose of marriage is to perpetuate the species and stabilize the adult personality. Marriage itself is an institution that includes the negotiation of marital roles (e.g., who should earn the money and who should nurture the children), companionship (e.g., hiking together, going to movies together), and resources (e.g., saving money for a house or spending money on consumable items). Depending on the goal of a specific marriage, some of these issues are more important than others. Prince Charles, the heir to the throne of England, was not allowed to marry anyone who was not a virgin and from a royal family. Undoubtedly, his son (Prince William) will face similar constraints in his selection of a partner. He is strongly encouraged to marry **endogamously** (i.e., within his social group) and refusing to do so could cost him his opportunity to be the King of England.

Americans also have mandates for endogamous marriages. For example, the marriage between the Onassis and Kennedy families assured that a large amount of wealth stayed in the control of those two families. **Exogamous** marriages occur between members of different social groups. Tribes have been known to encourage exogamous marriages to create peace between two conflicting groups. In the United States, marrying a member of a higher economic strata gives a partner access to more resources than would have otherwise been available to the lower economic family. In part, a mission of the Reverend Sun Myung Moon is to create world peace by performing marriages between people of different races and of different national origins.

A family in New York sent their daughter to Greece each summer to live with her extended family so that she would have the opportunity to meet and marry a Greek man, which she did. Ethnic similarity was more important to her family than residential propinquity (marrying a person from the same or an adjacent location). In some economic strata there are hopes that members will marry "up" financially. In the American culture, women are more often encouraged to marry "up" than are men, and typically that upward mobility is limited to one to two socioeconomic levels from the birth status. For the respondents who completed RELATE, however, 57% were similar to their partners in family income, and of the groups who differed in income there was no pattern of one gender marrying up more than another. Understandably, when someone does marry up or down in socioeconomic status it is not always as easy as it may appear. Consider the marriage of Maggie and Sol:

> Maggie and Sol worked through the difficulty of socializing with Sol's business associates. Maggie was born into a lower-middle-class family, and had little interest in college. Sol was from a middle-upper-class family, and his family was known for its wealth and generosity in its small town. A university education was expected in his family; for her, there was no family expectation that she should go beyond the twelfth grade. She did attend a community college for one semester before quitting and going to work full time. She was happy to be married and was anxious to begin her family. She had grown up believing that only very intelligent people had college degrees, and she did not consider herself to be very intelligent. She did, however, know that she was wise, and a good wife, and would be a good mother.
>
> When she described the problem concerning her husband's associates, she took pride in the idea that she had more manners than they

did. At first she felt like they were all smarter than she was, but after a while it was clear that when they were all together, rather than discussing topics requiring extreme intelligence they engaged in discussions that tapped their collegiate social experiences. As they would reminisce they would exclude this new wife from the discussion. She saw that her job was to be a part of Sol's social events, and she worked to redirect the discussions to areas in which she had experience and felt competent. She had decided to not allow the social network to interfere in her marriage, but at the same time she was angry at her husband for insisting they socialize with such rude friends. This network was very important to the husband, but so was Maggie's happiness. Social networks are powerful, and until this marriage Sol had not needed to look at his social network from the perspective of a woman or a working-class person.

Within which social group are you expected to select your partner? Are the members of your social network concerned about race, ethnicity, economic strata, or geography? What are the characteristics of potential partners who are in your **pool of eligibles** (that is, the group of people from which an individual can choose an appropriate partner for marriage)?

Choosing an Eligible Mate

Although arranged marriages are rare in the United States, families and friends often help to select partners for their members with introductions and blind dates. When that is unsuccessful, it is increasingly common for singles to reach out to some of the formal dating services that are widely available. Although they manifest in a number of ways, gender roles and culturally based behaviors underlie all of the behavioral strategizing that is used in developing a relationship that leads to marriage. The dating process is a filtering screen in which those whose attitudes and behaviors are similar have an opportunity to become more involved with each other, and those who are not similar are able to separate.

Throughout the media, through social activities, and through folklore, unmarried members of the culture are taught to view some persons as members of their pool of eligibles, and others as outside of that pool. It takes only a quick look around in any community to know what that profile looks like. The pool of eligibles is that narrowed population from which a particular person may select a partner. Breaking convention in marital choices and choosing outside of the pool of eligibles can cause difficulty throughout the extended family. A humorous portrayal of such difficulty was illustrated in the 1960s Sydney Poitier movie *Guess Who's Coming for Dinner?*, in which a white woman brought home an African American man to meet her family. The movie portrays the family's difficulty with initially receiving this guest and accepting the notion that their daughter has chosen a partner who is clearly outside of the pool of eligibles.

Children are fairly clear about the expectations of their parents, particularly in relation to the pool of eligibles. When children know that a partner is outside of their parents' approval they spend more time building up that partner to their parents before they introduce the partner in person and reveal the exogamous characteristics (Leslie, Huston, & Johnson, 1986).

Final mate selection is often based on the couple's feelings of love for each other. Their experiences of dating typically include intimate interactions that become increasingly interdependent until they have considerably overlapped (Levinger & Snoek, 1972). Out of those interactions grow interdependence and love. The American macroculture is romantic and expects premarital love to be romantic, containing passion, intimacy, and commitment. Other cultures, however, are more concerned with the practical aspects of love than the romance. A 30-year-old, religiously conservative husband described his partner selection this way:

> My wife didn't love me before we got married. She had received two proposals, and I was the more logical choice. I think that she loved the other guy more, but he wasn't very ambitious, and she knew I was a hard worker. We knew that we could fall in love later, so she picked me.

Some researchers have found that closeness and trust are most easily created between two persons of a common background (Sherman, Oresky, & Roundtree, 1991). Sherman and colleagues have also suggested that such similarity in marriage involves similarity in cultural heritage, socioeconomic status, level of acculturation, and degree of traditionalism. Homogamous couples share a number of similar attitudes, preferences, and personal characteristics prior to meeting each other, which facilitates the experience of being known. People tend to like others who are much like themselves, and tend to prefer to socialize with people who have similar values and attitudes, and with whom a common language and dialect is shared (Kelley, 1979).

Social support from friends and family is a positive predictor of later relationship quality, especially for women (Doxey & Holman, 2001). It is the social world that stabilizes the adult personality and supports or distracts from a relationship. The social world is effective because the approval or disapproval of others has an impact on the couple. With their approval or disapproval, social networks gain the compliance of their members, and that compliance generally results in marriage between members of the same social grouping. In cases where people marry others who are outside of that which would normally be accepted by their social world, they tend to be differentiated from their community and are prepared to proceed without the support of their friends and family. In fact, marriage between people of two different backgrounds or identities in some instances may represent a situation in which the members of the couple are trying to become differentiated from their family of origin, and selecting such a partner helps to establish boundaries of separation. These individuals may also be somewhat rebellious or adventurous or overreacting to the struggles they have had with their parents (McGoldrick, Preto, Hines, & Lee, 1991):

> A young, athletic couple came to a marriage and family therapist for help with moving their relationship toward marriage. The problem was clear

to them: Their families kept interfering in the relationship. Jane was a very reserved British subject, and Paul was a second-generation, passionate Italian American. The couple saw these differences as stimulating, but their parents were alarmed. The couple insisted that they enjoyed the difference they each brought to the marriage, although each community was doubtful that they would be successful in their union. The couple had a choice of finding ways of convincing the members of their families that this relationship was worth marrying outside of their prospective communities, or they could choose to stop listening to the objections. They had avoided many of the difficult discussions that their families thought were necessary to discuss. Their social network refused to overlook the differences in their relationship because their prospective cultures viewed the function of marriage to be the birth and socialization of a new generation, and they were doubtful of the ability of this couple to succeed in the face of adversity.

The couple chose not to interact with either side of the family during the first year of their marriage because to do so caused too many problems between them as a couple. Within the second year of marriage this couple began having difficulties, and attempted to turn to their families for assistance. They had not yet had children, and the families were not supportive of their commitment to their marriage. Several family members simply suggested that they divorce. The couple was isolated and needed to turn to professional help instead of family to resolve their difficulties. With time, their relationship improved despite their families' objections.

When couples match on a variety of characteristics it seems logical that there would be fewer day-to-day negotiations required; attitudes and preferences would be largely shared; and a basis for a well functioning relationship would be established. However, there are plenty of homogamous couples that find a multitude of opportunities to argue. Heterogamous marriages can be just as successful as those based on homogamy, even though the dissimilarity in experiences and attitudes presents a wider potential for conflicts of interest and necessity for problem solving. There is value in what is new and exciting, which makes dating others who are different in appearance and/or mannerisms quite attractive. These conflicts can actually contribute to a stimulating interaction style when they are addressed appropriately. As seen in Chapter 16, support from extended families can be pivotal for relationships during these times of disagreements. If the relationship meets the expectations of the social network, the latter is more likely to be supportive of the union and during difficult times create some barriers to dissolution. If the relationship is unsupported, or even opposed, the couple may need to look outside the family for support.

Difficulties for couples of different belief systems and different social groups can be somewhat expected during predictable transitions in the life cycle. When couples have a common heritage, some of those transitions can be enacted through

Positive support from friends and family is a predictor of later relationship quality.

cultural scripts that are shared. When the family operates with distinctly different cultural scripts, each problem requires renegotiation and effort. For example, when children become part of the family, couples from widely divergent backgrounds may have considerable difficulties in deciding on early family rituals (which holidays to celebrate, which beliefs to share, etc.) and rules to use to raise children:

> Kim and Paula had been married for two years when their baby was born. Kim moved out of their bedroom so that Paula could sleep by the baby. He had seen his family members do this, and found it horrifying that Paula would consider putting their babies by themselves in a bedroom before they were at least one year old. He also found it foolish that he and his wife should sleep in the same bed because he did not think that they both should have to wake up all night to care for children. Paula was surprised at his behavior and felt abandoned by him. She planned to have the baby in their room until she was two months old, and then move her to her own room and her own crib. The couple needed new strategies for working with their distinctly different expectations.

When children are present, cultural differences are often heightened. This may also be true with aging. Later in the life cycle people feel a greater need to reconnect with their cultural heritage, and that opportunity tends to be more available in homogamous marriages (McGoldrick, Preto, Hines, & Lee, 1991).

Couple Process

Scripts, or guidelines for relationship interaction, are learned within the context of social interaction. Behaviors for women and men in particular cultures are played out formally and informally, training members to fulfill expectations of the group. For example, traditionally oriented women are often part of a social network in which men are viewed as marital leaders. Some of the beliefs that are associated with traditionalism include partnership characteristics such as husbands who are older than their wives, have more education, and who are expected to generate more income than their wives. Often, the cultural ideal also includes physical appearance issues such as husbands needing to be taller than wives. When such guidelines are used they limit women's access to potential partners, particularly as women age (due to a natural sex-ratio imbalance favoring a greater number of women) or become more advanced in their careers. It is often expected that within couples men are the more powerful partners. When this marital expectation is violated, the result is a family in which a more powerful wife may actually feel the need to do more relationship maintenance in the family so that her husband does not feel threatened by her power (Blumstein & Schwartz, 1983). This concern is not reciprocated, however: More powerful husbands do not feel the need to restore equity with their increased contribution to relationship maintenance. Such traditional thoughts about marriage may be shifting, given the RELATE results: For 60% of the couples, the husband and wife share the same socioeconomic status, and in 26% of the couples the male has a higher status. In only 14% of the cases, however, the woman has the higher socioeconomic status.

Once a partnership has been established, cultural context again dictates the ways in which couples progress toward marriage. Asking the bride's parents for her hand in marriage is practiced in some very conservative subcultures, but is rare in the United States. Some formality is typically used in the engagement process and in the wedding ceremony (e.g., the father walking his daughter down the aisle), which functions to include the community in the union. With the variety of criteria that may be used to select a mate, and the various levels of role systems (e.g., traditional to egalitarian) that may be used among couples, it is truly amazing that couples actually function so similarly.

Group Identification

In the American culture biology is mixed with ethnic identity and social position to create belief systems that govern daily life. Birds of a feather do, to some extent, flock together. When groups are completely homogamous (same race, gender, and age), the members have similar experiences with members outside of the groups. For example, women are likely to have very similar experiences and dilemmas to other women. Often groups distinguish themselves based on physical characteristics, clothing, and habits, but sometimes what distinguishes group members is biology: race, gender, and age. Much has been written about the discrimination felt by people of color, women, and the elderly. While perspective taking can assist one in appreciating the experience of another, it is difficult for those who are not part of a particular social group to fully understand the experiences that others have simply based on their skin color or gender. Interactions affect behaviors and belief systems, some of which can be shared in marriage (e.g., those experienced through racial features in a homogamous marriage), while others must simply be understood (e.g., the different experiences of women and men in marriage).

Some experiences that are biologically based are actually dangerous. For example, a black man and his white wife had been in the military, stationed in the southeastern United States. He described a vacation in which he and his wife experienced great fear of danger from the members of communities encountered while driving from Virginia to Florida. They found their interracial marriage to be a point of considerable consternation to complete strangers. He explained that he and his wife felt so threatened as they drove through some of the more racist communities that when one was driving the other lay down in the back seat, keeping their interracial relationship out of sight. For those experiences that are based on social status or ethnicity, it is possible for members of the couple to "pass" so that they fit into the immediate situation. Where race or gender are the distinguishing characteristics there is very little chance for "passing," and the victimization that comes of racism and sexism is experienced. The environmental aspects of self (i.e., ethnic identity, socioeconomic strata, and sexual orientation) allow for "passing" in a way that biological aspects (i.e., gender and race) do not.

Biology and Marriage: Gender, Age, and Race

Gender, age, and race are fundamental to the creation of a worldview: We describe ourselves and those with whom we interact in these biological terms, and our interactions reflect how we have learned to understand others who fit into these descriptive categories. For example, expectant parents are often asked if the baby will be a boy or a girl. It is impossible to interact without taking gender, age, and race into account. Something as simple as a request to hold open a door would be understood differently given the gender, age, and race of the requestor.

Gender.   Gender differences are significant and can be a source of considerable difficulty in relationships. Consider, for example, the following description of roles for men and women that many couples still act on in their relationships. Historically, women and men have had very different experiences in dating and marriage, with men extending invitations for dates, and women waiting for the invitation and being the guest. Although the beginning of the relationship may differ now and include more group activities or "hanging out together," once the relationship becomes serious women often take primary responsibility for its maintenance.

Women tend to be the more pragmatic partners (Rubin, 1983), becoming involved later than men, and getting out of a relationship that is not likely to be satisfying first. Women's responsibilities for bearing and raising children create a need to stay cognizant of their age and childbearing opportunities (although the age at first birth has extended well into the thirties and early forties in many cases). Even nontraditional women may find their social sense of self influenced by their marriages. Men are stereotypically thought of as the primary wage earners, and even when the economy is depressed many men feel the expectations and stress of being ultimately responsible for the family's well-being. During times of relationship dissatisfaction women tend to be focused inside of the marriage to find a solution to the problem. Women are taught to connect emotionally with their family members, and to be keenly aware of the needs of their members. Men are often socialized to be problem solvers and wage earners, so when there are problems in the marriage they have a tendency to look outside of the marriage for the cure (e.g., they may put in more hours on the job, help neighbors, or engage in other projects). Men's behavior is geared toward protecting and caring for their families. Not surprisingly, some women believe that their partner's solutions exacerbate the difficulties and consequently decide that their husbands do not care enough about the marriage to be more available. Some men then consider their wife's disapproval as an indication that she doesn't appreciate his attempts to help.

It is unfortunate that men and women often forget to consider the meaning of their partners' behavior, and attribute negative intentions to the different ways of handling issues. Women and men do focus on different things during conflict, as would be expected given their socialization. Rubin, Peplau, and Hill (1981) found that when faced with conflict, women were more likely to make attributions to individual or relationship factors (e.g., differences in interest), whereas men primarily made attributions to things external to the relationship. Women and men made similar attributions in many areas of conflict (e.g., politics, religion, education), but they made different attributions when the conflict involved sexual attitudes and financial matters (Harvey, Wells, & Alverez, 1978). Rubin (1983) suggests that gender differences in relationship concerns are caused by cultural definitions of masculinity and femininity: Masculine is synonymous with independent and feminine is synonymous with dependent. The economic independence of men is mistakenly thought to indicate emotional independence, and the economic dependence of women is mistakenly thought to indicate emotional dependence. According to Rubin, these stereotypes are not consistent with people's inner needs. Instead, social barriers, such as women remaining economically and socially disadvantaged, maintain the status quo. Many self-help books have focused on communication strategies in an effort to help men and women read each other's behaviors and intentions. The greatest challenge is to teach couples to take the time to not only hear each other's words, although that alone is helpful, but to understand the social context of their lives. The exact same event may have very different meanings for women and for men because of the ways in which they have been taught to understand events as members of distinct subcultures.

Sexism.   Nontraditional partners may have a difficult time seeing themselves in this review of gender roles. After all, wives and husbands can decide between themselves how to handle inequities. Couples can be quite firm in their beliefs in equality although they are often nested within a larger community where their interactions as spouses, parents, and workers are affected by gender bias. Unfortunately, women's opportunities are often limited in the larger culture, and the men who marry them share in overcoming those obstacles. For example, if the wife is the primary wage earner, the husband experiences first hand the glass ceiling and the pay differential between women and men. If the husband is the wage earner, however, the wife shares in some of the privilege available to him.

Belief systems are based on interactions with others, and shape the ways women and men see themselves and judge their potential. These belief systems include the rules by which people live, and they are in line with the larger social groups within which families live. Not surprisingly, communities support their members in adopting thoughts, feelings, and behaviors that are in line with the cultural goals. Egalitarian couples, then, are forced to work within contexts that are not equitable and that influence families directly. The larger world of gendered discourse about relationships includes occupational and institutional structures and policies that are gendered and affect daily decisions of childcare, community support, and tradition. When partners reach decisions about household work and child-rearing they must make these decisions within the very real constraints of money, opportunity, and social supports—all of which are inextricably tied to gender (Gilbert, 1994). Some couples find themselves shifting from egalitarian to more traditional roles after the third month of the first pregnancy. In fact, egalitarian marriages have been said to be more of an ideal than a real situation, existing largely among professional couples without children.

Age. Age at marriage is consistently and highly related to later marital quality (Holman & Linford, 2001). Teenage marriages are considerably less stable than those that take place when couples are in their mid-twenties. Holman and his colleagues have offered the hypothesis that there are curvilinear age effects. This hypothesis has been verified by other researchers who suggest that the optimal time to marry is in the "mid to late twenties." Too much earlier or later than this can negatively influence relationship success, although age at marriage is only one of many factors that can affect relationships (Glenn & Marquardt, 2001). Marriages that take place too young, and those between first marrieds who are too far above the mean age for marriage (25 for women, and 27 for men), could be problematic. The concern is whether the members of the couple are mature enough to handle the stresses of marriage, and flexible enough in their preferred style of living to adjust to a predictably different set of needs and preferences.

"December–May" relationships are said to exist when one member of the couple is much older than the other. It is typical in the American culture for women to marry men older than themselves, so there is generally a greater tolerance for age differences in which the male is considerably older than the woman. When the woman is the older partner, age differences of as little as five years are cited as a problem. For either gender, however, a highly discrepant age premaritally is predictive of breakup (Rubin, Hill, & Peplau, 1981; Huber & Spitze, 1988; Meredith & Holman, 2001). Two issues appear to be particularly salient to these couples. First, their experiences in their cohort are significantly different from each other, limiting the degree to which they may be similar even if they are from similar backgrounds and similar cultural experiences. Next, it can be difficult for family members to cope with that which does not fit the status quo, as would be the case with stepparents who are younger than the stepchild, or sons-in-law who are older than the parents.

It is still unusual to see older women marrying younger men.

Age differences, then, could affect the social connections in families, and it is the support from family and social connections, along with age, that are two of the best predictors of couple permanence (Meredith & Holman, 2001).

Race.   Race is biologically determined. Members of each race are similar to others of their group because of some specific physical feature. Distinguishing physical characteristics of members of each race are often immediately obvious: Members of the Caucasian and Black race are often distinguished by skin color and hair texture. Persons of Asian decent are distinguished from other races by the shape of their eyes. There are probably a number of physical descriptors that can be used to distinguish the three races. When a Caucasian, a Black, and an Asian are together, there is generally no mistaking one for the other. If a Caucasian expresses a desire to pass as a member of the Black race, he or she will not be particularly successful. Some members of a race are very vocal about their concern that marriages be racially endogamous. Remarkably, until recently intermarriage was against the law in several American states (Sherman, Oresky, & Rountree, 1991). In many settings interracial couples will find that they experience discrimination in both direct and indirect ways. Interracial marriages can also create unique challenges for children:

> Jenny was a tall, slender adolescent. She was extremely intelligent, but having trouble adjusting to the rules of her father's home. Her mother and father had been divorced years before, and she had just moved in with her father. Her father was not sure what she was angry about, but suspected it had to do with her recent move and settling in with them.

Within a few weeks she had become increasingly disrespectful. He and his new wife had tried a number of parenting strategies, but none had worked. They entered therapy hoping to reverse her negative attitude and behaviors. As they explored the weeks that she had lived with her father, she insisted that everything was fine. Soon, however, the problem was clear. Her new friends had given her a nickname after learning that she was half Black and half Japanese. Her father and his new wife were Black, and that was the racial membership that she was claiming in Washington, D.C., where she lived. Her mother, however, was Japanese. Jenny had dark skin, and slender facial features. She had a beautiful, exotic look, and the other teenagers thought it was fun to call her "Red." The behavior that her father saw was anger at him and her mom, and her inability to pass in the African American culture as a Black woman.

The difficulties inherent in interracial relationships are certainly ones that can be managed, as is evident by the many couples who have successful interracial marriages. It is distressing that people are judged so readily by skin color and that these judgments can interfere with the happiness of many couples. It is clear that discrimination seems to be more significant and pronounced against interracial couples both within their families and from people in the community.

Environment and Marriage: Ethnicity, Socioeconomic Strata, and Geography

Environment and social network give meaning to gender, age, and race. In some countries there may not be distinctions among ethnic groups, whereas the same groups are considered quite different in another country. A Mexican immigrant told of her marriage to an African man. According to this woman, in her hometown there were light- and dark-skinned people, but not white and black. One year after they were married she and her husband moved back to his home in Oakland, California. Toward the end of her first pregnancy she was walking down the street to the grocery store and saw what she believed to be a Catholic procession. She stopped to pray. Her husband and his brothers, seeing her on the street, ran out of their apartment building, grabbed her, and carried her into their apartment. She was livid that he would interrupt her observance of this event until they impressed upon her that she was living in a Black neighborhood and the parade was the KKK, a group she had never seen before. She recalled that it was then that she realized she and her husband were an interracial couple.

Cultural differences emerge in language, personal space, values, and hierarchy (Berg & Jaya, 1993; Perli & Bernard, 1993; McGoldrick, Preto, Hines, & Lee, 1991). For example, there is no word for "privacy" in Chinese, Korean, or Japanese (Berg & Jaya, 1993). It is not uncommon for people to understand ethnicity and culture as synonymous because in so many ways they end up overlapping. **Ethnicity** refers to the identification of social groups based on their common ancestry, religion, and cultural history. Ethnicity can be both celebrated and devalued in the larger culture.

For marriages, ethnic identity underlines rules and rituals of the most intimate activity in family life. The greatest threat to ethnically diverse couples is the potential for misunderstanding some of the predictable ways of thinking, feeling, and behaving that are characteristic of the cultures.

Ethnicity is only one of the factors that underlie differences in language and meaning. Income, education, and occupation together make up socioeconomic status (SES). Within SES there are differences that affect a wide range of functions, not the least of which are marital roles and parenting strategies. Typically, people in your neighborhood are of the same socioeconomic stratum, and there is often little opportunity to socialize with others outside of that group. Marital roles tend to vary between members of the working class and the professional class, probably for reasons of pragmatics. Childcare is a great expense in families, and a working-class mother often has a difficult time earning enough in the marketplace to cover her childcare costs. Often the decision for a mother to stay home reflects the reality that blue-collar men often have a greater earning potential than do pink-collar women. Consider the case of Amy and Chuck, who were from a working-class background and were having problems with their work role expectations:

> Amy and Chuck were married for 10 years and had 4 children. They married in their early thirties, and both had been employed before they had their first child. Amy was firm that when she and Chuck decided to start their family, the two of them agreed to have a traditional family: It was Amy's job to care for the children, while Chuck was responsible for the income. Chuck had worked all of his adult life and was able to earn a reasonable amount of money, although he never really enjoyed working and he preferred to help with the children and maintain the home. Chuck had decided to "retire" early, and the marriage was in serious trouble. According to Amy, Chuck violated the contract of their marriage. It was not important to her that they had enough money to live on. It was important that he spent all day in her "work space" and she was furious.

The social expectation of some families is that the wives have legitimate power in the household, and husbands have legitimate power in the labor force. The roles are often clearly defined; the women have their own friends and leisure pursuits, and the husbands have theirs (Rubin, 1976). For this husband, in this socioeconomic stratum, to decide to retire early and not work to support the family was a violation of a basic cultural expectation of his wife's. Professional class marriages, on the other hand, are often based on companionship, with less focus on the stratification of marital roles and more focus on dividing up the roles based on talent and interest. This may be at least partially in response to a greater availability of resources to help make a variety of marital arrangements possible. Consider another situation in which stratified gender roles were not as clearly defined:

> Bernice and Mark both held professional positions in finance and marketing. They believed that it was important for a parent to be home

when children were babies, but it was not important to them to have the mother be that parent. Soon after the birth of their first child, Bernice's job became busy and she was required to do a substantial amount of traveling and work long hours. Mark, on the other hand, was between projects at his work, and he was able to arrange a situation where he would work from home primarily, and go into his office just a few hours per week. Bernice and Mark felt relieved that they were able to keep a parent with their child most of the time, and were pleased to have a babysitter they could trust during the other times.

RELATE includes a variety of questions in the Values section regarding marital roles, gender, and equality. These scales are crucial for couples to consider carefully. More traditional attitudes about the appropriate roles for males and females create a marital culture that would be very different from less traditional attitudes. In a more traditional relationship there might not be an expectation for the female to work outside of the home. Partners are likely to feel distressed if they end up marrying someone who expects them to be primarily concerned with the home and children when they have strong career aspirations. In contrast, someone who wants an egalitarian relationship with regard to decisions, finances, and child rearing will become dissatisfied with a partner who isn't interested in being involved in these issues.

Finally, where people reside affects the way they think about things, what is important to them, and even the type of schedules that they keep. Weather, hobbies, proximity to entertainment, and, often, proximity to family members are considerations affecting where people call home. Finding a place to live that is acceptable to both partners, and where the partners can find work in their areas of expertise, is challenging. Interestingly, there is a concept of **residential propinquity:** Typically, people fall in love with others who live near them. Clearly, others in your community (or apartment complex) have similar values, similar available income, and similar environmental influences. Not surprisingly, however, it makes sense that residential propinquity is a factor in relationships because it is simply easier to meet people who live near you. Long-distance partnerships show the difficulties that can exist when propinquity isn't part of a relationship. Although there are some success stories of relationships that flourish across many miles, typically it is easier to develop a relationship in close proximity, even if during the maintenance stage, when the commitment is already established, the relationship becomes a long-distance romance.

There is a different way of living in small towns versus big cities, and these differences can be fundamental. It is easy to underestimate the importance of agreement on leisure activities because premarital relationships are so influenced by convention (e.g., dinner and a movie) that it is sometimes easy to miss that one person requires an opportunity to "people watch" and the other needs time to work in a garden. Consider the geographic environment that you and your partner prefer. How would you feel living in a place where you have plenty of space to garden but there are only three months without frost per year? Could you live in a state that is all desert and no ocean? Which natural disasters can you live with? Are you a risk taker, willing to chance an earthquake? Are you comfortable with tornadoes? Can you live with the high-pitched buzz of a mosquito? Do you want to live and die within five miles of your parents and siblings? If you and your partner both value family to that degree, can you both get your needs met?

Some communities are known for their regional behavior. Think about the American South, and ideas of the Bible Belt and southern belles may come to mind. Or think about the Midwest, with farms and hard-working families, as compared with the Southern Californian relaxed lifestyle. Certainly these are stereotypes, but they also have meaning for the cultural expectations of people who are from those regions:

> Jane and Ben were living in California when they became engaged. Jane was from Ohio and she wanted to have the ceremony in her hometown. Ben wasn't too excited about a large wedding but he agreed to be married in a large church wedding closer to her family and friends. In a telephone conversation she assured her parents that she and Ben would be home for the marriage ceremony, and announced their preference for an early November wedding. At that point the parents became offended. Had their daughter been gone so long that she didn't remember that weekend to be one of the most important of the year? It was, you see, the opening of deer-hunting season, and all of the men of the family looked forward to opening their hunting cabins on the very day that these "Californians" were planning a wedding. The wedding date changed, and took place mid-summer—the most beautiful time of year, by anyone's account, in northern Ohio.

Weather, leisure pastimes, available employment, political belief systems, environmental issues, and consequently political ideology are tied to geography. Some families are tied to a harvest schedule; others are influenced by tourist seasons. Regions of the country where more of the families are tied to factories, mining, or logging have particular political concerns, while those influenced by shipping and trading, tourism, and farming have other concerns. These concerns translate into values and traditions that differentiate one region of the country from another.

Who Are You?

Americans may fluctuate between being considerably ethnocentric ("my way is the only way") to being xenocentric ("anything foreign must be better than what we have here"). Cultural idioms, style of dress, and moral codes become the anchor by which people know themselves and identify themselves to others. Some degree of difference is exciting, whereas differences in fundamentally important areas become frightening or off-putting.

Gender, race, and ethnicity are present at birth, yet an individual may move in and out of cultural contexts (Preli & Bernard, 1993). In fact, most people belong to more than one culture (e.g., the collegiate culture, the corporate culture, the regional culture) and often adopt differing interactional styles depending on the group within which they are interacting at the moment.

Culture is reinforced during interactions with others, where support is obtained for appropriate choices and sanctions are applied for those choices that are not approved. In one situation, tattoos and tongue piercing are common and appreciated. In another situation, only a conservative suit and modest self-presentation are acceptable. The context of culture involves the personal, interpersonal, and structural levels of values, behaviors, and belief systems. The culturally connected couple knows its own cultural identification and the cultural identity of each partner, and purposefully works to integrate those two experiences in a way that helps both of them differentiate themselves from their families of origin and become interdependent with their partner.

Interaction Effect That Compounds the Struggle

If you and your partner are heterogeneous in one area (e.g., from different regions of the country), yet match closely in family of origin, socioeconomic stratum, and ethnicity, the differences between you may be relatively minor. If, however, you find yourself racially different, ethnically different, from different regions of the world, and from different socioeconomic strata, the potential for difficulty is greater. The challenge, always, is to make sense of your partner's behavior so that it can be seen lovingly and with good intentions. Then, and only then, can reasonable solutions to seemingly huge impasses be developed. McGoldrick and her colleagues (1991, p. 571) have outlined four areas for couples to consider as they develop their couple relationship:

1. **Communication Style.** What is the style of communication that you and your partner use? Are you verbal, taciturn, rational, or dramatically expressive?
2. **Conflict Style.** As you observe your style of handling conflict, do you more often argue, reason, withdraw, tease, or offer an indirect response?
3. **Attitudes.** Attitudes toward intimacy and dependence are also culturally bound, with some people displaying more or less positive, fearful, assertive, demanding, or withholding behaviors.
4. **Emotional Expression.** Finally, the ways in which different cultures express grief and sadness can be a very important issue in marriage. Are you or your partner more stoic, expressive, emotional, denying, or angry?

As you identify your differences, ask yourself if you are willing to work through your differences. Is your tolerance level for individual differences high, or do you feel personally humiliated when a partner's behavior differs from what you would expect of yourself? Finally, consider how much work your relationship will require over your life span. It is important to be willing to work on relationships, but overall, relationships should be fun and rewarding. A relationship that begins as hard work will rarely become less difficult. There are predictable difficulties that all couples experience during their lives together. When you start a relationship with fun and rewarding experiences you have something to remember for those dark, albeit infrequent, days when you need to remember why you married in the first place.

11

Spirituality and Religiosity

The main question, which has tormented me consciously or unconsciously throughout my entire life—the existence of God . . . the nature of man is correlative to the nature of God; if there is no God, there is also no man.

—Fyodor Dostoevsky

Philosophers, poets, politicians, psychologists, and people of every walk of life struggle with the deeper questions of life. How did we come to exist? What is the purpose of it all? Is there a God? What happens after death? Do my behaviors really matter in the larger scheme of things? Dostoevsky struggled with these questions for his entire life and seems to have concluded that God does exist and is closely connected with humanity. Others struggle with the same questions and decide that God is only a belief and not a reality. These questions are much broader than a chapter or even an entire book could contain, yet the answers that each of us has to these questions often influence how we feel about our lives and relationships. Spirituality and religiosity, although usually very personal matters, are discussed in the social context because often people's spirituality is partially defined by the social groups they belong to. In addition, spirituality and religiosity can be two of the primary determinants of mate selection and relationship satisfaction. Some people consider the spirituality and religious beliefs of others to be the most important characteristic of a future partner. Even those who do not adhere to a specific belief system are often looking for partners with a particular spiritual view of life. In any case, views on spirituality often become quite important after the birth of a child, so it is an essential component of premarital and early marital education.

Defining Spirituality and Religiosity

When people say that something was spiritually moving or that they had a spiritual experience, they are often speaking of moments in life that were sacred and of a

Prayer is a common source of spiritual strength for many people.

deeper nature than the usual day-to-day experiences. Definitions associated with "spiritual" are "of the spirit or soul as distinguished from the body," "showing much refinement of thought or feeling," or "of religion . . . sacred, devotional" (Guralnik, 1982, p. 1373). Spirituality thus can be considered refined thoughts and experiences of a sacred nature having to do with the spirit or soul or deity. Some couples speak of the love and companionship that they share with each other as being very spiritual and sacred. Sometimes spiritual experiences are facilitated and felt within a religious context or setting and other times they are not.

"Religious" is defined as that which is "characterized by adherence to religion or a religion" and "religion" is defined as "any specific system of belief, worship, conduct, etc., often involving a code of ethics and a philosophy" (Guralnik, p. 1200). Therefore, the religiosity of a person is connected to one or more religions and is not necessarily synonymous with spirituality.

Influence on Dating and Marriage

Religiosity and spirituality can be an influence for improving behaviors and relationships, but some have used these principles to demean and try to force others to behave in certain ways. Using religion in an oppressive way has been a tool of much destruction in the history of humanity both inside and outside of families. However, this has almost always occurred because those with power have violated the very principles they are trying to *force* others to adopt. Any belief system can be oppressively enforced by those in power, whether it is religiously oriented or not. These instances of oppression between groups of people and among family members can create a strong reactivity in some to anything that appears to be religious or appears to propose a "right way" of conducting life. Nevertheless, it would be as inappropriate to stereotype religion or spirituality as fanatical, dogmatic, oppressive, repressive, or any other negative label as it would be to stereotype a group of people as oppressive because historically some members of the group have hurt others. Millions of people continue to find religion and spirituality to be helpful and uplifting endeavors that enrich and improve the quality of their lives.

How does the spirituality or religiosity of people influence their dating and marital experiences? Table 11.1 includes several indicators of couples' spirituality and religiosity. For those who have taken RELATE, spirituality is important for almost all of them and so is religion and religiosity. Women are more consistent in their desire for spirituality and in their religious behaviors than are men. For a few people these principles have little if any influence on their lives and relationships. Nevertheless, from the RELATE data it is clear that most people attend religious services and consider spirituality an important part of life. It is very likely that family members of dating partners will consider these issues to be very important even if the couple does not. For example, the approval of family members of their children's dating and marriage partners is consistently higher when the partners are more spiritual and religious.

Spirituality and religiosity can help relationships and partners when both members of the couple have desires to include religion and spirituality in their lives. Spirituality and religiosity have a stronger influence on values than any of the other contexts, according to the RELATE data. Those who emphasize religion and spirituality are much more likely to see marriage and family life as top priorities and they are more likely to have more conservative views regarding sexuality and birth control. Spirituality may influence males and females differently. If a male is more religious and concerned about spirituality, he is more likely to be kind, happy, empathic, and loving and less likely to be violent, critical, and immature. Females are also more likely to be satisfied with partners who are more religious, and religious females are more likely to be empathic and loving in their relationships.

TABLE 11.1 *Some Indicators of Religiosity and Spirituality from the RELATE Data*

Indicator	Males	Females
Percentage of people who consider spirituality important	80%	87%
Percentage of people who pray at least sometime	68%	81%
Percentage of people who attend church at least annually	88%	91%
Percentage of people who attend church at least monthly	64%	65%
Percentage of people who belong to a religious denomination	92%	92%

These findings certainly do not mean that people who do not feel strongly about religion and spirituality are going to be poorer partners and have more distressed relationships. Most of us have known people who strongly valued religion but were not good partners and most have known people who were not interested in spirituality but were very loving spouses. The idea that religion may help some people improve their behavior does not mean that good people are concentrated only in religious groups.

The primary religions in the United States and the world are listed in Table 11.2 (Wright, 2000). This table illustrates that in the world there are more people who are members of non-Christian religions, but in the United States 85% of the population is a member of a Christian denomination. Table 11.3 gives more details of the almost 40% of the U.S. population who are Christian but not Catholics. There are many different religions in the United States and in the world and the odds are increasing that those who are potential dating partners may belong to a different religion or have no religious beliefs at all. While some religions may be very close to others in terms of the doctrines and practices of its members, other religions can be very distinct. The religion of a potential partner may be a primary filter that determines whether someone will be asked on a date or eligible to become a spouse.

Since most religions include extensive value systems that suggest how people can make sense of the world and how people can act in ways that are supposed to bring increased happiness, it is difficult for many to date or marry someone without these values. This is more a reflection of preferences and identification with a belief system than it is a bias against others. It is very crucial for dating partners to consider how important a particular belief system is to them and to evaluate whether this is likely to be a source of shared experiences or disagreement. Many couples that marry even though they are strongly dedicated to different religious beliefs find that

TABLE 11.2 *Percentage of the U.S. and World Populations Belonging to Religious Groups*

Group	United States	World
Roman Catholic	21%	19%
Protestant	23%	6%
Orthodox Catholic	2%	4%
Other Christian	39%	5%
Buddhist	1%	6%
Chinese Folk	0%	6%
Hindu	0%	13%
Muslim	2%	20%
Jewish	1%	0%
Other Non-Christian	1%	6%
Nonreligious	10%	15%

TABLE 11.3 *The Largest Christian Religions in the United Sates Other Than Roman Catholic*

Religion	Number of Members in Millions
Southern Baptist	15.7
United Methodist	8.4
Church of God in Christ	5.5
Evangelical Lutheran	5.2
Church of Jesus Christ of Latter-Day Saints	4.9
National Baptist	3.5
Lutheran–Missouri Synod	2.6
African Methodist Episcopal	2.5
Assembly of God	2.5
Progressive National Baptist	2.5
National Missionary Baptist	2.5

there is substantial conflict throughout their lives. Often the serious differences that can emerge between partners who hold very different beliefs do not become apparent until child-rearing begins. As parents decide what values to use to help them manage the challenging task of raising children, there must be enough common ground to send consistent messages to children.

Additional struggles will emerge for couples who have different belief systems when they interact with family members who expected and hoped that each partner would marry someone with the same beliefs. These struggles can make it very difficult for spouses to find acceptance and satisfaction in relationships with in-laws. Weddings can often be very tense when certain religious settings are selected over those that were desired by parents and extended family members. Holidays, too, can turn from opportunities for enjoyment to tense and stressful experiences when families have differing expectations for traditions and activities based on their religious beliefs. Even the school or university that children attend can become a point of intense conflict when parents or grandparents expect a child to attend an institution with a religious focus.

Some couples are willing and able to negotiate the difficult paths that result from interfaith marriages and some are not. The success that couples have with these struggles is at least partially dependent upon the importance of the religious system to family members and the married partners. If partners and family members are only loosely associated with their religions, conflict or distress may be minimal.

The struggles inherent in interfaith marriages also influence the interaction of the couple with the larger social context. Where a couple decides to live can have very different meanings for partners if one location has a good support system for one religion but not the other. One of the best ways that involvement with religions can strengthen couple relationships is the provision of a support system (Gottman, 1999). There are usually couple and family activities, workshops on child-rearing and marital communication, and opportunities during religious meetings to interact with others who believe the same way. However, if spouses and children feel that they must regularly give up one support system to be in another, religion may turn into one of the most divisive and destructive elements of family life rather than one of the most powerful ways of supporting families and helping them improve.

Sharing Spirituality as a Couple

Spirituality is about connection. Some find that added spirituality comes to their lives through enhancing connection to nature. Others find an increase in spirituality through becoming more connected to people. Ideally, if individuals have a commitment to spirituality, they would find their marriage partner to be a primary source for discussions about the deeper questions of life and some of their shared activities would be designed to help them experience greater spirituality.

Working at becoming more connected to God is another pathway to improve spirituality. Yet spirituality is not something that automatically comes to people just because they decide to take a scenic drive or spend time with someone they love or read sacred texts. These activities can help people feel more spiritual, but usually there is something more involved.

Elizabeth Barret Browning wrote, "Earth's crammed with heaven, And every common bush afire with God; And only he who sees takes off his shoes" (Bartlett, 1937, p. 431). Spirituality involves a degree of work, persistence, meditation, and a particular mindset that allows people to see beyond themselves. Without that ability to see, bushes are just common bushes, mountains are just common mountains, and people are just common people. The struggle to become more connected through concentrated effort and thought allows that which is common to become deeply moving and significant.

Usually spiritual experiences are preceded by difficulties, struggles, deep questions and pondering, and perhaps long periods of time with unanswered questions or dilemmas. Because these difficulties make us stop and think and try something different, we move outside the daily routine and try to understand our lives from a larger perspective. Just as many of the great texts of spirituality describe people who must struggle for months or years (e.g., Abraham, Muhammad, Christ), often forgoing comforts and the habits of normal life for a pathway or pilgrimage that includes great difficulties, relationships too must include regular episodes of struggle and discomfort in order to increase intimacy and connection. "A wonderful marriage doesn't make life easy or painless. It just makes the work sweeter and the pain more meaningful" (Schnarch, 1997, p. 403).

Comfort or Growth

Growth in relationships is not automatic. All people spend their lives in two circles: the comfort circle, and the growth/change circle (Schnarch, 1997). The pathway from the comfort circle to the growth/change circle is called "risk." Only through challenging ourselves to be more open, vulnerable, and clear can we experience growth and change. However, all growth and change creates some degree of discomfort and anxiety. As a result, often before we are able to grow and progress as we need to in our relationships, we fall back into the comfort circle that is built on our habitual behaviors and our safe conversations.

The growth circle can be a spiritual experience for couples. Supporting each other through difficult periods of growth and change can be the most challenging giving that a person is asked to provide. Spirituality is about connection, and marriage is the "crucible of connection" (Schnarch, 1997). A crucible is literally a container that can withstand great heat, which is used to separate precious ore such as gold from the dross or nonprecious elements. Marriage will create enough heat, enough friction, enough struggle, enough desire, to separate what is good about you from what needs improvement. However, if couples do not have a strong commitment to each other, or they expect marriage to be relatively easy or trouble free, the spiritual growth that could occur will be sacrificed for comfort or the relationship will be abandoned for something else.

Love and Death

Love and spirituality are often connected or synonymous in religious texts. Sometimes God is referred to as Love. In other instances loving others is described as the sign of someone's spirituality. Death is also a common process that is central to many spiritual or religious systems. To love is to die beautifully. Parts of us must die and be discarded if we are to become more connected and experience deeper love and greater spirituality. The selfish person must become selfless; the conceited person must become more humble; the immature person must learn to act more responsibly. We often will not make difficult, usually painful, change unless we see the negative effects of our mistakes in the lives of those we love. We become frustrated with ourselves and desire to become something more. We let parts of us die that are not serving us well and that are interfering with our ability to be intimate. This process of being in a relationship, noticing how we are hurting or disappointing others, and trying to improve, can bring significant spiritual experiences as the connection with others deepens.

It is also true that all of us have death hanging over our heads, and for some people this is terrible knowledge that can be debilitating. Some people who have lost loved ones in a shocking, sudden manner never want to feel such pain again in their lives and choose not to risk anew. Many of us hold back different aspects of ourselves to keep from being hurt by those we love should they decide to leave us or be disloyal to us. Whatever the reason, the knowledge that relationships can and do end suddenly, that they die, can haunt us to the point where the very relationship we hope to never lose is lost due to the fear of losing it.

It is when we hold back and choose comfort and safety because we might be hurt that our relationships cannot grow, that they begin to die through starvation. Starvation is a slow, painful demise that distorts the body while the mind fades into a fog. In contrast, living, risking, and growing is invigorating, and should death occur, though shocking, happiness is the last taste in the mouth, the final memory to roll upon the minds of those who remain. Loving, then, giving all of ourselves to another, is learning to die beautifully.

Couples can enjoy spiritual growth and share spiritual moments as part of their relationship if this is their orientation and desire. Those who are in the premarital stage would do well to carefully evaluate this often neglected dimension of relationships by first considering how important spirituality is to them and, second, considering how much they want this to be a part of their marriage. There can be few aspects of life as rewarding as having spiritual experiences and sharing this with someone you love. In contrast, it can be very disconcerting and create high levels of dissatisfaction to experience spirituality in life and not feel that it is helpful, permissible, or possible to share these experiences with the most important person in your life. If spirituality and religion are important to you, the dating stage is a perfect time to attempt to share this part of your life with partners in order to ascertain their acceptance of this worldview and their desire to participate in this aspect of life. As is the case in many other areas of relationships, couples too often think that love will persuade a partner to adopt a certain spiritual outlook on life and change over time. Spirituality and religious worship seem to be areas that are particularly vulnerable to this type of unrealistic expectation and the accompanying dissatisfaction that occurs when the hoped-for change never happens.

A Dynamic and Confusing Issue

In classes conducted by the authors it has been intriguing to see the ways that religion and spirituality can influence couples. For some people, religiosity is a very important, if not *the* most important, aspect of relationships. These strongly religious people would not dream of marrying or even dating someone who didn't feel the same way. For others, religion is something of minor importance and would never be a reason to exclude someone from the pool of potential partners. In fact, some people find the idea of not marrying someone you loved because of their religious orientation to be very offensive. Yet we have found that many if not most people appreciate the idea of spirituality and have experienced some events that they consider spiritual. Most also want to share spirituality with their future spouse. However, it is not uncommon for some to express that spirituality is enhanced in religion while others think that religion detracts from "true spirituality." Many aren't sure what pathway to choose to enhance their spirituality. Much confusion about these issues exists in the minds of many people. For some people, clarity regarding spirituality and religiosity may not come until after many years of searching, experimenting, and learning. While agreement on these issues is often elusive in classes, it is clear due to the nature of the debate and the intensity of feelings that are expressed that religion and spirituality are very crucial issues to be discussed early on in relationships.

Your Preferred and Actual Couple Style

His name was George F. Babbit. He was forty-six years old now. . . . He was not fat but exceedingly well-fed. He seemed prosperous, extremely married, and unromantic. . . . Myra Babbit was definitely mature. She had creases from the corners of her mouth to the bottom of her chin, and her plump neck sagged. She had become so dully habituated to married life that in her full matronliness she was as sexless as an anemic nun.

—Sinclair Lewis

While none of us would wish for a style of marriage like the Babbits's, their dull avoidant marriage is what they have adjusted to and accepted as married life. In the course of Sinclair Lewis's novel it becomes clear that the Babbits have avoided conflict and even their own interests and passions in exchange for outward peace and material comforts. However, because this is not George's preferred style, eventually trouble brews and the plot thickens.

Each person brings a unique personality, background, behavioral habits, and culture to the table of marriage and tries to mix it with the unique qualities of the partner so that the end result is a pleasing full-course meal that is nourishing and healthy. Sometimes one person prefers Italian fare while the other person prefers French food. Though there can be some turn taking so that on Monday French food is selected and on Tuesday Italian is the choice, most often the relationship represents a merging of both styles over time until something entirely new is created. This merging together of personalities and behaviors is no small feat and is complicated by overarching social norms as well as the personalities of forthcoming children and families of origin. For example, in the previously mentioned novel by Sinclair Lewis, George tries to break out of his dullness only to find that the social forces pressuring him to conform are too powerful, so he returns to his routine marriage.

The development of a unique relationship has been called the "cocreation of a shared reality" (Levine & Busby, 1997; Reiss, 1981; Wamboldt & Reiss, 1989). It is a fascinating process to experience the merging of two distinct realities and backgrounds into one new relationship and family. Over time, spouses adopt parts of each other's habits, language, thinking, and preferences. Although developing a relationship together can be stimulating and fun, the difficult nature of such a task is one reason for the high divorce rate. Some people find that their commitment is too weak to sustain them through difficult times. Some are unaware that the transition is going to include difficult times. This unrealistic expectation creates a sense of disillusionment when problems arise. Other people find that their partner is so different that it seems impossible to make even small decisions without explosive arguments. The best way to allow the cocreation of a shared reality to emerge is to avoid rushing into marriage (Larson, 2000).

A primary purpose of dating is to get beyond the surface with someone and explore what it is like to create a shared relationship. Each dating relationship is really an experiment with many possible outcomes. Some dating relationships might end with the realization that though you are very attracted to one another, it

Each couple develops a unique style of interacting with each other.

is simply too hard to get along when the passion dies down. Other relationships might end with the awareness that though friendship is there, passion is absent. Another relationship may end because your life trajectories are so different that you drift into different directions.

Being patient with this process and being honest with both yourself and your partners can be quite challenging. Fortunately, many couples endure the transitions of married life and find that the end result is something much more beautiful than either of them could have achieved on their own. These successful couples live happier, healthier, more prosperous, and more productive lives than their single or divorced counterparts (Waite & Gallagher, 2000).

When considering all the areas of a couple relationship that must be negotiated, the degree of change individuals must undertake to develop and maintain a long-term relationship is astonishing. Partners must decide what traditions from their families of origin to adopt, adapt, or discard for new traditions. They must decide what to do about competing career choices. Compromises must be made regarding recreational activities, when and if children are going to be a part of the family, what values and religious organizations are to be adopted, and how to handle money, meals, friends, and so on. Even the day-to-day behaviors such as how to stay in touch with each other while at work, how to communicate when together, and how to make decisions, must include compromise and negotiation. Each of these negotiations is complicated by the fact that individuals have unique preferences, habits, and behaviors that to them seem like the "right way to do things."

Preferences Regarding Conflict

Of all the different preferences a person brings to a relationship, perhaps the most important preferences are about how conflict is managed. During those serious arguments that nearly all couples have, deep injuries can be inflicted and long-term trouble can develop, or problems can be addressed and the relationship can continue to grow. Unfortunately, partners often have different expectations regarding how conflict will be handled, so the same behavior that might mean something positive to one person is interpreted as disrespectful to another. One person might have experienced a style of conflict in his background that was "avoidant." That is, he might have learned to avoid arguments and disagreements whatever the cost. He might be expecting that with time, and through the process of nonconflictual discussions, problems would work themselves out. In contrast, his partner may have come from a background that handled conflict more like debates: People were expected to voice their disagreements openly and forcefully and arguments were considered a healthy way to resolve issues. Consider how these two partners might interpret the same behaviors differently. During their first major argument he tries to calm things down and avoid disagreement, while she keeps trying to forcefully express her views. She might interpret his behaviors as a sign that he lacks backbone or courage or he is unclear about his beliefs, while he might interpret her as domineering and mean. Either style of conflict management can be a good workable style if *both* partners find it satisfying. However, if one person is labeled negatively when she or he tries to work through conflict in her or his natural way, problems will consistently crop up for the couple. It may be possible for the male in this example to be a little more forthcoming and the female to withhold some of what she would normally say, but this kind of compromise may not be sustainable during times of high emotion and intensity. Most people can communicate in ways that are acceptable to their partner under nonstressful circumstances and during conversations about unimportant matters. What matters is the preferred, habitual way that partners relate to each other during intense, highly charged conversations.

The four most common approaches to couple conflict were listed in Table 7.1, from the RELATE instrument. These conflict styles have been extensively researched by Gottman (1994, 1999) and others, and are good predictors of relationship satisfaction (Busby & Taniguchi, 2000; Holman & Jarvis, 2000). Three of these styles—volatile, avoidant, and validating—can lead to sustained relationships that are satisfying to couples. The hostile approach is an unstable and destructive style of conflict management. Many couples erroneously assume that the validating style is the ideal that all people should pursue. Most frequently individuals, families, and cultures tend to prefer one of the three successful ways of handling conflict. Some questions to ask yourself in order to assess what might be your preferred style are the following:

- Do I really dislike conflict? Do I try to reduce it whenever I experience it? Have I learned that fighting over issues just does not do much good?
- Do I find that I have strong opinions and views? Do I feel it is inappropriate to back down when expressing these views? Do I respect people who stand up for themselves and who like a healthy debate? Is it true that most of the things that I get involved with I do with vigor and high levels of energy?
- Am I pretty good at compromising and negotiating? Do I usually find ways of saying things that are not likely to cause conflict or make people upset? Can I often see when arguments are getting heated and then find a way to slow things down without necessarily giving up my perspective?
- Am I hot-headed and explosive? Is it hard for me to stay calm when others disagree with me? Do I sometimes say or do mean things in the heat of an argument?

If you found yourself answering yes to questions under #1, you are probably someone who prefers an avoidant style. If you found yourself answering yes to questions under #2, you probably prefer the volatile approach. If you related more to the questions under #3, you will most likely prefer the validating approach. If the questions under #4 are more your style, you may be in the hostile category. It is also important to know how people you are in a relationship with would rate you. Sometimes we think that we are calmer and more compromising than others experience us.

The crucial issue for dating couples to determine and understand is their conflict management style: the style they learned in their families and the style they use most often. Couples often find that they have few serious disagreements during the dating stage of their relationship and some couples do not become involved in intense disagreements until after they are married. This can cause serious problems because the couple may be mismatched in their style of managing conflict, which will cause relationship satisfaction difficulties when disagreements cannot be discussed and resolved acceptably.

Each person should carefully consider his or her regular way of handling conflict. More people typically say they are validating when in fact they are not, as this is overly idealized in the United States. It may be useful to specifically think of the last arguments you had with someone, not necessarily a romantic partner, and consider how you handled it. Did you find yourself trying to escape and avoid the conflict? Did the conflict make you very uncomfortable and uneasy? You may be accustomed to an avoidant style. However, you may have found yourself more calm and willing to compromise and able to listen to someone who disagreed with you without much distress. This may suggest you are accustomed to a validating style. Conversely, you may be a little more "hot-headed" and prone to make your point with vigor and passion, hence the probability that you are accustomed to the volatile style. Whatever your style, it is likely to be frustrating to you if you are matched with someone who does not prefer the same style or who sees your style as dysfunctional.

The Actual Styles of Couples

Figure 12.1 illustrates how nonmarried respondents who took RELATE scored on the Conflict Style questions. Fifty-five percent of the couples either did not score high in any of the four styles, were mixed, or were hostile. Each of these situations creates a need for further attention. The mixed couples scored high on more than

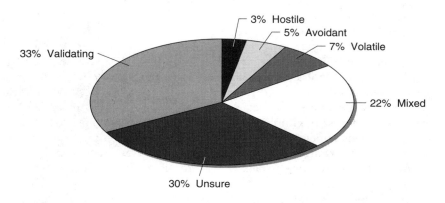

FIGURE 12.1 *Percentage of Couples Who Scored High on Couple Conflict Style Questions*

one style, whereas the unsure couples did not score high on any scale and may not have experienced enough conflict to actually know their style.

Unsure Couples

The concern for the unsure couples is that, should they get married or engaged without knowing their couple style of conflict management, they may experience serious problems if they are mismatched. Yet, it is not possible to fake an argument just to see what your conflict style is as a couple, or to practice arguing to establish a couple style. It may take some time before the relationship is serious enough, the issues are significant enough, and your emotions are strong enough for conflict to occur. It is not necessary to have serious conflict prior to getting married. It is possible to evaluate your own style and that of your partner based upon previous conflict with other people. This may give you at least a reasonably good guess as to your style and help you avoid mismatches or problems.

Mixed Couples

Certain mixes are better than others. Of those couples who were mixed in Figure 12.1, about 10% scored high on both avoidant and volatile, 13% scored high on both volatile and hostile, 51% scored high on both validating and avoidant, and 26% scored high on both validating and volatile.

The avoidant and volatile mix is one of the styles that is most likely to be toxic (Gottman, 1999). This is because one person prefers to avoid conflict while the other partner prefers to work things out openly with a volatile, passionate approach. Inevitably, both partners are likely to feel that conflicts do not lead to an acceptable resolution, not necessarily because problems are not solved, but rather because the feelings toward the partner that result from conflict will undermine commitment, trust, and love. A person who prefers to avoid conflict will become emotionally flooded when the partner uses her or his normal volatile style to discuss problems. This may result in an even higher level of avoidance, which may cause the volatile partner to be even more frustrated and potentially hostile.

The volatile and hostile mix is another combination that may prove to be lethal to the relationship. It is not uncommon for some volatile couples to turn into hostile couples (Gottman, 1994). The key to remaining volatile rather than hostile is the ability to soothe self or the partner during intense conflict, and the commitment to continue the positive activities and behaviors that counteract the arguments. Soothing refers to the ability to calm down and use words that reduce criticism, contempt, or defensiveness. As stated earlier, for a relationship to stay healthy partners need to experience five positive interactions for every one negative interaction. If a couple's style of handling conflict is volatile, the negative feelings that emerge during arguments might make positive behaviors less likely. Couples should contemplate how they respond to negativity. If one or both partners is prone to holding a grudge or takes a long time to calm down and let go of negative interactions, the volatile approach would be likely to lead to hostility. It may be that when one partner moves from a volatile to a hostile approach it is because the volatile approach is already contrary to the preferred style. Flooding and frustration are a part of most conflict and these feelings can lead to hostile acts.

Hostile Couples

Any premarital relationship that already has even one partner who is labeling the conflict style hostile should consider the relationship vulnerable to breakup and at risk for much difficulty. Hostility is not likely to spontaneously improve due to marriage, children, or other changes. More likely, hostility will lead to violence, higher levels of substance abuse, and relationship dissolution (Busby & Taniguchi, 2000). As a warning sign of serious relationship trouble, when one or both partners describe the couple style as hostile, the relationship is typically brittle and sometimes dangerous. This result on the RELATE inventory should be handled in the same regard as if someone was diagnosed with cancer, heart disease, or some other life-threatening illness. Couples who are describing their relationship as hostile would be wise to employ professional relationship help.

Stable Conflict Styles

Couples who describe their conflict style as avoidant, volatile, or validating are more likely to be in a stable satisfying relationship when both partners prefer the same style. It is not necessary for all couples to talk through all their difficulties. An avoidant style is functional as long as neither person is resentful or desires a more open approach to problems. Couples are also not doomed to a dissatisfying relationship if they are more volatile and argumentative, as long as they do not slide into the hostile style and begin to feel contempt or defensiveness. Couples who are characterized by one of the stable styles must maintain a much higher number of positive interactions than negative interactions. It is not enough to just avoid arguments: Total avoidance would be considered stonewalling or withdrawal and is a sign of severe distress. Rewarding interactions in which couples share positive feelings toward one another, experience satisfying physical intimacy, solve daily problems without conflict, or participate in enjoyable recreational activities are the glue that holds any relationship together.

Natural Changes

It is helpful for any couple to carefully analyze the style of conflict and the overall experience of positive and negative interactions. Sometimes, developmentally, people change and grow and prefer different styles than what was acceptable during the early years of a relationship. It is not uncommon for younger or less committed couples to find any conflict quite distressing so they might be prone to avoid conflict as much as possible. Over time, though, as they become more comfortable with each other and discover that it is okay to express opinions openly, it may be that a validating or volatile style is more fulfilling. These changes in couple style can occur so gradually that neither partner notices until it becomes obvious that there are more arguments or difficult discussions occurring than was common earlier in the relationship. This increase in arguments is not necessarily a sign of impending doom. The partners must be aware that they are testing a new way of exploring conflict, and be willing to de-escalate the conflict before one or both of them become emotionally flooded.

Stress can be another cause of change in the couple conflict style. Every relationship goes through times when the external stress is high and arguments are more likely. This can occur during times of transition such as graduating from college, changing careers, the birth of a new child, a promotion, a serious illness, or the death of a parent. These significant life events affect the normal way of interacting and reduce one's patience. Healthy couples will attribute this change to the external stress and avoid taking the partners' behaviors and words literally. When the stress is prolonged and conflict remains high for many months, damage can occur in the relationship. Couples going through highly stressful events must find positive experiences to share so that the relationship can find equilibrium again. Even a few dates or enjoyable activities can be refreshing enough to hold the couple together through intense stress.

13

Negative Communication Patterns

In civilized life domestic hatred usually expresses itself by saying things which would appear quite harmless on paper . . . but in such a voice, or at such a moment, that they are not far short of a blow in the face . . . I have had patients of my own so well in hand that they could be turned at a moment's notice from impassioned prayer for a wife's or son's "soul" to beating or insulting the real wife or son without a qualm.

—C. S. Lewis

Here we listen to the advice of one dark angel to another in *The Screwtape Letters* on how to keep people from getting along. Their strategy is to lead people to communicate in destructive ways and to act with duplicity by taking extreme offense at others who communicate in the same manner. It seems that their approach may be working better than we wish!

There is a self-perpetuating, accelerating, and expanding quality to the downward spiral of negative communication. None of us has fully escaped the whirlpool. We each know what it is like to get pulled into these destructive arguments. Sometimes critical exchanges seem to have more power than our own will and we almost helplessly find ourselves falling into what we promised ourselves we would avoid. If the spirals happen too often and with increased negativity, most people will withdraw and avoid intimate conversation. Although this solution seems better than more arguing, in the end it is just another step in the downward spiral that leads to divorce or separation.

Negative communication patterns are surprisingly predictable and consistent across couples. Although each couple may have unique hot buttons or topics that they argue about, the downward spiral has similar steps and behaviors for most couples that fall down it. Thankfully, many couples, although they have occasional arguments and negative feelings, do not travel down the spiral very often. This illustrates the very important point that all couples argue, criticize, and get defensive, yet many couples would not be characterized as being in a hostile or distressed relationship.

We Have Found the Enemy and It Is Not Negative Feelings

There is a danger in a chapter such as this one to implicitly send the message that negative feelings are not good for a relationship. Feelings are not the problem in relationships, whether positive, negative, or neutral. If a partner perceives that only one type of feeling can be expressed in a relationship, over time the relationship will become restrictive and suffocating. The negative feelings that are experienced by partners are diagnostic in that they are a sign that something needs to be discussed or changed. Often negative feelings accompany the growth and change that is necessary and healthy but difficult. Who wants to be told that they are not nice, or that they are often grumpy, or that they are too quiet, or that a particular behavior is rude or distasteful to others? Most of us would prefer to avoid hearing such things. Yet negative statements from a partner may be the only way that someone becomes aware of a problem and may be the only way change can occur.

Still, there are many ways to express a negative feeling. You might say to a partner, "I want to smack you when you do that" or "I wish you would stop doing that" or "Sometimes I think you're stupid when you keep doing that over and over again" or "It bothers me when you keep interrupting me and taking over the conversation." Each message would engender a different reaction from the partner though they all might be "true" and about the same irritating behavior. In addition, if a partner tended to only notice mistakes and problems and didn't express positive feelings, even a few negative statements would be harder to hear by others. Finally, if your partner was very sensitive about weight and you mentioned it regularly, it would have a stronger negative influence on the relationship than if you mentioned something your partner wasn't as sensitive about, like keeping the room clean. Hence the negative nature of certain feelings is not the problem; rather, it is the manner in which they are expressed, the frequency with which they are expressed in relation to positive statements, and the influence the particular negative expression is likely to have on the partner.

Reciprocating Negativity

When someone is negative to us we are more likely to be negative back. Although this is nothing new to most people, it may be news that reciprocating negativity is one of the best discriminators between couples who will have a lasting marriage and those who will divorce. In fact, the tendency to reciprocate negativity is more important than the amount of negativity in a relationship (Gottman, 1994; 1999). In couples that stay happily married, partners are more able to break out of negative

Reciprocating negative behaviors in marriage is one of the best predictors of divorce.

cycles by responding with a positive or at least a neutral response when the conversation starts spiraling downward. This does not mean that partners try to discount the negativity of the partner or ignore the problem. What it means is that satisfied couples learn that it is okay that partners have negative feelings. A partner's expression of something negative is not a sign that the relationship is in trouble or that someone is worthless or failing. In fact, because negative feelings are often harder for many people to express, it is possible to even see the expression of something negative as a greater sign of trust and openness than the expression of positive sentiments. In other words, when a partner expresses negative affect to you it is an *invitation for intimacy and closeness* rather than an invitation for distance and distress. Many of us do not automatically see negative expressions by others as an invitation for intimacy. Learning to see negativity in this light requires a degree of maturity and self-confidence that takes experience and time. In fact, for those who have taken RELATE, over sixty percent feel attacked when their partner expresses something negative. Females and males are similar in their tendency to interpret negative comments by partners in a defensive manner.

There is a strong logic to seeing negativity as an invitation for intimacy. Working through our frustrations or disappointments is one of the quickest ways to improve our feelings about ourselves and about the people around us. Conversely, pent-up frustration can lead to unpredictable explosions, depression, and distance. It is also clear that if a person finally decides to express certain frustrations and negative feelings to a partner and then the partner explodes, withdraws, or criticizes, chances are that similar feelings will not be expressed in the future and intimacy will be more evasive.

The Cascade to Isolation and Divorce

Not Accepting Influence from the Partner

The first step in the cascade to isolation and divorce (see Figure 13.1) is that one person, most often the male, does not accept influence from the partner (Gottman, 1999). This means that when a person, usually the female, tries to change things, have a say in matters, or influence the relationship in one way or another, she feels rebuffed, ignored, powerless, irrelevant, or dismissed. The male may not be purposely trying to ignore his partner. It may be that his nonverbal behaviors and the

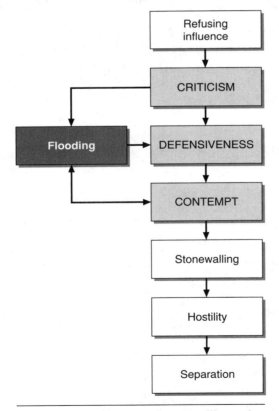

FIGURE 13.1   *The Cascade to Hostility and Separation*

lack of change after communication send an implicit message that, over time, leads his partner to feel that she has little influence on what happens in the relationship. One measure of not accepting influence (from the RELATE questionnaire) is the degree to which females perceive their partners as being good at listening and understanding them. The Empathy Scale is a measure of these attributes. When a female rates her partner as someone who is low on empathy it is likely that she will also perceive that there is inequality in the relationship. Low empathy and inequality in a relationship lead to the second step in the cascade.

Criticism

When a person feels that he or she has little influence on what happens, that person is more likely to criticize. Sometimes people have learned to be critical in their interpersonal relationships regardless of how much influence they think they have. Others are critical only when they get fatigued, frustrated, or are feeling depressed.

What is criticism? The dictionary defines it as "the act of finding fault, censuring, or disapproval" (Guralnik, 1982, p. 336). All of us say negative things at times, but all negative comments are not necessarily criticism. For example, if you said "I'm not happy with the way our relationship is going," this is negative, but because you have not found fault, censored, or expressed disapproval, it is not criticism. On the other hand, if you said "This relationship isn't going well because you're too selfish," clearly this is finding fault and is criticism. People naturally react more defensively to criticism and it has a way of undermining positive feelings of compassion and love.

Nevertheless, all people at times lapse into critical statements about others. This is to be expected in busy lives filled with many disappointments and much stress. Criticism is not lethal to the relationship in small doses, but it moves the couple down the negative cascade that can lead to more difficult problems.

Flooding

One of the most detrimental side effects of criticism is a principle called flooding. Researchers who developed this term say that a person is flooded when emotions become so strong and prevalent that they dominate a person's emotional world (Ekman, 1984). A flooded person is having such intense feelings that she or he cannot think as clearly as usual and is more likely to react and say things that are not helpful. When flooded, people may feel heart pounding, face flushing, an increase in perspiration, and other physiological signs of distress or excitement (Gottman, 1994). Throughout the negative cascade that leads to separation, flooding is a primary result of criticism and other types of negativity and is a cause of strong feelings that lead to defensive reactions and the desire to isolate oneself.

Each person has a different baseline of flooding, in that some are much more likely to react physiologically to criticism or threats than others. Researchers from the RELATE Institute have found that a person's natural tendency to act impulsive or feel anxious are closely related to the tendency to experience flooding (Busby &

Taniguchi, 2000). It may be that there is little a person can do regarding an innate tendency to feel flooded, but there is much that can be done to reduce the duration and intensity of emotional flooding. Interventions that reduce flooding and help arrest the negative cascade will be briefly mentioned at the end of this chapter and other strategies to prevent this negative cascade will be discussed in the next chapter.

Defensiveness

Most people who are criticized and become flooded are likely to respond in defensive or reactive ways. In times of calm it is easy to recognize that responding defensively only makes matters worse, but such thinking is too rational for most of us when we are flooded. Defensive responses are more than offering an alternative or different perspective; they are responses that lash back at the partner either through the words that are used, the tone of the voice, or both. However, when a partner is criticizing, she or he might be so upset that any attempt to discuss a different perspective may make matters worse and may be perceived as defensive. At times, when people are on a "criticism roll," just letting them vent for a short while is the only response available. The first response to criticism by a partner is a very crucial response that can lead to worse arguments or a resolution. Defensive responses are sure to lead to the next step in the cascade.

Contempt

Perhaps the most destructive and unique aspect of the cascade to separation is contempt. Gottman reports that contempt is not a part of healthy relationships as is some degree of criticism and defensiveness (Gottman, 1999). This suggests that once contempt is reached, a couple has passed a threshold from normal arguing and fighting to severe problems.

Contempt is different from criticism. The dictionary defines contempt as the "condition of being despised or scorned" (Guralnik, 1982, p. 306). Here it is clear that although criticism is saying something negative about someone else, contempt is something much worse. All criticism is not necessarily laced with contempt, though most contemptuous statements include some criticism. However, some contempt does not even include words, as some people are experts at conveying contempt through a look of scorn or hatred. The defining characteristics of contempt are the strong feelings that convey to the partner that she or he is worthless, irrelevant, or inferior. Typically, partners can recognize when they have reached the contemptuous stage because their feelings are so intensely negative and their fights are so brutal that it is clear to everyone that the relationship creates a punishing, hostile environment. Whereas some couples can stop their contemptuous remarks and heal, this is often the stage at which things are said that may leave a lasting negative impression that is hard to overcome. To avoid these contemptuous exchanges and strong feelings, couples usually escape to the next step in the cascade.

Stonewalling

Stonewalling is where one or both partners put up a seemingly impervious wall that blocks the other person out. Most of us, if confronted by others who are extremely negative and contemptuous, will leave or refuse to be involved any longer. Married couples live together and must continue to be in close proximity as long as the relationship lasts. Stonewalling, then, is an escape without physically escaping; it is the emotional withdrawal from a relationship so that the partner cannot penetrate the defenses. Males are more likely to stonewall or withdraw, whereas females are more likely to keep pounding away at the wall and criticizing (Gottman, 1994). When one partner has stonewalled, the couple is in the last death throes of the relationship and is likely to end up separated before long.

Hostility and Separation

A couple that engages in high rates of criticism, defensiveness, and contempt is by definition in a hostile relationship. Close on the heels of hostility are separation, sometimes violence, depression, and increased alcohol or other drug use (Busby & Taniguchi, 2000). As discussed in Chapter 12, hostile couples are inflicting wound after wound on partner and self and children. Sometimes, though, couples who have reached the stonewalling stage are actually less hostile and conflictual, because they have created such impervious barriers and avoid one another so thoroughly that interactions are minimized. Whether the couple fades into extreme distance that is characterized by silence or hostility is of little consequence because the end result is the same: the termination of the relationship. The following two descriptions illustrate how different, but equally tragic, are these two ways of drifting apart:

A Woman's Description of Her Stonewalling Relationship:
We got to the point where he slept in the basement and I slept in the bedroom. We never ate together, traveled together, or did any of the daily chores in the same room where the other person was. We just naturally found ways of going to work at different times and arriving home at different times. In fact the only time we were in the same place together was when we had to go to work functions and put on our happy faces and pretend we were a married couple again. I don't know what we would have done had the kids still been at home as that would have made our deafening silence impossible to enforce. I can remember weeks passing where I never heard his voice and he never heard mine. It isn't mysterious at all why both of us started looking outside the relationship for love.

A Man's Description of His Hostile Relationship:
We would fight long into the night, throwing insult after insult at each other in our sleep-deprived stupor. We were like two pit bulls who refused to unlock their jaws until one died. Oh, how I hated her and

myself! Those things we said to each other that were so awful, words I never imagined would come out of my mouth—vile, vulgar insults day after day. Even now after several years I get angry just thinking about some of the things she said to me and I want to call her up and blast her again. It is a miracle we didn't kill each other before the divorce.

Such can be the horrifying end to what were once loving relationships after couples have allowed themselves to drift down the cascade of negative communication patterns. The good news is that the next chapter will describe many of the ways couples can keep from getting to such places in their relationships by practicing positive communication. However, a few words need to be added regarding how to arrest the progress down the cascade to separation.

Resisting the Pull of Gravity

Many if not most couples resist the downward pull of these negative communication patterns and find a way to turn their relationship in a positive direction. Some people have a strong resistance to destructive communication and were given good roles models so they know when and how to provide a soothing word or to acknowledge fault so that defenses are no longer necessary. A key to resisting the negative cascade is catching negative interactions early and noticing when you or your partner is flooded.

The very first instance of criticism in a discussion can be a key moment. Cognitive therapists have described a technique for years that is very effective at reducing someone's critical remarks and resolving angry outbursts (Burns, 1999). This technique has five steps that can be taken when someone else is critical or angry:

1. Listen nondefensively to what is said and find something to agree with.
2. Express appreciation for the person's honesty and agree with a part of what was said.
3. Attempt to begin a resolution of the issue by seeking more clarification or asking for suggestions.
4. Ask if there is anything else that is bothering the person about the situation or about you. Go back to step 1 if necessary.
5. Disengage from the person if steps 1–4 only lead to increased hostility.

The following example illustrates how this process might look in an argument with a couple.

>**H:** (said in an angry voice after looking at the mail) Sometimes you are just so forgetful it makes me crazy! You write things down and still you don't follow through. Now the electric company is going to shut off the electricity because the bill wasn't paid again.

W: (in a calm tone of voice) I make myself crazy sometimes too, but this wasn't my fault (she slips into a slightly defensive mode).

H: (now very upset) How can you say that! The bill hasn't been paid for almost three months! Surely you must have realized that our checking account had more money in it than usual.

W: You're right. I knew the bill hadn't been paid and I should have called them up immediately and found out what I could do about it.

H: (much less upset). Well are you going to call them today?

W: I already have, that's what I meant when I said it wasn't my fault. They had us mixed up with another family with the same last name so our bill last month was sent to a different address and we never received it. That doesn't excuse me from getting on it more quickly but it made it easier for me to put it off.

H: (now as calm as she is). So are they going to shut off the power like they said?

W: No; I paid the bill over the phone and they have our correct address now. Do you have any ideas how we could handle the bills differently? I was thinking the other day that maybe I should keep the checkbook balanced and you should be the one that pays the bills. I am getting a little tired of keeping on top of the bills.

H: I don't mind doing the bills, but I hate reconciling the checkbook. As long as you can get it balanced before I need to pay bills it should work out.

W: Is there anything else that's bothering you?

H: (said in jest) Yeah—could you make another $50,000 a year so we won't need to worry about how much is left in the checking account?

Although this technique can help reduce angry exchanges, it only works as long as one partner remembers to stay calm enough to use it. Inevitably, both people will get upset to the point that the steps are not followed and arguments ensue. A crucial key to stopping an argument once it begins is for the couple to become adept at recognizing when someone is flooded.

Because of the physiological responses that occur when someone is flooded, clear rational discussions cannot be accomplished for a considerable amount of time afterward. The heart rate, blood pressure, and accompanying hormones that course through the body can keep a flooded person more hypervigilant and less able to think clearly for up to several hours after an argument (Gottman, 1999). This means that once an argument is going full blast it is necessary to disengage and calm down for some time before attempting to address the issues. Yet if partners have not acknowledged this reality and the need to calm down, they might pursue each other instead of disengaging and thereby make the argument last longer and increase the risk of additional problems.

Learning how to detect whether you are flooded or your partner might be flooded is crucial to stopping these arguments. Though difficult, it is possible to notice the earliest signs of being flooded, such as a tightness in the chest, angry feelings, a physical sensation of being blushed or hot, or stomach distress. If you can agree that when either person notices these signs in self or other a time-out will be taken, many arguments can be stopped before they lead to worse behaviors. It is best not to suggest, though, that the conversation should be stopped because you notice your partner is too upset. This will only encourage a denial or more intense feelings in your partner. It is most effective to just say, "I'm getting too upset about this right now. I need some time to calm down before I can talk about it any more"—even if you think your partner is more upset than you are! A word of caution, though: If someone is always stopping conversations and not getting back to the issues, it is probably more about avoidance than about being flooded and this will need to be discussed. Also, if your partner or you find yourself angry enough to hit or say very destructive things almost instantly, without warning, you may need some additional help from medical or psychological professionals to discover what can be done to reduce the intensity and rapidity of your feelings.

There are many approaches to calming yourself down—from relaxation training, to meditation, listening to music, or participating in nonintensive exercises. Each person can usually discover several ways to soothe feelings and reduce the heart rate. What is more difficult is consistently finding the willpower to stop negative interactions and to become self-aware enough to use the relaxation techniques when they are needed.

14

Positive Communication Patterns

Mutual empathy is the great unsung human gift. We are all born with the possibility of engaging in it. Out of it flows mutual empowerment.

—Miller & Stiver

A basic principle of the communication literature is that you **cannot not** communicate. People generally prefer to interact with others who like them, and evidence of liking is gathered from verbal and nonverbal communication that indicates genuine positive regard. Estimates are that most communication is nonverbal, which means that much of the information that one has about being liked is sent nonverbally.

Positive communication involves appropriate wording and effective problem-solving strategies, but it involves more, too. Positive communication involves a positive attitude that results in positive causal attributions: The partner's intentions toward oneself and the relationship are understood to be good. The belief system that underlies positive communication patterns is one in which a wide range of behavioral options are acceptable, and the overall approach to such relationship interaction is genuine and loving. Couples who communicate positively are able to look beyond inevitable human failings and focus their faith in the essential goodness of their partners. In these couples, competition gives way to collaboration, "I told you so" is replaced with kindness (e.g., "I'm sorry it didn't work out the way you wanted it to"), and "I want" is replaced with "we need." As the old joke goes, a good marriage is one that couples go into with their eyes wide open, and stay in with their eyes half shut. Positive communication is that which allows for a safe, full discourse in advance of behaviors, and allows for processing and connection after an event. In positive communication, the nonverbal message gives validity to a congruent verbal message that conveys "I believe in you and me."

According to Carl Rogers (1965), the keys to a positive relationship are warmth, genuine positive regard, and honesty. In this chapter we will look at the five key rules of positive communication patterns that help to create that relation-ship: (1) positive thoughts about your partner, (2) positive reframing of events to give partners the benefit of the doubt, (3) acceptance of a wide range of partner thoughts and behaviors, (4) willingness to let go of differences, and (5) a mutual appreciation for and acknowledgment of trust in the relationship.

Positive Thoughts About Your Partner

In any relationship there are some behaviors that are more appreciated than others. It is fairly predictable that some behaviors that are enjoyed early in a relationship become more difficult to tolerate as the relationship progresses. According to Harriet Lerner (2001), much of the early behavior in intimate relationships involves a pur-poseful avoidance of areas of annoyance so that the illusion of a perfect match between two persons is not crushed. For example, a person may have a habit of not replacing the caps on items after using them, and that trait may be "sweet" in the eyes of the new partner. Over time, there is the potential for the attribution of "sweet" to become one of "rude." Many jokes have been made about the disagree-ments that newlyweds can have over toothpaste caps and toilet paper rolls (although for many newlyweds this dilemma is anything but funny). The disagree-ments begin as issues about a misplaced cap, but they can quickly accelerate to issues about the meaning that nonreplacement has for the person who feels com-pelled to clean up behind the absent-minded partner. Meanings that events have for relationships begin at the behavioral level ("He left the cap off the toothpaste."), ascend to the normative level of meaning ("This is behavior that I would/would not expect from an appropriate spouse."), and end at the dispositional level ("A spouse who leaves the toothpaste cap off is charming/rude.") (Braiker & Kelley, 1979). The acceleration to negative dispositions is held in check by positive communication pat-terns, and the negative behavior does not result in a negative attribution but is seen as an exception to the stable, positive disposition of the partner.

In close relationships, thoughts about one's partner are eventually communi-cated, even if it is through nonverbal communication. If I learn that my partner has a habit of not replacing caps, and I believe he is thoughtful and kind, I will develop a solution for myself that involves a partner who does not replace the caps, or we will negotiate a compromise where he learns to replace caps or I have my own tooth-paste. If, however, I believe that my partner's neglect in replacing caps is an ex-ample of his thoughtlessness and arrogance, I will become angry. The attribution to thoughtlessness and arrogance provides the battleground for a power struggle over a toothpaste cap. My nonverbal behavior will be affected by my thoughts about my partner's disposition, and he will likely reciprocate the behavior he experiences from my *nonverbal* behavior.

Positive thoughts, then, consist of a willingness to look for the good in the be-haviors of, and interactions with, a partner. The communication with the partner is not as a cheerleader who chants a predictable cheer despite a losing score, but more like the coach who acknowledges the team's fundamental talents despite a need to work on timing. It is warm, positive, and realistic. In positive communication the partners do not ignore difficulties, but create an experience of positive regard such that problems are viewed as being outside of the nature of the partner, and hence are viewed as changeable. This, according to Gottman (1999), becomes a fundamental repair technique: Couples become their own therapists by finding the healthy and positive aspects of their communication and responding to that part of the communication, rather than reciprocating what is negative. The balance of positives in the relationship keeps partners from emotional flooding and the subsequent risk of contempt and stonewalling.

Attention and Connection

Positive communication is fundamentally reciprocal. That means that positive communication strategies involve both partners' attention to the needs and thoughts of the other. Others learn of our feelings toward them through behavior and words, including the ways in which we respond to their bids for attention and the ways we use nonverbal attending behaviors. A key part of this reciprocity is listening for what is said and for what is unsaid. According to John Gottman, people make bids for their partner's attention that can take the form of affectionate touching, facial expressions, playful touching, affiliating gestures (e.g., opening a door), or vocalizing. Depending on the partner's response to those bids, the couple can feel closer or

Nonverbal attending behaviors are simple to include in interactions, and make a big difference in the ways in which the experience is felt.

more distant (Gottman & Declaire, 2001). Partners who hear each other's bids and respond to the bids by turning *toward* their partner (e.g., attending to the concern or interest in the sender's message) have more satisfying relationships than those who either ignore the bids or meet the bids with antagonism. Those who turn *away* from bids (are preoccupied, disregard the concern, or interrupt) give the impression that they are uncaring about their partner's concern. Those who turn *against* the bid may be rude or contradictory, and give the impression of being mean or hostile.

Being liked is an important component of the loving relationship because liking is a component of love (Braiker & Kelley, 1979). Attention to a partner bid is important, yet sometimes, as in the case of turning away from a bid, it is simply a lack of appropriate attending behavior that makes the partner feel unimportant. Other times attending to a bid can become overwhelming because a complaint or criticism is feared. When that happens, partners often want to turn away or fight back.

Nonverbal attending behaviors are simple to include in interactions, can be done in a way that is soothing, and can make the difference in a partner feeling important or unimportant. For example, nonverbal attending behavior such as eye contact and head nodding tell the bidder that you are acknowledging the bid. Keeping an open body position, smiling, or adding minimal vocal responses (e.g., mmm, I see, huh) show communication effort without usurping the speaker. Finally, minimizing distracting behaviors by not playing with keys, change, hair, or jewelry tells the partner that she or he has your full attention. When flooding is occurring, partners should take extra care to purposely slow down head nodding, and focus on keeping breathing at a slow and even pace. It is necessary to find a way to self-soothe so that you can be present for your partner, and yet keep yourself from becoming overwhelmed. Also, because partners will synchronize with you, you can soothe your partner by remaining soothed yourself. For example,

> *Judy:*   Bill, Can I talk to you about my mother's birthday present?
>
> *Bill:*   Hmmm (deep breath), I'm not sure, I have an uneasy feeling right now that this could get ugly.
>
> *Judy:*   Yeah, we're having some trouble about this and I feel pretty firm about what I'm thinking. We can do this.
>
> *Bill:*   OK (nodding head, slowly).

Bill took some time to answer, while taking a deep relaxation breath. Then, he used head nodding to keep a slow pace. Judy, who recognizes flooding in her partner, gives him both time (waits for him to be ready for the conversation) and encouragement ("We can do this."). Bill makes it rewarding for his partner to be patient by having the conversation even if he's uncomfortable. After the bid is an opportunity to experience connection and fuel positive affect in the relationship. Such stockpiling of positives buffers the relationship against the potential negatives.

There are times in which members of the couple do not attend to the communication no matter how clearly the bid is sent. It is more difficult to be ignored than it is to be disagreed with, because at least in disagreement the interpersonal connection is validated. The partner derives meaning from inattention, ranging from understanding the possibility that the partner is preoccupied to feeling ignored and disconnected. The way in which the listener completes that piece of the puzzle has much to do with the overall quality of the relationship. When ignoring is present, the connection is unavailable, and fear is prevalent. A partner may think, "He is just too wrapped up in what he is doing; I'll have to get his attention another way." In contrast, the partner might attribute disagreement or disrespect, causing another layer of communication difficulty (e.g., "Well at least suggest a better idea, don't just turn away from me.").

In summary, positive thoughts about a partner influence the relationship by creating a frame of reference within which to process the partner's behavior, and by establishing the reciprocal experiences that are beneficial to the relationship. Partners may bid for the other's attention in a number of ways, and how that bid is acknowledged makes a difference in the relationship satisfaction. Sometimes, despite the best efforts, events occur that are not satisfying to the sender, the receiver, or both. At these times, events can be framed—or reframed—in a way that gives the partner the benefit of the doubt.

Positive Reframing of Events to Give Partners the Benefit of the Doubt

Positive communication patterns involve a tendency to use positive reframing of events when necessary to give a partner the benefit of the doubt. Positive reframing of events involves objectively observing an interaction and noticing anything outside of the situation that could help the couple rethink the event in a way that makes attributions to positive dispositions logical. For example, if a woman wants to go out dancing on a Friday night, and her partner suggests a different activity instead, she has at least two choices of how to think about his suggestion. She may become upset and think that he is trying to control her. Alternatively, she may reframe the situation and tell herself that her partner is also invested in the relationship and he has given serious thought to what they might want to do together. The reframe changes how one might see the situation and intentions, and gives it another "spin" so that an event can be viewed in a more relationship-friendly way. Rather than being a power struggle, it is an issue of both persons making an effort. The latter is much more enriching for the overall relationship feeling.

Reframing requires understanding yourself well enough to know what you are reacting to, reviewing the situation objectively, and stepping back to find a way of understanding the situation from a completely fresh lens. Reframing events is particularly helpful when one is on the receiving side of an abrupt, or impolite, message. For example, imagine that Craig has been very distracted with his work and tonight Sandy is hosting an important dinner at their home. Sandy asked Craig to be sure to come home early so that he could help her with the last-minute details. Craig agreed to be home by 6:00, but at 6:30 he still has not arrived. Sandy was deciding which things to take care of, and which to forget about when Craig finally arrived. Sandy caught herself being sarcastic and saying, "Gee, thanks for the help." Craig snapped back, "You're welcome!" This is the beginning of a potentially tense evening that can easily become a power struggle over what time he should have been home, the number of times in the past he has not measured up, and a critique about his response. Keep in mind that "it's not what you say but how you say it." Effective feedback skills help to avoid some of the pitfalls of using disagreeable responses, and help turn around unhelpful statements after they are made.

The situation can be diffused by the use of a reframe that allows for a positive attribution of the other and a new look at the situation that takes into account the experience of the other. When the situation is reframed Sandy can calm down. When she is calm, she can think in nondefensive ways and look at the bright side of things. It is easier to be validating when you are not feeling defensive so you will have the energy to take responsibility for that which is your responsibility, and compliment your partner for her or his contribution to your relationship.

In the former example, Sandy may think about the effort that Craig made to be home when he was, the difficulty for him of switching from worker to host so quickly, and possibly decide that the tasks she wanted Craig to do could be left in his hands and he would manage. Taking his perspective, and attributing to him positive intentions, a reframe of the situation can turn a potential power struggle into a connection. She may decide that he is thoughtful of her and that he does what he can to comply with her requests.

Specific skills are important in positive communication so that the intention of the sender and the understanding of the listener are clear and manageable. Even though the verbal message is a small part of the message, it is important. The best intentions in the world can be hidden by an inappropriate choice of words; appropriate words make what is experienced tangible and manageable. It is not a message of disagreement or unhappiness that makes a message negative, but the method of delivering that message.

Manageability is an important tool in turning a situation around before it becomes a major negative event. A self-disclosing statement helps diffuse a negative event because the sender has the opportunity to reframe the message to take into account the effect of the circumstances on both partners' behavior. In the previous situation, Sandy may feel the need to tell Craig how angry she was that he did not arrive earlier to help her. By taking responsibility for her anger, she might say, "I realize that you are here to help with the party, and I can use the help. I am not feeling very happy right now because I need to work through my anger that you were not here when I was expecting you."

Effective Self-Disclosure

Reframing events occurs when one is able to step back from a problem and look at it from a fresh perspective. Ownership of the problem allows that stepping back to occur. Some problems are his, some are hers, and some are theirs. The focus of effective self-disclosure is on the part of the problem that belongs to the speaker. The primary component of self-disclosure is ownership of thoughts, feelings, and behaviors. Problems are stated as "I" statements, giving any information to the listener that is relevant to the speaker's experience in the specific instance.

Effective self-disclosure is a brief statement with three components: affect, situation, and action. The affect is the feeling word that is associated with the event. Some examples of words that describe affect are happy, delighted, anxious, sad, angry (see Table 14.1 for more affect word choices). The situation is a short phrase that helps the listener distinguish the context that caused the event to be a problem for the speaker at this time. The action is a short phrase that describes the event in behavioral terms. Behavioral descriptions focus on that which is observable and countable. One way to deliver a self-disclosing statement is to fill in the blanks in the following formula: I feel (affect) because/about (situation, action). For example, "I feel angry because I was planning to leave at 8:00 and you arrived at 8:30." Self-disclosure is often regarding something that has gone wrong, but it can be used for positive messages as well. For example, "I feel pleased because I wanted to finish cleaning the house and you helped with the chores that needed to be finished."

The most difficult part of learning to use effective self-disclosure is to learn to own one's thoughts, feelings, and behaviors. In fact, it is so tempting to blame a partner under the pretense of using an "I" message that such mistakes have a name: disguised "you" messages. Placing the blame or responsibility on a partner can be done directly as a "you" message (e.g., "You are wrong!"), or indirectly as a disguised "you" message (e.g., "I feel like you are wrong!"). Notice that an early sign that a disguised "you" message is coming is that a cognition word is used instead of a feeling word. "I feel *like*" begins a thought, whereas "I feel angry" is a feeling. If the speaker is very careful to use an affect statement at the beginning of the phrase, "I feel _____," it will be more difficult to create a "you" message.

Providing the extra information that is needed to communicate the dilemma or understand the circumstantial information is most efficiently done with the use of "I" messages. The most difficult part of "I" messages is the urge to assign blame to a partner for transgressions, in which case "I" messages are delivered as "you" messages. When faced with a "you" message partners feel judged, which is counterproductive when the goal is to maintain positive communication in a relationship.

TABLE 14.1   *Affect Words*

Happiness	*Sadness*	*Fear*	*Uncertainty*	*Anger*
Happy	Discouraged	Scared	Puzzled	Upset
Pleased	Disappointed	Anxious	Confused	Frustrated
Satisfied	Hurt	Frightened	Unsure	Bothered
Glad	Despairing	Defensive	Uncertain	Annoyed
Optimistic	Depressed	Threatened	Skeptical	Irritated
Good	Disillusioned	Afraid	Doubtful	Resentful
Relaxed	Dismayed	Tense	Undecided	Mad
Content	Pessimistic	Nervous	Bewildered	Outraged
Cheerful	Miserable	Uptight	Mistrustful	Hassled
Thrilled	Unhappy	Uneasy	Insecure	Offended
Delighted	Hopeless	Worried	Bothered	Angry
Excited	Lonely	Panicked	Disoriented	Furious

When a partner feels judged, defensiveness and power struggles typically result. It is a short descent from defensiveness to contempt and then to stonewalling (Gottman, 1999).

There are times, of course, when couples disagree, and the most carefully constructed "I" messages do not alleviate the dilemma. In some situations, couples must decide to accept the partner's thoughts and behaviors, and know that understanding a partner and agreeing with a partner are two completely separate issues.

Acceptance of a Wide Range of Partner Thoughts and Behaviors

Carl Rogers made famous the notion that all that is truly necessary for a therapeutic relationship to exist is genuineness and unconditional acceptance. Although most family therapists today would insist on using more than those communication skills in a session, most clinicians use empathic listening to convey understanding and acceptance of their clients. Couples with positive communication send and receive accurate messages from their partners, and those messages communicate genuineness, warmth, and unconditional positive regard. Does that sound easy to you? Given the short self-disclosure phrase presented in the previous section, it should be relatively easy to communicate acceptance. Unfortunately, sometimes the words that a partner uses are "I accept you," but the whole message communicated indicates that the partner's thoughts and behaviors are *not* accepted. Couples with positive communication are able to accept a wide range of partner thoughts and behaviors, and they communicate that acceptance at several levels of a single message.

There are at least three levels on which all messages are communicated: direct, meta, and meta-meta. The direct message involves the actual words that are spoken. The meta level includes the meaning that the words have for a receiver. The meta-meta level is the attribution the receiver makes about her or his value to the speaker. A genuine message of acceptance is clear at each of the levels of communication, and in positive communication, the direct level of the message is kind and nonblaming. It takes into account the effect the words will have on the other person. The message can be positive or negative, but extra care is taken to assure that any negative feedback is focused on behavior rather than disposition, and on that which has a reasonable chance for improvement.

For communication to be positive, the beliefs underlying the message also must be positive. Hence, positive interpersonal communication has as its fundamental principle a belief in the essential goodness of the partner. If you believe that your partner is good, and has good intentions, even when you are disappointed in him or her you communicate that belief. If you believe your partner is bad and has poor intentions, your words similarly will communicate that. Imagine that you believe that all convenience store cashiers will try to "get away with" short-changing you. If you go into a convenience store to buy a soda, and the cashier gives you the incorrect change, how might you respond? If you were expecting to be cheated you may be angry and triumphant that you caught the cheat at his own game. Now imagine that you were once a convenience store clerk and remember it as one of the most difficult jobs of your career because of the poor treatment you experienced from complete strangers. You expect the cashier to be an honest, hard worker. When a mistake is made you are probably going to be understanding and work patiently to correct the error. Your thoughts about the circumstances and intentions surrounding the error influence your response to the problem.

In positive communication the nonverbal and verbal messages are congruent, so the meaning at the meta level is the same as at the direct level. When the speaker says, "I am angry about the mess in the living room," with an angry look and an angry voice tone, the listener understands the message to be "He is angry with the mess that I made." The listener attends to the speaker's whole message with little interference from extraneous information, and there is clear understanding between the sender and the receiver. When the words and the body language are in disagreement, however, the most carefully chosen words are little competition for the nonverbal message. When I tell my partner "I *am* being patient," with my teeth clenched and my voice rising, the message that he will hear is the nonverbal, vocal tone message: "I have lost my patience!" Since only one of the messages can be true, the listener can choose to believe either the verbal or the nonverbal message, and the nonverbal is typically more influential.

At the meta level of communication, the words spoken take on different meanings depending on the situation and on the nonverbal language of the sender. The nonverbal language includes body language and vocal utterances that do not constitute words but have meaning nonetheless. In the American culture, head nodding, eye contact, open body positioning, smiling, minimizing distracting behaviors, and minimal responses are all attending behaviors that provide information at the meta level of communication. The direct level of communication may be "I have time to talk with you about this," and the nonverbal message may be "I am looking at my watch continually because I really have someplace else to go." Nonverbal language also includes silence. Silence is extremely meaningful in most interpersonal communication. It can mean "I won't give you the satisfaction of making a comment right now," or it can mean "I am thinking about your concerns and developing my response so that I can be helpful in this relationship." In positive communication all of these skills are used to increase the likelihood of a discussion occurring, rather than as an attempt to manipulate the situation.

When the nonverbal and verbal messages are incongruent, meaning is established by the listener using interpersonal attributions to fill in the missing information. Interpersonal attributions are reasons that are attached to personality or disposition. In a strong relationship, when meaning is unclear, the attributional choice is typically positive (e.g., concerned, worried, ambitious). With dissatisfied couples, the attributional choice is more often to ascribe negative intentions (e.g., nosey, obsessed, bossy). The attribution selected greatly influences the listener's probable responses to the sender.

At the meta-meta level the message has meaning for the listener about the listener. In positive communication the listener experiences genuine positive regard—for example, "I am important to my partner." Such a message is communicated in body language that is consistent with the overall message, and interpersonally connected. In relationships that are strong, couples make positive attributions, assume positive speaker intention, and search for meaning when there are exceptions to those experiences. In dissatisfied relationships, couples use the discomfort at the meta-meta level as evidence that the partner intends ill will.

The verbal message is the most tangible part of communication. When there is a problem at the direct level of communication it is relatively easy to repair. When the problem is at the meta level, it is human nature to search for the meaning of any communication to determine how the other feels about the listener. This is the information at the meta-meta level that provides the foundation for future relationship attributions: We like others who like us, and we treat others in ways reciprocal to how they treat us. Oddly, while it is self-disclosure that sends information about acceptance from the speaker to the listener, it is the empathic listening that one does that helps the partner to feel understood and accepted.

Empathic Listening

The empathy scale on the RELATE instrument is consistently either the most important or one of the three most important scales in predicting relationship satisfaction, depending on what other scales are used. If there is any one communication area that couples should focus on to the exclusion of others, it would be learning to express empathy more regularly.

Empathic listening involves two necessary components: (1) the ability to understand and accept another person, and (2) the ability to convey understanding and acceptance back to the other. The goal with empathic listening is to recognize, in a short phrase, the sender's entire message. The sender is the person who is speaking, or sending a message nonverbally. For example, the partner who says, "I am really trying to be on time to this party," is sending a verbal message, while the partner who stands at the door, coat in hand and staring at his watch, is similarly sending a message about timeliness. The listener is the person for whom the communication is intended. Although the listener articulates an empathic response, for the sake of this example, she is still called the listener. Most simply, the listener may use a minimal response and genuine body language to say, "I understand you are anxious." When a minimal response is not enough, a verbal phrase that is very similar to the self-disclosing statement may be used. The listener might say, "You feel (affect) because/about (situation, action). For example, "You are ready and anxious to go, and I'm holding you up."

There are different opinions about how empathy should be expressed. Research by Gottman (1999) has challenged this use of empathic listening because he has not found it to be usually used by healthy couples. They may, for example, be more likely to say, "I know you want to leave soon and I'm doing my best to get ready." Conversely, in clinical situations (i.e., couples who have come to therapy with the complaint that they are having trouble communicating), it is extremely

A therapist can slow down the couple's communication so that they are able to understand the needs and concerns of one another.

helpful to slow the couple down so that they are really hearing and understanding each other before either proceeding with the next issue or offering countercomplaints. The formal process of expressing self-disclosure and empathy helps couples to understand the concept of ownership of thoughts, feelings, and behaviors, and gives the partners experiences of being heard. While they may vary from the formula once they have learned to convey their empathy, generally at the beginning of learning that skill it is a good idea to stay close to the formula.

Timeliness is one of those perpetual problems that Gottman (1999) talks about that conveys basic differences in partners' personalities or in needs that are central to their concepts of who they are as people. It is tempting to "fix" problems when partners are upset, and make promises to change behavior that may not be possible. For example, you may be tempted to say, "Okay, I'll do my best to be on time because I know it's important to you." The focus with empathy is on hearing the speaker's whole message, so the feeling word is one that represents the feeling of the speaker, not of the listener. In positive communication, the speaker feels understood and accepted, and that experience prevents the speaker from escalating, and reiterating the complaint. It is helpful when partners focus on the feeling and do not make any promises that can't be kept, while avoiding anything that might create more hurt. Once the complaint is understood, both the speaker and listener can move on to the next point of business. Notice the following examples, and try to point out where the speaker felt understood and accepted.

Situation One:

Speaker: "I am waiting to go meet our friends, hurry up."

Listener: "I am almost done, hold on."

Speaker: "I've been holding on for 15 minutes!"

Listener: "I can hear you are anxious. I am going as quickly as I can."

Speaker: "I'm going to wait in the car."

Situation Two:

Speaker: "I am waiting to go meet our friends, hurry up."

Listener: "I am almost done, hold on."

Speaker: "I've been holding on for 15 minutes!"

Listener: "You could do something constructive instead of just waiting for me."

Speaker: "I don't want to do something constructive, I want you to hurry up."

Listener: "I *am* hurrying up. I *know* you're waiting."

Speaker: "Right, but you're still late! I'm going to wait in the car."

The phrase that indicated understanding and acceptance included the feeling of the speaker in the response statement. It is in knowing how the speaker feels, and identifying the behavioral and situational reason for the feeling that helps one to get beyond the complaint. That is done in Situation One, "I can hear you are anxious." When an empathic statement is done well, the speaker does not need to pursue a complaint. When an issue is pursued long after it has occurred, there is a good chance that the speaker does not feel understood, and will continue to bring the discussion back to the event until she or he feels adequately understood. When perpetual problems continue to arise, partners become more and more hurt until they agree to disagree. If the listener gives advice or makes promises, it is difficult to get to the point of agreeing on what can reasonably be expected in the particular situation. In Situation Two it is quite likely that the conversation in the car will continue the disagreement (i.e., whether the speaker was reasonable in his expectations, or the receiver in her response). Empathic responses have the potential to work well in soothing partners and resolving issues. It sometimes feels incomplete to listeners to limit themselves to simple empathic statements, yet when information is added beyond empathy, such as including a judgment ("If you don't stop being so Type A you are going to have a heart attack!"), the empathy can be lost.

David Johnson (2000), in his book *Reaching Out*, recommends that listeners stay away from four common, yet dangerous, responses. Very often in close relationships it is tempting to try to fix the problem of our partner. If a partner is taking the risk to share a problem, it feels somewhat incomplete to simply understand and accept her or his experiences. Often, a cleanly articulated empathic statement is augmented by the use of advice, interpretation, probing, or support by a well-meaning listener. Those four techniques, however, change the communication from understanding and acceptance to something very different. An advising statement sends the message of judgment, that a decision is conveyed about the speaker's situation. For example, a listener who may say, "Just relax, we'll get there when we get there," is giving advice, and misses the speaker's complaint: "I feel uncomfortable when I am late." A listener who uses interpretation may try to help the speaker understand her or his own reaction better. She may say, "You are anxious because you care too much about what other people think." Interpretation disregards the speaker's dilemma in the present, and adds to the problem by introducing other areas in which the speaker could feel misunderstood or unaccepted. Probing, by its very nature, indicates a lack of understanding, because questions are asked when clarification is needed.

Finally, supportive responses do not require any understanding. Whether my closest friend—or a complete stranger—is crying, I can pat her on the back, tell her "Don't worry, it'll be OK," and walk away. The same supportive response is appropriate to a wide variety of experiences, and simply choosing one of them (e.g., "Don't let it get to you.") does not provide empathy. Supportive responses can provide sympathy, and sometimes sympathy and empathy are confused with each other. Empathy is strictly the understanding and acceptance of another, while sympathy is feeling sorry for another. In sympathy you offer comfort and solace. In empathy you offer understanding and acknowledgment. The supportive response does not have to change from one person to the next because it does not require understanding. The understanding response must change from situation to situation. In positive communication empathic responses are used frequently to convey understanding and acceptance of a wide range of partner thoughts and behaviors.

Willingness to Let Go of Differences

It is possible that some behavior of partners will fall outside of even the widest range of partner acceptance. Positive communication strategies involve a system of problem ownership such that couples decide who owns the problem, and can wisely choose which problems have a reasonable chance of being resolved. For those problems that do not have a reasonable chance of resolution, couples with positive communication skills choose agreeing to disagree and decide to forgive themselves and their partner for their perceived loss.

Relationships often begin in romantic love, which is frequently a situation of being in love with love. Partners in romantic love see the aspects of their partners that are exciting and endearing, and tend to disregard those qualities that end up emerging over time that may not meet their expectations in the relationship. For example, a romantic partner who is the life of the party spends time paying attention to a number of people. Over time it becomes clear that to attend to a number of other people means that little time is spent with each person, and often the least amount of time is spent with the romantic partner. This characteristic that was available for noticing at the beginning of the relationship persists as a relationship quality throughout the relationship. Behaviors that may or may not have been noticed before a relationship became serious are noticed and take on new meaning after a relationship becomes serious. These characteristics are referred to as "latent" because they are enduring qualities that are truly part of the partner, yet simply not noticed. Problems with latent characteristics are articulated as a "change." Partners may say, "You've changed now that we are married," when in fact there is often more of an emergence and a noticing than an actual change. The chance of resolving such dilemmas is not very good. The outgoing partner may promise to spend more time with her date, the date may agree to be a little less demanding, but often the couple will struggle as each of them receives less than is desirable from their social life.

A willingness to let go of a partner's transgressions begins with honesty about what is a transgression, and what is simply a difference of opinion about how a situation looks or a difference in personalities. Partners who communicate positively begin with honesty with themselves and each other, and expect to receive only what the other can reasonably be expected to deliver. Positive communication strategies center on a willingness to overlook some interpersonal differences and to eventually either solve the problems or agree to disagree.

Effective Problem Solving

You cannot find the answer to the problem by focusing on the problem. The answer to a problem is embedded in what the situation will look like when there's no problem. The answer to a problem of preferences is in the mutually accepted relationship goals, not in the relationship dilemmas. If your goal is to always arrive on time, and your partner is habitually late, focusing on punctuality is a recipe for failure. The solution to arriving on time is to give yourself ample time to make the journey, and to be comfortable making the journey alone when others need to arrive later. If your goal is to always arrive with your partner on time, and your partner is habitually late, then the goal cannot be obtained. Some couples argue about this emotionally charged dilemma for years, turning it into a struggle for control. They forget about goal assessment and problem ownership. Problems that are not resolvable are typically issues in which the person wanting the change is not the person actually required to change.

In summary, a willingness to accept differences includes problem ownership, defining the problem in relationship terms, a willingness to accept the wants and needs of the partner, and a willingness to be flexible in finding a solution to the dilemma. See the inset *Mutual Problem Solving* for a guide to putting these communication skills together to reach a common goal.

Trust

Communication includes behavior, words, and intentions. Positive communication is built over time in a relationship, and is built upon a foundation of trust as well as being the source of that trust. The degree of confidence that you feel when you

Mutual Problem Solving

Although problem solving comes under a variety of labels (e.g., conflict resolution, mediation, compromise) it consistently refers to the attempt to come to a mutually acceptable solution for problems created when one's desired goals interfere with another person's desired goals. The task is to find a way that both persons can achieve their goals and remain in the current relationship.

Steps to Mutual Problem Solving
1. Explore the problem area in relationship terms.
2. State the goal in relationship terms.
3. Generate alternative solutions.
4. Select and implement a solution.

Explore the Problem Area in Relationship Terms
1. Take responsibility for your own thoughts, feelings, and behaviors by using an "I" message: "I feel (affect) because/about (action, situation)."

2. Keep your exploration focused so that partners are safe to take risks. The following guidelines will help:
   - Focus on behavior, not personality.
   - Focus on description rather than judgments.
   - Focus on "here and now."
   - Focus on something that can change.
   - Focus on one conflict area at a time.

3. After each self-disclosure/feedback, the partner should respond with an empathic statement before moving on. This is where couples can really improve their chances of being generally satisfied with their relationships. Strong couples generally meet complaints with acknowledgment. Couples who are less satisfied tend to countercomplain—that is, meet each complaint with a new complaint.

   Julie: I feel frustrated because I am trying to get ready to go out and you are watching television.

   Daniel: You feel frustrated because you are getting ready to go out and I am watching television.

   Julie: Exactly.

   Daniel: I feel angry because I want to watch sports and you are trying to get me to go out.

   Julie: You feel angry because I am trying to get you moving and that is not what you want to do.

   Daniel: That's right.

Be sure that you take time to hear your partner's complaint: When Daniel begins to talk before Julie has finished, it is a clear sign that Daniel has not really listened to Julie: You cannot listen and prepare your statement simultaneously. It should take you a few seconds to formulate your response when your partner has finished talking.

(continued)

Mutual Problem Solving (continued)

State the Goal in Relationship Terms

Relationship problems occur because two people have differing preferences about what should occur. Compromising generally is *not* effective for problem solving because it means that each person gets a little bit less than what they want, rather than being completely satisfied with the solution.

> *Julie:*   I want the house clean.
>
> *Daniel:*   So do I, but I don't want to have to pass the white glove test all the time.

It takes longer to find a goal that will work for both persons, but it tends to be more successful in the long run. Stating a goal that would make both persons satisfied creates a picture of what things will look like when the problem is solved.

> *Julie:*   I feel frustrated because I just cleaned the house and you threw your socks on the floor.
>
> *Daniel:*   You feel frustrated because you think the house is dirty when my socks are on the floor.
>
> *Julie:*   Exactly.
>
> *Daniel:*   Okay, we need a way that you can feel like the house is clean and I can feel comfortable in my own home.
>
> *Julie:*   Right.

Generate Alternative Solutions

Sometimes you have time to finish problem solving, and sometimes things are too rushed. This is a good place to leave off and come back to if you need some time and/or space away from your problem. During a break each person can come up with as many options to solve the problem as possible. It also works out well to generate the alternatives together. However you choose to do it, have fun with it. Think of options that would never work, some that might work, and some that have always worked in the past. One couple was able to resolve their bathroom dilemma by her agreeing to not wear her glasses when she used that bathroom because she could not see very well without them. The resolution worked for them.

Many times people are stuck on the problem because they are focused on the problem when *the solution that will work has nothing to do with the problem.* Keep focusing on the relationship goal rather than the stated problem.

1. Make lists of alternatives
2. Cross off anything that is completely unacceptable to either person.
3. Keep thinking until you come up with at least four options that you could both live with.

Select and Implement a Solution

Congratulations!!! Now you have something to try out. Implement your new idea for at least a week, or long enough to give it a chance to work. If the new strategy doesn't work for *either* partner for *any* reason, then:

1. Explore the problem area in relationship terms.
2. State the goal in relationship terms.
3. Generate alternative solutions.
4. Select and implement a solution.

Even in the best of relationships, problem solving is a life-long process. Although you may come up with wonderful solutions for the issues presented today, things may look very different tomorrow. In time this process will become a very useful habit for maintaining a relationship in which needs are met and concerns are addressed.

think about a relationship is the level of trust that exists. Self-disclosures are risks taken by one partner to give the other insight into thoughts, feelings, and behaviors that affect a current relationship. Empathy refers to an understanding response that conveys understanding and acceptance. When self-disclosures are forthcoming, and empathy is abundantly available in the relationship, trust is the product. Trust is built from predictability, which is the ability to foretell a partner's specific behavior. A partner may arrive home at 6:00 PM sharp, every day. That partner's arrival time is predictable.

Trust expands to dependability when couples have established predictable ways of interacting and providing support. Dependability grows out of risk and personal vulnerability. Dependability is that sense that when there is a problem, the partner can be depended on to do what is right. For example, a partner who is typically home at 6:00 may arrive at 6:30 one day. When dependability is established, the waiting partner does not wonder, "What is she up to?" but rather is confident that there is a good reason for the late arrival.

Finally, trust builds to faith. Faith is the component of mutual appreciation for each other, and acknowledgment of the boundaries of the relationship that enable partners to go beyond the available evidence and feel secure that a partner will continue to be responsive and caring. Positive communication strategies at the helm allow a relationship to grow until confidence is gained and risks are safe.

15

Emotional and Physical Intimacy

The truth is, when our mothers held us, rocked us, stroked our heads—none of us ever got enough of that. We all yearn in some way to return to those days when we were completely taken care of—unconditional love, unconditional attention. Most of us didn't get enough.

—Morrie Schwartz

To be emotionally and physically close to your partner is to be *intimate*. Intimacy is the product of reciprocal risk taking in an ongoing relationship; it is a quality of interpersonal relatedness in which individuals are able to know each other deeply and extensively (Heller & Wood, 1998); and it is what separates a good love story from a great one. Intimacy is the extra twist in a relationship that transforms thinking from "me" and "you" to "us" (Doherty, 2002). The development and maintenance of intimacy requires a balance of self-assurance, timing, and coordinating needs, all in the context of a single ongoing close relationship. When a relationship is intimate partners feel close, safe, and replenished in their interactions with the other.

Emotionally Intimate Relationships

The process of developing intimacy is like exploring uncharted territory. It begins by deciding what to share with a partner and by having a sense of how much to share at any one time. With a wide range of potential ways of knowing one another, intimate relationships begin with low-intensity sharing of thoughts, feelings, and emotions, and proceed to a particularly intense depth in which partners share parts of their unique selves that are not typically available to others. Eventually the couple relationship becomes a unique blend of breadth and depth, interpersonal knowing and emotional intensity. The task for the couple is to become wholly connected. It is not surprising that couples begin their journeys by being fully consumed with each other.

Couples experience each other intensely around issues of personality, values, attitudes, family life experiences, and sexuality. In intimate relationships one person's experiences often contain meaning for the other. Partners negotiate distance and develop relational rules about how to use their knowledge of each other in their daily lives. The intimate relationship is dynamic and intentional (Doherty, 2002); it is continually growing and developing. The ability to confide in one another is at its foundation. Intimate partners learn about themselves in ways that they could not know themselves alone and are known by each other in ways that are unique from any other person. As intimacy progresses, partners find ways to be vulnerable and to accept each other's influence. To do this they must perceive each other to be nonthreatening (Gottman & Notarius, 2000). Couples risk new behaviors, making changes in their preferred behaviors (called *transformations*) such that they are no longer able to think only of themselves; they begin to also think about how their behavior affects their partners. Sometimes, even before they realize it, partners begin to make alternative choices that would not be made if they were considering their pleasures alone. By considering their relationship, partners find that shared pleasurable activities become more pleasurable overall, and nonpreferred activities also become more pleasurable (Kelley, 1979).

In intimate communication, partners use all of their senses (sight, sound, touch, and smell) to know each other beyond the words that are spoken. In that comprehensive communication they create shared visions for the future.

Safety

Ray and Mary enjoy their relationship and have learned to grow together. After having some minor disagreements they began to discover each other's "hot spots." They even found some sensitivity that they themselves did not know they had. They found that Ray became upset when Mary used a "teacher" voice, and Mary became upset when Ray walked out of the room when they were disagreeing. Each partner interpreted the other partner's behaviors as evidence that they needed to protect themselves.

They decided to make an effort to connect with each other in the mornings to talk about their hopes and concerns for the day. Mary learned to own her communication with "I" messages and to think about what she needed when she was tempted to become Ray's "teacher." Ray learned to self-soothe before he presented a complaint to Mary so that he did not need to walk away to soothe himself during the discussion. Even though it is not always easy to make the time to connect as a couple, they have found it helpful in redirecting their own self-protection habits. By checking in at the beginning of the day they have the opportunity to clear up any misunderstandings, and learn about their partner's concerns before small issues become large.

Negative communication patterns had begun to interfere with Ray and Mary's relationship because they were unable to feel safe with one another. When Ray and Mary's communication became unsafe it had profound implications for the potential for intimacy in the relationship. Without safety, intimacy is not possible. Sometimes all that is needed is communication skills training, and the couples learn to speak with and listen to their partners in more helpful ways. In such situations the relationship is quickly repaired. Other times, for instance when a partner is ambivalent about emotional intimacy, the solution involves more than simple communication training. Negative communication patterns play a role in regulating the intensity of relationships. Some couples become stuck using negative skills as ways of keeping themselves safe from intimacy. They keep the relationship cooled down, and the partners at a safe distance, until the intensity is at a level that they can manage.

Not all partners are at the same level of readiness to risk intimacy. Coordinating intimacy desire (the willingness to share risk) and ability (a level of risk that is comfortable) can be difficult. Imagine that your idea of taking a risk is to stay at a Best Western hotel in Iowa, and your partner is scheduling you for a safari in Africa. Although you are willing to take a risk, the level of risk taking required by your partner may be too much. Mismatched desire for intimacy can be more problematic than agreement on intimacy, even if the level agreed upon is very low. Once a partner has taken a risk in the presence of the other, there is an expectation of reciprocity. When members of the couple have different ideas about what risk is—for example, what information is personal and what can be shared—the least risk-taking partner may feel unable to confide very personal thoughts and feelings in the other. Couples may also differ in their displays of intimacy, the breadth of intimate behavior they are willing to engage in, and the depth of information they are willing to share with others. What one considers a risk the other may consider inconsequential. In these cases it can be difficult for couples to become synchronized with each other's intimacy needs (Heller & Wood, 1998):

> Sophie was concerned about her relationship with Bill. She felt close to him, and felt love for him, but she was somewhat uncomfortable with how much Bill shared with her. She enjoyed listening to him talk, and was interested in the way that he thought about things. She, however, preferred to think issues out by herself. She did not want to share her innermost thoughts even though Bill readily shared his thoughts and feelings with her. She was a good listener, and would offer supportive comments. She did not feel able to reciprocate the sharing, and it was beginning to be a problem for Bill. Bill was offering opportunities for intimacy and was receiving nurturance in return.

Nurturance is sometimes confused with intimacy. Nurturance is one sided. I can go from my comfort zone to nurture you, and retreat back into my space. You can come into my space to nurture me, and return to your comfort zone. Nurturance is unbalanced: Parents nurture children; mentors nurture new professionals. Nurturers experience little personal risk. Their job is to take care of the risks incurred by others. Intimacy, however, is balanced. It involves a reciprocal experience of acceptance and self-disclosure, a sharing of sexual expression, a balance of autonomy and fusion in the course of the relationship, and intellectual, physical, and emotional closeness (Heller & Wood, 1998). Not surprisingly, intimate relationships can be intimidating, and unbalanced relationships can be frustrating.

Ray and Mary found that they had similar ideas, but they needed to improve their communication skills so that they could maintain a balance of self-disclosure and safety. Sophie and Bill did not have the same needs in closeness. Couples evolve interactional patterns, like a signature dance, that include rules of validation, timing of sharing, and coordination of connection. It is through this foundation of safety and confidence that the context for risk taking can be fully established.

Relationship Risk Taking

Allowing yourself to share intimately is risky because you cannot become unknown in a relationship. If I have a thought that is unkind, but I rethink what I want to say and begin again, I can present myself more thoughtfully. If I blurt out my first thoughts without editing my presentation, I will be known according to my impulsive words that cannot be taken back. Once spoken, the words that are chosen influence subsequent interactions. In some cases, partners will be satisfied that their choices were the best they could do in a given situation. They can objectively assess their own interactions and they serve as their own source of validation. In other cases, the opinions of others are tremendously important. These partners do not feel able to assess their own interactions. They allow the judgment of the other to take priority over their own judgment of themselves, leaving them unequipped to manage the insecurities that can be aroused in the intimate relationship. Partners who are well differentiated can do both. They can judge and validate their own interactions while using feedback from their partners to make adjustments as necessary. Differentiation allows for greater freedom to take risks because there is a greater ability to stay emotionally safe.

Taking risks in relationships is also influenced by partners' experiences. Partners need the confidence that they will be able to manage the impact of their partner's emotional experiences. For example, if Jim has a need to avoid intense sadness, and Leslie is experiencing intense sadness, Jim may have a difficult time with Leslie's sharing. At a time when Leslie is unable to use herself to soothe Jim, he may need to be soothed. Such a situation may result in Leslie being less willing to share her experience in the future when she needs comforting. Jim and Leslie learn to avoid sharing intense, negative emotions. By being able to hear a partner's upset, and know that the emotion belongs to the partner, the intensity can be managed. When intensity is managed, barriers to intimacy (flooding and distancing) are diminished.

The timing of risk taking tends to be sequential. When there is a choice, partners take one major risk on at a time. Babies crawl before they walk, and they walk before they run. When couples enter into physically intense relationships they are less likely to take emotional risks than couples who first share risks emotionally. Relationships where the risks are physical but not emotional can be very difficult when partners are feeling vulnerable and need emotional connectedness. When the context of the emotionally supportive relationship has not been established, partners address their relationship needs as individuals rather than as a couple. For example, the partners may talk to their friends about the problems in the relationship rather than talking to the other partner. Active listening helps to keep the intimate experiences shared, and the understanding of the partner clear (Heller & Wood, 1998). Individuals who are able to be empathic stay present without experiencing reactivity. They can allow their partners to have their own experiences within the context of the relationship without simultaneously experiencing the same emotion (Long, Angera, Carter, Nakamoto, & Kalso, 1999). Consequently, the level of disclosure can stay equitable, and the partnership experiences a comfortable rate of sharing.

In the RELATE questionnaire, couples are asked to assess themselves and their partners in their abilities to be empathic and to express clear sending messages. Empathy requires an ability to differentiate self from other and to understand one's partner: Empathic behaviors are the essence of behaviors that contribute to intimacy. Similarly, the ability to state one's needs clearly in a nonblaming way allows the partner to participate in developing intimacy without having to defend her- or himself.

Like the comforting aroma of a family home before a holiday meal, there is a tempo that is expected in intimate relationships. Intimate behaviors do not occur in every movement; in fact they are noticed more in their absence than in their presence. Couples may automatically kiss each other hello, and be particularly aware if the kiss on any one day was different from what they expected. It is in the context of expectation and values that opportunities for behavioral and emotional intimacy are evaluated.

Some relationships stay casual because the partners are not ready for a serious relationship. Partners interact in relationships with expectations for the level of intimacy that would be appropriate for them. When people are ready for Mr. or Ms. Right, they will be more likely to attend to the rhythm of developing intimacy in the relationship. If an individual has future plans that do not include a spouse, that person may be more likely to overlook opportunities to develop intimacy. Decisions about emotional and sexual intimacy, then, often fulfill individuals' needs for timing serious relationships.

Early in relationships, physiological passion is high and intimacy is low. Separating oneself from the emotional experience of the partner is easier when there is less expectation for fulfilling each other's needs, as is the case in earlier stages of dating. As intimacy is developed over time, the passion (which is focused on one's own needs) tends to decrease and intimacy (the connection and depth of the relationship) increases. Each risk that is taken contributes to an ever-expanding area of feedback about the partnership and the relationship. The feedback shapes a relationship identity with information about strengths and weaknesses, and influences the very core of the relationship. Intimate relationships, based on a set of risks, sustain relationships over difficult times and allow partners to put the needs of each other first and create the experience of being soul mates.

Intimacy Journey

What does it take to be able to progress along the intimacy journey? According to Schnarch (1991), intimacy is dependent on partners' abilities to validate themselves so that they can feel safe in the context of a risky relationship. Intimate relationships require independent and differentiated partners who can risk increasingly deeper levels of self-disclosure (Heller & Wood, 1998). Partners who are better able to validate themselves and handle the emotions of the partner use a wide range of sources of validation. Such partners tend to be older and independent from their families of origin. They have personalities that allow them to be discriminating in the opinions of others and do not require as much nurturing in interactions. For those persons who must look to the other to validate them, or to help them feel secure, intimacy is more risky because security is dependent upon pleasing the partner. In intimate relationships there are a lot of areas of upset and hurt that have nothing to do with the partner beyond the expectation to have the partner listen and be available. When a caring partner is not able to separate him- or herself from a hurt partner's stories, the caring partner may attempt to take away the hurt, or to take the hurt personally (e.g., "How could you still be hurt about your former lover, am I not good enough for you?").

Relational scripts, such as those prescribed through gender, sometimes make it difficult for partners to maintain their strength and confidence. For example, women often lose their voices in the context of intimate relationships. Women experience their value through their relationships, so they often become "we" instead of "I" in the context of a serious relationship. Partners can be self-assured and open to risk, or unsure of themselves and in need of validation that they are good enough and that others like them. There are times when no matter how much we want our partners to confirm for us that their angst is not our fault, they may not be able to do that for us. Those who require approval from their partners have a more difficult time being open because they remain concerned about the meaning of their partner's response. Consider how self and other validation works in this relationship with Colleen and George as it changes in levels of seriousness:

> Colleen was a strong, opinionated woman. George fell in love with her because of her willingness to speak her mind. When they began dating he would need to give her ample notice for an evening out because she would not consider changing her plans with her friends to go out with him, although she would allow him to come along with her and her friends. When she felt discounted by him she made it clear that his behavior was unacceptable to her. She set clear limits on what she would

and would not accept in her relationship. He thought she was fun, interesting, and challenging.

The longer they dated, the more difficulty Colleen experienced in saying what was on her mind. She was continually concerned about whether George agreed with her and whether he was happy. She watched carefully for signs of approval, and often interpreted his nonverbal behavior as disapproving of her. Soon, Colleen was complaining about his lack of thoughtfulness and accusing him of changing.

Colleen was more differentiated and sure of herself in casual dating than during serious dating. She knew herself better outside of the context of a serious relationship and her risk taking was more available to her earlier in the relationship. At the beginning of the relationship Colleen's vision of how she should behave validated her competence in taking care of herself and being confident. Rather than continuing to validate herself and her ability to take care of herself, Colleen began thinking about "we" (what he and I want from the relationship), and was not able to integrate the two sets of needs.

Women often abdicate their right to meet their own needs in intimate relationships. They tend to focus on their partners' wants and needs. At times this process feels suffocating to the partner, who becomes too ingratiated and subsequently angry with the other partner for becoming a martyr. The challenge is to make the transition from casual dating to serious relationship such that the focus goes from thinking about *me* to thinking about *you-and-I ("us")* instead of the thinking going from *me* to *you*.

After experiencing hurt in their attempts to become intimate, partners may protect themselves by maintaining tighter control over the risks they take. Hence, partners' levels of self-confidence may change during relationships. They may be extremely confident in their ability to validate themselves and take risks, but after some negative relationship experiences begin to doubt themselves and limit their risks. They learn from a series of interactions that being known is unsafe.

Coordination of Connection

Often, couples will complain that they and their partners do not communicate or that they are "too distant." Gottman and Notarius (2000) have reported that this experience of interpersonal distance is more about the feel of the relationship than about the communication. That is, when people are not feeling accepted and close to their partners they complain that they are not communicating, when actually, the dilemma is that they are communicating difficult messages: They do not feel valued and accepted. Heller and Wood (1998) have noted that couples experience more mutual intimacy when a spouse's knowledge of her or his partner is accurate and that accuracy is conveyed back to the spouse. In the RELATE report, couples respond to questions about their personal characteristics and values, and about their thoughts on their partner's personality characteristics and values. Couples learn about how

Sexual intimacy involves more than sexual intercourse.

their partners know them in areas of personal characteristics (such as kindness, ma- turity, and self-esteem) and values (such as togetherness and sexuality). This is often an opportunity for couples to explore the meaning of these characteristics in their relationship.

Comfort with Intimacy

As a group, women are more comfortable with emotional intimacy than are men, and have more tolerance for defining themselves in the context of relationships. Of course there are individual differences in which some women are less emotional than some men, but overall most women have been socialized to be the emotional leaders in families. Men, on the other hand, have been socialized to be the eco- nomic leaders in families, and tend to define themselves in terms of autonomy and work (Heller & Wood, 1998). Women more often want connection and intimacy than do men. Even in problem solving, women are more affiliative and men are more coercive (Gottman & Notarius, 2000). Why do women and men operate dif- ferently? Boys are taught to separate from their mothers much earlier than are girls, sensitivity is discouraged, and cultural rewards for men are present in the labor force more than within families. Men, therefore, have different expressions in their needs for closeness than do women. There is some thought that this difference in displays of intimacy are maintained as the result of power imbalances between women and men. For example, the person with the most power does the least amount of maintenance behaviors, which means that men who are more powerful than their female partners (which is the most frequent situation in romantic relationships) do not need to learn relationship maintenance behaviors because their partners have been socialized to acquire and use them (Blumstein & Shwartz, 1983). It is also possible that men do engage in intimacy strategies that are not noticed because of a cultural bias that measures only women's expressions of intimacy. Even now, women are typically viewed as the emotional experts in relationships and men's ways of connecting with their partners tend to go unrecognized. The challenge in a relationship is to develop a system of intimacy in which the members of the couple experience each other's presence, and are able to regulate the exchange of intimacy so that it fits their needs. To get a couple started in their discussions of intimacy, they may ask themselves the following questions:

- What would help me feel emotionally intimate with my partner?
- What do I need to know about my partner before I can be fully open?
- Do my partner and I expect the same degree of intimacy now or is one of us less willing to be intimate?
- Do I expect that my partner will share everything with me at some point?
- How soon do I expect to learn about the difficult issues my partner is dealing with?

Sexual Intimacy

Is sexual intercourse intimate? Sexual relationships may be referred to as intimate relationships, but not all sexual relationships are intimate. You may intend to have sexual relations with a partner, and you may be ready to experience sexual intercourse with a partner, but you may not have the ingredients to create intimacy from physical sexual relations. The United States has been called one of the most sexually repressive cultures in history (Stayton, 1996), and puritanical views are enforced through guilt, fear, and the denial of sex as pleasure (particularly for highly religious individuals). When there are sexual difficulties in healthy, intimate relationships, these cultural beliefs are quickly blamed. Sexual difficulties influence relationship satisfaction, and sexual dissatisfaction is a predictor of marital dissolution (Christopher & Sprecher, 2000).

Sexual behavior is "sanctioned in marriage, it is often explored in dating, and it is an intricate part of other committed romantic relationships" (Christopher & Sprecher, 2000, p. 999). Some couples express the belief that sexual intercourse provides an opportunity for them to get to know each other better. Other people have numerous sexual partners in search of "sexual chemistry." Schnarch (1991) has commented about sexual chemistry that "If partners can maintain their sexual excitement through the disillusionment, anger, and desperate struggle for autonomy that follows 'instant intimacy,' they may succeed in discovering an alternative formula for sexual chemistry . . . the equation for sustaining intimacy and sexuality." Others concur that early sexual behavior in a relationship increases the potential for conflict and that this is important because of the strong relationship between premarital conflict and lower levels of marital satisfaction (Christopher & Sprecher, 2000; Long, Cate, Fehsenfeld, & Williams, 1996). Sexual intimacy is influenced by the connection that you have with your partner and, paradoxically, when experienced too early in the relationship, sexual relationships interfere with the development of emotional intimacy. Sexual intimacy does not replace the cognitive work in a relationship. While it may be a bonding experience, it is a weaker predictor of love or general relationship quality than are other forms of intimacy. Better predictors of love are the degree of affection expressed and the supportive communication experienced (Christopher & Sprecher, 2000). Sexual intercourse causes relationships that may otherwise have ended at the early signs of serious problems to continue longer than would otherwise occur, acting as a barrier to relationship dissolution.

Sex in a Developed Relationship: Passion, Intimacy, Commitment

When sex is experienced in an intimate relationship, some of the knowing in the relationship may decrease the passion experienced. For example, if you and your partner have been planning a sexually exciting evening and your partner becomes worried about her or his work, the concern is a shared concern and the sexual interest decreases as the couple works on restoring the members' emotional well-being. Casual relationships have less focus on both persons' emotional well-being, and more emphasis on sexual satisfaction. Although there are a variety of opinions about when sexual intercourse should occur in casual dating relationships, one finding is clear: Sex guilt, particularly for women and highly religious partners, is very powerful. For this reason it is imperative that a couple's sexual decisions are congruent with their own sexual values, and that couples realize the long-term relational difficulties that arise when sexual intercourse is the result of partner pressure (Long, Cate, Fehsenfeld, & Williams, 1996).

Rules About Sexuality

For all partners, some level of sexuality is involved in the process of getting to know a partner (e.g., physiological attraction). As relationships are explored cognitively, they also are explored physically. Handholding, eye gazing, and kissing: These are all sexual behaviors. New couples, wanting to know every inch of their partner, make decisions early on about whether or not they will engage in sexual intercourse. For some people, sexual intercourse is exclusively available in marriage. Other partners decide to wait to have sexual intercourse until they have committed to marriage. Still other couples do not wait at all to become sexually involved.

For all relationships, emotional and physical intimacies are connected in such a way that when couples are taking sexual risks they are less available to take emotional risks with their partners. Relationships in which sexual intercourse takes place very early in the relationship are qualitatively different from those in which sex takes place after the couple has developed emotional intimacy. This may not be an issue for the person who believes that sex is a physical act analogous to sneezing, but for those who believe that sexual intercourse is a special sharing that is part of an ongoing relationship, it is important.

Clearly, some partners engage in sexual intercourse outside of a relationship and believe that sex should be enjoyed for the physical pleasure without the expectations of a close emotional relationship. For some people sexual intimacy is confused with emotional intimacy, and they continue having sexual relations with a variety of partners, looking for the connection of an emotionally intimate relationship. Such people are the recipients of much heartbreak, as the risks are high and the potential for finding love is low.

Changes in Intimacy

In marriage therapy, a frequent complaint from couples experiencing trouble is that their intimacy has decreased over time. Intimacy does change over time, making that which may have seemed easy at the beginning increasingly difficult as the relationship deepens. Romantic relationships begin with long periods of eye gazing and information exchange. Intimacy can feel more available during these times because the behavior is plentiful and the risk is relatively low. Exchanging information and increasingly knowing one's partner are essential first steps in building a relationship (Heller & Wood, 1998). On the other hand, intimacy may seem painfully unavailable for couples later because being understood by one's partner becomes more salient in the intimacy process than is simply exchanging information. The original intimacy does not become "lost" any more than you can "un-know" a partner. When couples stop growing, the experience of intimacy may decrease or become stagnant. Perhaps that is why the development of intimacy in a relationship is so wonderful, and the experience of loss of intimacy so painful. You cannot become un-intimate, but you can become frightened about how a partner will use your intimacy.

Emotional and physical intimacy is rewarding and frightening, taking on different meanings at different stages of relationships. Interestingly, marital sexual intimacy can become difficult for people who have experienced strong prohibitions against premarital sex. In *Fighting for Your Marriage*, there is a helpful chapter that addresses marital sexuality and the unique dilemmas that some couples face (Markman, Stanley, and Blumberg, 1994).

Intimacy is a basic, reflexive, human process that involves accepting and knowing oneself in the context of a relationship. You can know someone with whom you are not intimate, and you can feel intimate with someone you really do not know (for example, a member of an on-line chat group whom you have never met). You can have sex with someone with whom you are not intimate, and you can have intimacy with someone without having a sexual relationship. Really knowing a partner requires a well-timed dance in which each partner is allowed to be present, and then to retreat as needed to protect themselves. Partners "lose" their intimacy when the risks that they take are met with a painful response. Not surprisingly, sexual intimacy is not insulated from dilemmas that may occur in other areas of relationships. As couples explore their sexuality in their relationships, they might want to ask themselves the following questions:

- When is sex appropriate in a relationship?
- Will I participate in sex before I feel ready if my partner wants to?
- What sexual behaviors are appropriate for a more casual relationship versus a committed relationship?
- If I have sex with someone, does it change how I think about the relationship?
- Do I need to be sexually exclusive before I can expect to be emotionally intimate with someone?
- Do I need alcohol to help me feel comfortable being sexual? If so, what does this mean?

Threats to Intimacy

Intimacy is keenly important, yet frightfully elusive in close relationships. Many engaged couples would characterize their relationships as "intimate." At the beginning of a dating relationship couples talk for hours about their hopes, desires, accomplishments, and disappointments. They feel close, and begin to feel known by another person in ways that are often different from the ways that parents know their children or best friends know each other. Intimacy is the ultimate mind game: Everyone can feel like a pro at the beginning, but it is more difficult to move from "pretty good" at being intimate to risking more as they invest more and have more to lose. The threat of losing makes the game more difficult, and the players stay keyed into any potential for loss. The following are some threats to emotional and sexual intimacy, and some suggestions for addressing those threats:

- **Family history of shaming.** Think about how you learned to think about yourself in your family. Choose three things about yourself that you believe you bring to an intimate relationship with another person. Choose three other things about yourself that you want from an intimate relationship. Write down how you will know when you have been successful in addressing those wants.
- **Personal history of having been abused (physically or sexually).** Abuse interferes with the ability to trust another person. You may need to spend a lot of time at each level of trust. Begin to notice when your internal warning signs are activated because of something that is occurring in the present, or because of a memory of something in the past. Work with your partner on a strategy for allowing you to work through your memory and keeping it as your own dilemma, rather than something your partner fixes.

- **Personal history of having seen others being abused (physically or sexually).** It is often surprising to people that witnessing abuse can be as upsetting and damaging as actually experiencing the abuse yourself. Acknowledge when those memories are being erected and address them as something outside of the relationship that is having an impact on your relationship.
- **High stress outside of the relationship.** Take time in the relationship to relax. Intimacy does not always have to be made up of intense conversation. Some of the most intimate experiences are in sharing quiet, soothing moments.

16

Problem Areas, Disapproval from Others, and Violence

> *There is value, when choosing a long-term partner, in realizing that you will inevitably be choosing a particular set of unsolvable problems that you'll be grappling with for the next ten, twenty, or fifty years.*
>
> —Dan Wile

Although it may be entirely unromantic to consider a partner as a set of unsolvable problems, it is probably wise to ponder the meaning of this statement by an expert on marriage (Wile, 1993). Many couples either do not seriously consider their problems prior to the wedding or they assume that these problems will naturally improve as a result of being married. Either stance can lead to unnecessary disenchantment and the assumption that your partner is not the same person he or she was prior to marriage.

Unsolvable Problems

Are many problems really unsolvable in marriage? In this respect, marriage is not different from any other aspect of life. There are always problems that can be resolved and there are problems that have to be lived with, sometimes for the rest of our lives. For example, you might really want to be an Air Force pilot but your eyesight is so poor that you will not be able to pursue that goal. This poor eyesight, though correctable to some degree, will be a problem that must be coped with all your life. Another example: Perhaps you fell in love with your partner because of his wonderful sense of humor. Over time you realize that he has a hard time determining when it is not appropriate to be humorous, and his seemingly endless supply of jokes can become irritating. It may be possible to discuss this and he might become more serious in certain situations. Yet his nature is more jovial and fun-loving than most, so he could not give up his sense of humor any more than you can give up how tall you are. This problem, of not knowing when to take things seriously, will probably always be a part of your relationship, though it might improve a little. One of the primary tasks in the early years of marriage is discovering which problems are solvable and which are not. A strategy that couples may find necessary is to eliminate the unrealistic expectation that marriage and time will automatically resolve all the significant struggles in a relationship.

Most of the unsolvable problems in a relationship have to do with differences in core personality traits, basic abilities, and personal likes and dislikes. It is no small feat to learn to live with a foreigner, and that is exactly what each marriage is. Learning to live with someone who came from a different location, with a different set of values, a different genetic makeup, a different gender, a different set of childhood experiences, a different culture, different, different, different. . . . Yes, it is surely the case that new habits can be learned, new values can be adopted, and new likes can be developed. Nevertheless, when we pressure our partners, or ourselves, to become something that person is not, in terms of basic worldviews, abilities, personalities, and preferences, we are walking on dangerous ground. If we have strong mathematical abilities and we really enjoy playing strategy games, but our partner is more verbally oriented and enjoys playing word games, why do we pressure each other to try and play something again and again that is not enjoyable? Surely part of marriage is learning to give and compromise, but it really will not be all that enjoyable to play strategy games with someone who does not enjoy them and who does poorly at them time after time; nevertheless, this is what many partners do anyway. It can be hard for us to give up on the ideal that we will share everything with our partners.

It is not going to be necessary to search for these unsolvable problems. Once married, and sometimes even before marriage, the unsolvable problems will emerge again and again. The key is finding a strategy for handling problems in such a way that they do not destroy the relationship. Most successful couples learn to recognize these problems and one or both partners intervene in the arguments before too much damage is done (Gottman, 1999). It is as if a warning bell goes off in the couple's minds and they say to themselves, "Here we go again. I've been down that road too many times and I know we aren't going to resolve this so I'm going to do something to keep us from getting too ugly with one another." This approach is different from resignation or giving up. It is recognition of a complex, unsolvable problem and a commitment to help the situation by reducing the negative spiral. These interventions by each person to stop negative communication patterns are called repair attempts (Gottman, 1999). Repair attempts are often small behaviors by one or both partners that may include acknowledging that someone else is right, accepting responsibility for something that caused pain to another, apologizing, agreeing with at least part of what the other person is saying, encouraging the partner to be honest about something that seems to be festering, recognizing that sometimes problems aren't going to go away easily, saying something to lighten up the moment, expressing hope, showing empathy, and so on. Repair attempts are one of the most important strategies that satisfied couples use that distinguishes them from dissatisfied couples (Gottman, 1999).

Prior to marriage it may be necessary to think seriously about some of the minor problems that already exist and imagine how it might be to live with these problems for many years. With some couples who expend large amounts of time in primarily positive activities and experiences, it may not be possible to identify any significant problems. This is not necessarily a warning sign, as some validating couples are not going to have significant problems early on. Still, it could indicate that an insufficient amount of time and personal disclosure have occurred to reveal the relationship difficulties. If it is too early to know which problems you are facing, it is also too early yet to know whether this relationship will last.

Problem Areas Checklist

The "Problem Areas Checklist" from RELATE is one source that can be used to identify some of the unsolvable problems in a relationship. However, the specific areas such as communication, raising children, finances, and intimacy should not be labeled unsolvable problems because these are just the content areas that provide clues as to where you should look deeper. For example, if a couple most often has problems with "communication," this is not really very helpful information. Communication is the most commonly identified problem of both premarital and marital couples (see Table 16.1). However, knowing that communication is the most common problem area in your relationship can help you identify where to look a little closer to find out the unsolvable problems. Is communication a problem because one of you does not feel consistently understood, that one partner is too quiet and does not share much, or is it that a partner cannot be disagreed with without getting angry? The specific type of communication pattern that does not work for you is

TABLE 16.1 *Rank Order of Problem Areas That Have Significant Influence on Relationship Satisfaction for Premarital and Marital Couples*

Problem Area	Premarital		Marital	
	Males	Females	Males	Females
Communication	1	1	1	1
Time Spent Together	2	3	4	3
Intimacy/Sexuality	4	2	2	2
Substance Abuse	3	4	7	5
Who's in Charge	5	5	3	*
Roles (Who Does What)	*	*	5	6
Having Children	*	*	6	*
Rearing Children	*	*	*	4

Note: 1 = The problem area with the strongest influence on relationship satisfaction.
*Not a significant problem for that group.

what is most likely to be an indication of a long-term pattern. If your partner is quiet and does not communicate as much as you like or need, he or she is not likely to spontaneously become gregarious. Improvements can be made and more communication can occur, but it is probably better to ask yourself, "If my partner continues to be a much quieter communicator than I am during the next 20 years, can I live with this and be satisfied in this relationship?" Complaining to your partner will probably not be particularly helpful, at least in identifying unsolvable problems at the premarital stage, as she or he will probably try harder over the short term to be much more communicative. You may then feel much better about your relationship, only to find that over time your partner returns to a quieter pattern that is his or her natural style. If you get in the habit of pressuring your partner for more communication and see that short-term gains occur, but over time the problem is the same, you will need to decide whether you will be comfortable applying pressure for the next 20 years or whether you will be more comfortable with a quiet partner. Two other options are that you find friends who are more talkative so that you can value your partner for other reasons, or that you find a different partner who is not so quiet. The important point at the premarital stage is to identify these differences and consider what it will be like living with them year after year.

Table 16.1 illustrates something else about the problem areas that may develop in your relationship. After marriage, issues emerge that are not present premaritally. The primary differences between the two groups are that issues around children emerge for married couples, as do concerns about who is in charge and what roles people take. These differences are logical, as premarital couples are not usually sharing all of their resources yet and spending time managing the same household or worrying about children, so role sharing is not as common and who is in charge does not come up as often. It may be helpful for premarital couples to discuss the future and consider issues surrounding parenting, children, roles, and control. These discussions may bring up values and preferences that can cause considerable problems when partners are not in agreement. It might be very distressing after five years of marriage to find out that your partner does not really want to have children for a long time, if ever.

The other important finding from the RELATE data is that problem areas are much more important for married couples than premarital couples. Said in another way, premarital couples do not get too concerned about the problem areas, but for married couples these problem areas influence satisfaction twice as much. This suggests that the unsolvable problems do start to emerge later in the relationship and can cause considerable distress for couples. Females are more likely to list problems prior to marriage, but after marriage both sexes are about equal in the number of problems they describe and the influence these problems have on their relationships.

Problems with finances are one of the most commonly listed problems for couples both prior to and after the marriage, almost as common as communication. However, it is interesting that financial problems do not seem to have any significant influence on relationship satisfaction for either group, hence the reason that finances are omitted from Table 16.1. It may be that because both samples are relatively young, the problem with finances is more an issue of poverty than conflict between the partners. This assumption is borne out by the fact that the average income for both groups is less than $30,000 a year. Over time, though, it is clear that money is one of the top reasons listed by couples as a problem that leads to divorce (Berry & Williams, 1987). Because money is one of the clearest symbols of power and control in our society, it is an issue that deserves special attention and discussion for all couples. Personality styles that are impulsive or controlling may interact in troublesome ways with financial issues and create lethal problems that lead to divorce.

Certain problems may not be solvable but they also may not be something that one or both of you can live with for the rest of your life. Ideally, these kinds of problems will be discovered prior to marriage, but this is not always possible. Most of the problems that cannot be tolerated have to do with more extreme behaviors and core values. Some people insist on living life according to a particular moral code and will not be able to tolerate a partner who does not agree to live by the same code. Other people have learned to dominate partners through either emotional or physical abuse. This controlling behavior is something that can be hidden quite effectively by partners until after the marriage ceremony. Sometimes the opinions or impressions of friends or family members are the only indications that there may be deeper problems that have the potential to be dangerous to your future.

Disapproval from Others

Disapproval from others can be a very important warning sign. Strong disapproval may be suggestive of serious problems such as a very possessive partner who may end up being violent. It is often the case that family members are able to pick up on warning signs of controlling behaviors better than partners. Their wisdom should not be discounted. It is difficult to determine, however, whether a family member or friend is being overly protective or whether there is some problem that requires attention. In other instances, family and friends may have particular biases that keep them from seeing potential in-laws in a clear way, such as "He's too old," "She's not the right race," "He doesn't make enough money." The only way to clearly determine whether disapproval from family and friends is a serious concern is to make sure that your partner has repeated and numerous experiences with your preexisting friends and your family. This will allow you to discover whether the problems are inherent biases in your peer and family group or whether your partner has some issues that might cause serious difficulties down the road.

If you generally found your family and friends to be helpful and wise in their evaluations prior to your current partner and now they do not like your partner very much, this should be a clear danger sign. It is also important to remember that marriage is not just between two individuals—it is between two or more families. A person marries both the spouse and the spouse's family. This new family will be a part of the rest of your life and will be a source of either conflict or support. Some adjustment problems are always going to exist when new families merge, but serious problems at the premarital stage are clearly signs of much difficulty in the future.

The approval patterns for respondents who completed RELATE are intriguing. Table 16.2 indicates that females' parents have the lowest approval levels and that females' friends have the highest approval ratings. According to the respondents, fathers and mothers have similar levels of approval. In fact, 70% of the time the approval rating is the same for both parents. However, the female's mother is likely to have the lowest level of approval of the couple relationship. Perhaps there is something to the cliché that mothers-in-law are harder to get along with. The reasons for this lower level of approval by the female's mother are not clear. It may be that they have the strongest relationship and that the mother feels more protective of her daughter, or that the mother anticipates a great loss in her relationship with her daughter when her daughter begins a family of her own. Another explanation may be that the mother is more perceptive of relationship dynamics and might pick up on problems more readily than others do.

Not apparent in Table 16.2 is the influence these approval ratings have on the stability of the couple relationship. One would expect that when disapproval is stronger the relationship of the couple would be less stable. The findings support this hypothesis, but more for females than for males. The male's perception of approval from family and friends has only a low relationship to his ratings of relationship stability, whereas for females the relationship is moderate. Perhaps males do not listen to the feedback of others as readily as do females. Some studies show that males tend to have fewer friendships and share less information with family and friends than do females (Waite & Gallagher, 2000). This may be why approval ratings of others do not influence the male's relationship very much. Females are more sensitive to feedback from friends, but not from parents. A female's friends have a consistently significant influence on her relationship stability. Because females tend to have more friendships and share more with their friends, they may value the approval or disapproval more than males. It is interesting that the female friends' approval ratings also have the strongest influence on relationship *stability* of all the different approval scores. It appears that a male must win over not only the female, but also her group of friends.

TABLE 16.2 *Mean Approval Rates of the Premarital Couple for Parents and Friends of Both Females and Males*

Person Approving	Females	Males
Father	3.78*MF	3.86MF
Mother	3.57*F	3.71
Friends	3.67	3.68

*Significantly different from the male mean in the same row.
M Significantly different from the mother's mean in the same column.
F Significantly different from the friend's mean in the same column.
1 = low approval; 5 = high approval.

Violence between Partners

One particularly troublesome problem that couples might experience is violence. Violence can take many forms and may occur very seldom or very often. In some relationships both partners hit one another; in others only one partner uses physical force. Sometimes the violence might include sexual coercion and even rape. In many instances when there are problems with violence there are also problems with alcohol (Busby, 2000).

Physical Violence

Physical violence is far too common in couple relationships today. Estimates on violence rates suggest that between 30% and 50% of couples have experienced at least moderate violence (Killian & Busby, 1996). One of the most alarming statistics regarding violence is that in 40% to 80% of the cases the occurrence of a violent incident did not change the couple's perceptions of the quality of their relationship prior to marriage in a negative manner (Cate, Henton, Koval, Christopher, & Lloyd, 1982). This is alarming because violence tends to increase after marriage and couples may not be taking this problem seriously enough when they are dating.

Table 16.3 contains the violence rates for couples who have taken RELATE. These results indicate that about 16% of the females and 10% of the males are violent, according to both self and partner reports. It is likely that these rates are not accurate, though, because there are higher rates of denial with violence than with other negative behaviors.

The higher rate of female to male violence is consistent with other studies (Bernard & Bernard, 1983; Thompson, 1991). However, although females may slap or hit more than males, it is rare that this violence creates serious harm. Male violence is much more likely to inflict serious injury, whereas female violence is often in response to male violence. It may be that neither gender takes female violence very seriously. This could be a serious mistake as hitting begets hitting and female violence could become an excuse for males to hit.

Violence from a male, whether it causes serious injury or not, will carry a different meaning for the victim. Knowing that your partner is stronger and bigger than you are creates a natural innate fear that causes the smaller person to interpret

TABLE 16.3 *Percentages of Males and Females Who Report Physical and Sexual Coercion in Their Premarital Relationships*

Violence Statements	Males	Females
Your partner was physically violent toward you.	15%	10%
You were physically violent toward your partner.	10%	16%
Your partner pressured you to be sexual against your will.	15%	20%
You pressured your partner to be sexual against her/his will.	28%	9%

Unfortunately violence is a common problem in many relation-ships, even before marriage.

the very same behaviors differently than will someone who is larger. This means that males have a greater responsibility, in general, than females for ensuring that violence does not exist in relationships. The effects of their aggression will be greater and carry stronger implications to the victims than does violence from females to males.

The positive findings from the RELATE data are that even though violence has happened in at least 15% of the relationships, almost all of this violence is occurring rarely. This suggests that most couples who are violent have only experienced a few incidents and they may not be trapped in relationships that are regularly violent. Still, once certain boundaries are crossed they are easier to cross again, so violence is much more likely to reoccur for couples even if it has happened only once. Any couple who has experienced violence prior to marriage should seek professional help and may want to seriously question the viability of their relationship. This is especially the case if there is a partner who is possessive or jealous, who has a history of violence toward strangers and other partners, who has a pattern of substance abuse, who has values that are accepting of violence as a way of solving problems, or who has strong insecurities and low self-esteem. A partner with some or most of the preceding characteristics who has been violent even once is very likely to be abusive in the future. It may be difficult to safely leave such a partner without help from a shelter, friends, and family.

Sexual Violence or Coercion

As is clear from Table 16.3, sexual coercion is more common with premarital couples than is physical violence. Surprisingly, males' reports of their own sexual coercion are higher than their partners' reports of their coercion. It may be that males interpret some of their behavior as coercive when their partners do not, or it may be that their partners are more willing to overlook coercive behaviors. Either way, almost 30% of the couples who have taken RELATE report sexual coercion in their relationship. This issue of pressuring partners to be sexual against their will, which is how the question is worded in the RELATE questionnaire, is a serious matter. The dating scene at many colleges is fraught with danger for women. The culture is often one where attendance at parties is expected, as is the consumption of alcohol and the participation in sexual behaviors with people who are only casual friends.

Some women are also coercive in their attempts to be sexual with a partner. About 10% of the women report that they are coercive to their partners and about 13% of the men report that their partners are sexually coercive. However, after one of the authors of this book interviewed couples in which the woman was reported as being sexually aggressive, it was clear that females' coercive attempts were different from males'. The females encouraged sex through verbal pressure, such as saying it was a sign of love or saying they would leave if their partner refused. Males, however, were much more likely to use verbal pressure and then follow this up with physical force if necessary to get their way. Although both psychological and physical threats are damaging, when both are combined the effects are exponentially more negative. In the end, women are almost always the victims of sexual aggression and thousands of them carry the emotional and psychological scars of this trauma for many years.

Informal surveys in courtship and marriage classes have resulted in the following list of suggestions to help reduce the threat of sexual trauma:

- Avoid alcohol and avoid being alone with someone who is inebriated.
- Avoid parties where alcohol and other drugs are readily available.
- Use a buddy system at parties so someone knows where you are and who you are with at all times. This will help reduce the risk of being involuntarily incapacitated by drugs or alcohol that are put in drinks or food by others.
- Ask about potential dating partners from people who have gone out with the person before.
- Be clear with a partner about your sexual boundaries as soon as possible.
- Express a zero tolerance for sexual pressure at the verbal level. Leave the situation and do not date the individual again.

- Double date until you really trust your partner.
- Do not participate even in milder forms of sexuality such as necking when you do not want to. Some people interpret these mild forms of sexuality as an implicit agreement to proceed to intercourse.

Substance Abuse

The issue of substance abuse is an important issue to include in a chapter on problems and violence. Alcohol and other drugs are a part of approximately 70% of the instances of violence and sexual abuse (Killian & Busby, 1996). Not only are the perpetrators likely to become less capable of controlling their violent and sexual tendencies, but victims who have used mind-altering drugs are less able to perceive threats and find ways of escaping. When these threats are combined with the additional problems of legal complications, deteriorating health, unwanted pregnancies, and the potential disasters that accompany drinking and driving, it is counterintuitive that alcohol and other drugs continue to be such a common part of the dating experience. Perhaps the discomfort in getting to know other people and the fantasy that drugs act as a social lubricant continue to make them popular with people of all ages.

Regardless of the reasons for substance abuse, it is a serious problem at all stages of the courtship and marriage process. Table 16.1 illustrates this reality for those who have completed RELATE. It is true that substance abuse is less likely after marriage, as almost all high-risk behaviors diminish for married couples compared with singles (Waite & Gallagher, 2000). There is a settling down that occurs for many people when they decide to marry. Yet this finding should not be misinterpreted to mean that your or your partner's problems with substance abuse will spontaneously improve after marriage. Letting go of addictive drugs, which includes alcohol, is one of the most challenging habits to break. Countless marriages and families are destroyed because of one person's addiction that everyone hoped would get better with time. It is best to eliminate these problems prior to even forming a steady dating relationship so that minds are clearer and wiser decisions can be made. However, even if someone has already overcome a substance abuse problem, this is something to carefully consider as a significant perpetual problem. Alcoholism can be a lifelong struggle even if a person has had many years of sobriety.

17

Satisfaction, Stability, and Marriage

We can live safe and avoid pain. Or we can embrace risk, laughing well and crying hard and living big.

—Linamen, 2001

What would you think about being in a romantic relationship that is fulfilling? In this relationship you would have what you want and what you need, given your personality characteristics and your values. Your partner would have what she or he wants and needs, and you would be able to share with each other love and support that is respectful and energizing. Outside of your fulfilling relationship you would be supported by a concerned and healthy social network—one that provides enough support for the two of you to make it through your dilemmas, and enough wisdom to make the two of you responsible to each other. These may be the optimum qualities in strong relationships: satisfaction, intimacy, and stability.

If asked to choose just one of those qualities (satisfaction, intimacy, or stability), which would you choose? In relationships you probably can have it all, but not all of it all at once, and not without a lot of work (and a little luck). Strong relationships evolve over time, beginning with a focus on oneself and one's own needs, changing to concern for the other partner, and then the relationship is placed in a social context that can create smooth sailing or rough waters. The success of the journey is dependent on the skills of the ship's crew and its determination to do whatever is necessary to stay afloat.

Ideally, satisfaction, intimacy, and stability are all substantially present in serious relationships. They make up three sides of a single relationship triangle (see Figure 17.1). There is no reason to believe that the three sides will be equally present in all relationships. Some relationships, while being very intimate and satisfying, are

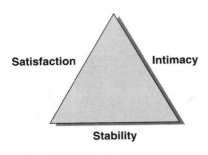

FIGURE 17.1   *Three Elements of Relationship Well-Being*

between partners who have no expectation that the relationship will last. Other couples may be fully committed to their relationship, but are missing satisfaction and intimacy. Each couple's relationship triangle is unique, and its shape continues to change throughout the duration of the relationship. Relationships may have more or less satisfaction, more or less stability, and more or less intimacy. A little of each side must be present at all times, however, so that it remains a triangle and not just a flat line.

Depending on the length of a relationship and its seriousness (e.g., casual dating, steady dating, serious dating, engagement), some of these elements of relationships are more of a focus than others. Relationships often begin with a focus on satisfaction and intimacy, with fairly limited stability concerns. As the relationship matures and the partners take more risks with each other, stability (which is a reflection of the commitment that the couple has in the relationship) becomes an important focus.

As couples assess their relationships, it is important to consider the question of how serious the relationship has become. Has the relationship changed stages of seriousness (e.g., gone from casual dating to serious dating), and does the relationship meet each partner's personal needs at this stage? Will the relationship be able to meet the participants' needs as it progresses?

As couples engage in deeper levels of relationship exploration, notice where their focus is in terms of the intimacy that is possible in relationships. Relationships actually involve more than the two partners and it is helpful to look back over each partner's personal histories and consider the influence of these histories on the relationship. Can the past be used in healthy ways? How will past traumas be experienced in the current relationship? Each of these questions provides information about what is expected of the relationship and whether the relationship will be able to fulfill those expectations.

Partners' assessments of satisfaction and their decisions to either focus on the current relationship or continue looking until a more appropriate relationship is available are influenced by the degree to which their expectations are met in the relationship and whether or not expectations are realistic.

Satisfaction

Satisfaction is a barometer of the extent to which you are receiving relationship rewards. If you were measuring the character size of letters in a book you would use a ruler. If, however, you wanted to measure the character size of letters on a building, you might use a tape measure. Relationship satisfaction works similarly: The amount of satisfaction needed to detect its presence from a distance is dependent on its size relative to what is expected. If you are measuring a current relationship against a standard of abusive relationships, you may only need the slightest indication of positive affect to have a measurable amount of positives that meet your expectations. If, however, you have always been in rewarding, loving relationships, you may require much more indication of positive affect for it to register on your satisfaction tape measure.

Early in relationships when members of a couple are deciding whether to become serious partners, the focus of evaluating levels of satisfaction is oneself. For example, when you first see your partner you may be very aware of your personal experience of excitement and anticipation. Although your partner may very well experience the same feelings, you are most aware of what it is like for you. Not surprisingly, relationships that are solely based on one's own satisfaction are fragile. Imagine that you enjoy stopping at your partner's place of work to say "hello" during the day. You become excited to see your partner. For her, however, your visits are uncomfortable. At her workplace she wants to be viewed as a professional, and if she greets you in the way to which you are accustomed she feels that her self-presentation at work is compromised. When you come into her workspace she feels frustrated. If you continue to come into the room and only notice your own high levels of satisfaction, the relationship will quickly suffer. As you might imagine, there are differences between couples in which one member is very satisfied and another is dissatisfied, as compared with couples where both are somewhat satisfied. Only at the beginning of an intimate relationship would it be appropriate to expect the individual's satisfaction to be more important than the shared satisfaction between the couple. As relationships become more serious, the expectation that one partner will change her or his behavior to increase the satisfaction of the other increases.

It is human nature to like what is new and exciting, and to become less satisfied with that to which we are accustomed. Over time, a partner's behaviors that were initially charming may become annoying. Imagine that before you were dating you enjoyed listening to your partner's hearty laugh. When she laughed, most of the people around her would stop and look at her. It was also cute at the beginning of the relationship, but now in the third month of dating it has become embarrassing. You would be more satisfied with a smile or a grin, and a softer laugh. As needs change, so do those things that are perceived as satisfying. Unfortunately, our partners are sometimes unaware that our satisfaction needs have changed, and they may continue doing what is no longer perceived as rewarding. In successful intimate relationships, partners learn to monitor their level of satisfaction and communicate with their partners before their satisfaction level gets too low. For example, prior to serious dating or engagement, a woman may be thrilled by receiving a dozen roses. While planning for marriage, however, she may prefer that her partner bring her less expensive flowers, bring a single rose, or pick a wildflower. In such a case the woman might tell her partner that she appreciates his thoughtfulness, and that she would be equally flattered with one of the lower cost alternatives. Often, just knowing that an experience is becoming uncomfortable for one member is enough information for the other to modify behaviors. This is, in Kelley's words (1979), a transformation. Each partner's behaviors become somewhat modified to meet the needs of the other.

Finally, the experience of satisfaction in a relationship influences, and is influenced by, the level of intimacy experienced by the couple. As you recall, intimacy is a form of risk taking. If I am going to risk loving you, I need to know that my risk is well taken. If I need behavior that is different from how you would prefer to act, whether or not you are willing to behave in the way requested provides tremendous information to me about the relationship. The modification of your behavior to increase my satisfaction, and my subsequent modifications to increase your satisfaction, result in the exchanges of intimacy and lead to the development of another side of the triangle. This simple idea is not foreign at all to couples who have remained in satisfying relationships for decades. It does tend to surprise people in short-term relationships, or in serial marriages, who hold the belief that they should take care of their own needs first and resist making changes on behalf of others.

Expectations and Experiences

Now ask yourself what it is that you expect in your relationship. Do you expect to be very happy most of the time? Are you expecting some peaks and valleys? Are you expecting to get your needs met quickly and efficiently? Your ability to maintain realistic expectations has a great impact on your relationship satisfaction. As you think about a past or current relationship, ask yourself whether you get your needs met about as often as you would expect, more often, or less often than you would expect. Your expectations are influenced by the belief systems and values you learned by virtue of your gender, race, ethnicity, and spirituality. You may want to consider whether your expectations are realistic and whether they are in line with your behaviors. For example, if you expect that your partner will not know what you need unless you tell her or him, but then refuse to tell him or her because "if they love me they should know," your behaviors and belief systems are not in line with each other (Gordon, 2001).

Expectations are based on experiences that are developed either in relationship with actual partners (past and present) or vicariously from the experiences of others. Those vicarious experiences are subject to romanticism coming from media, the social appearance of other couples, or an awareness of alternative partners outside of the current relationship. For instance, perhaps you have observed the marital relationships of your parents and your grandparents, and you expect your own romantic relationships to be similar. This provides a standard to which you hold your current relationship accountable. If you have seen husbands and wives who greet each other at the end of the day with a big kiss and fifteen minutes of intimate conversation, and are dating someone who prefers blowing a kiss and running to check her e-mail, you will find yourself quite dissatisfied. When people receive what they expect or more than they expect in their relationships, they are satisfied.

You probably know people whose expectations are unrealistic. A commonly held myth of close relationships is that romantic partners can meet all of each other's needs (Larson, 2000). When unrealistic expectations are the standard to which the relationship is compared, the real relationship cannot possibly measure up. Although some partners settle for being treated very poorly, with the expectation that they do not deserve better treatment, most people fall somewhere between unrealistically high and very low expectations.

If a relationship perfectly meets your expectations for the satisfaction level you should receive, why would you ever decide to leave? We live in a culture of overindulgence. It is not uncommon to want more than you have, even when what you have is sufficient. If there is a relationship available that supplies more satisfaction than that experienced in the current relationship, even though the current relationship supplies the necessary level of satisfaction, discontent can grow. Competition raises the expectations for satisfaction. Doherty (2002) calls this consumerism in marriage.

Competition that changes the expectation level can be tangible or intangible. When the competition is another real person who is available to objectively assess, some of the romanticizing of a different partner can be challenged. The person who was fantastic looking and debonair on the first meeting may commit social errors during the second meeting, creating a more human impression than what was originally seen. When the competition is intangible, as coming from the media or Internet chat rooms, partners who promise more are not truly available for scrutiny, causing relationship expectations to be unrealistically high.

Expectations are sometimes so common that they tend to be overlooked. When some women complain that their partners do not meet their expectations for communication, they refer to their greater comfort in talking with their girlfriends about issues that are bothering them. Men, on the other hand, may complain that their partners do not meet their expectations for communication when they do not let things drop, like their buddies can. Expectations are based on experiences of what is possible in relationships outside of the romantic relationship. The Golden Rule, "Do unto others as you would have others do unto you" is generally good advice; however, when following such a rule women end up trying to engage their partners in more conversation (because that is what they would like done unto them) and men end up letting issues drop quickly (which is what they would like done unto them). It can be a vicious cycle of misunderstanding. Perhaps The Golden Rule for Couples should be, "Do unto others as they tell you they would have others do unto them." What you would need from your partner may not be exactly the same as what your partner needs from you. That is where good communication skills are very helpful. Knowing what questions to ask, and how to listen, is a more realistic goal than expecting yourself to have all of the answers.

Interdependence

The ability to sustain a level of satisfaction in the relationship that meets or exceeds the expectations of both partners takes work. A level of satisfaction that is achieved initially in a relationship is much different from that which is based on anticipated future satisfaction of a long-term relationship. The relationship work begins with a willingness to understand and take responsibility both for your own feelings of satisfaction and for the effect of your behavior on your partner's satisfaction.

For example, imagine that it is Saturday afternoon and that you are content to be watching the basketball game on television as your partner cleans the house and begins to prepare supper. You may be quite satisfied. At half time, however, as you enter the kitchen for a cool drink you notice that your partner is particularly quiet and grumpy looking, and you discover that his level of satisfaction is quite low. In fact, he is not satisfied to be taking care of the household responsibilities while you enjoy the game. Your level of satisfaction in the current situation will probably begin to change. You will be less satisfied to sit and watch the game because that behavior has a cost to your partner, and that cost has meaning to you. When your partner experiences a negative cost it decreases the satisfaction that you would have felt had you been looking at your rewards alone. Some readers may find this too calculated—surely love relationships are not based on tit for tat. As a matter of fact, they often are. Not only do couples tend to "keep score" in relationships so that they notice the relative contributions of each partner on an ongoing basis, they actually bring in their score cards from other relationships and hold their current partners accountable for past debts (Gordon, 2001). Couples may not be aware of their score

Couples sometimes take turns choosing leisure activities so that both partners have the opportunity to enjoy their preferred activity while spending time together.

keeping at first, but when relationships become unsatisfying, couples are readily able to report the number and types of costs they have incurred in the current relationship.

There is something more about the example, of course. Chances are, you may have been expecting the basketball fan to be a man, and the unhappy homemaker to be a woman. Is gender relevant to the discussion of satisfaction? Absolutely. Again, it is the family and social context that creates the vision of what is possible, and what is probable, in the relationship. Unfortunately, gender sometimes masks issues of satisfaction because intimate relationships are steeped in gender roles. Should the woman feel entitled to continue enjoying the basketball game even though her partner is unhappy? What would you think if the roles were reversed? Would it have mattered? We get into habits of using our own personal lens of expectations, from our own perspective of roles and privilege, rather than looking at our partners' experience. The experiences of women and men in close relationships can be quite different from each other. Their expectations are nested in their gender, race, and other areas of socialization.

Partners eventually begin predicting their future satisfaction from their daily experiences. When a partner understands and appreciates the relational efforts of the other and expects that both people will give to each more or less equally over time, temporary dissatisfaction is tolerable. If, on the other hand, the future prediction is that the same person will be experiencing leisure while the other works each day of the relationship, the satisfaction will be lower for the less benefited partner. Imagine the relationship when the basketball fan expresses gratitude for the partner's labor, and confirms the partner's expectations that she will be contributing to the household labor at a later time (or is actually folding laundry during the game!), as opposed to one in which one member expects the other to perform all of the labor in the household. Interdependence is a pattern of sharing that is based on continual feedback between two people. Partners share happiness, concerns, physical labor, emotional closeness, physical resources, and more.

Transformations are the basis on which partners begin to predict the likelihood of receiving relationship rewards in the future. In intimate relationships, satisfaction is less influenced by what is immediately available than by what is expected to be available in the future. Predicting positive future outcomes typically depends on the perception that a partner is genuine, loving, and thoughtful. On the RELATE report, two items assess predictions of future outcomes: How kind is your partner, and how kind does your partner think that you are? Kind people will be thoughtful, may delay some of their own needs to meet the needs of their partners, and will be emotionally available. Without kindness, future negative outcomes are likely. Any time people are able to predict pain, they find ways to protect themselves. For a couple in a committed (e.g., engaged or married) relationship in which those future positive outcomes cannot be predicted, the future is likely to include a distant, dissatisfying relationship.

In summary, we begin relationships using our own experiences and expectations to assess satisfaction. As the relationship progresses we begin widening our vision to include our partner's experiences, and ours, in and outside of the relationship. Satisfaction is based on whether our experiences and our expectations are similar. Couples begin changing how they behave to increase both their risk and their benefits in the relationship. Based on experiences of partners making changes for each other, current satisfaction begins to be predictive of future satisfaction.

In RELATE, a number of areas of potential satisfaction are assessed. There are satisfaction questions on physical intimacy, the love experienced, the ways in which conflicts are resolved, the amount of equality experienced, the amount of time together, the quality of the communication, and the overall relationship. For both males and females, the most influential area of the relationship on the overall satisfaction is the love experienced, followed by communication and equality. The amount of time spent together and how conflicts are resolved are not strongly related to overall satisfaction for either gender. Because the RELATE respondents are primarily younger couples, much conflict and time constraints that are experienced by older couples with children are not yet problematic for them. Physical intimacy is not strongly related to overall satisfaction, but it is strongly related to respondents' answers about their satisfaction with the amount of love they experience.

Stability

Stability simply refers to the number of times that members of the couple have considered leaving the relationship or have actually left the relationship. Stability has a great deal to do with your values about relationships. If you believe that marriage is a permanent arrangement, you will work harder to stay married than if you believe that you can get divorced and start over. Your commitment to a relationship has everything to do with how hard you are willing to work to make the relationship succeed.

Simply staying married, however, is not the same as staying in a relationship. Some couples are very stable and completely miserable. These couples may have all commitment and no satisfaction or intimacy. They have a "relationship" as far as the legal paperwork and perhaps the physical residence, but they are not intimate partners. Whereas maintaining a relationship requires commitment from both people to succeed, unfortunately, ending a relationship requires only one person.

Stability in marriage is like a building on the California earthquake fault line: constructed with the hope for permanence and dependent on the strength and flexibility of the foundation. Stability is part commitment and part alternatives. At the beginning of a relationship partners are independent and can find equal or greater satisfaction in relationships outside of the current relationship. Each partner's satisfaction is dependent primarily on her or his own rewards. When partners are interdependent the relationship is more stable. Personal satisfaction is affected by partner's satisfaction, and there is more invested in the relationship. Such interdependence in the current relationship fulfills enough of a partner's needs to require an even greater alternative to warrant making a change. This is the glue that holds relationships together through the difficult times that relationships are bound to experience, and provides stability while the couple works to repair and redirect the relationship.

Some relationship dependence is a result of limited alternatives that are actually available outside of the current relationship. When the pool of eligibles for a particular person is sufficiently restricted and there does not seem to be a possibility of becoming part of a new relationship if the current relationship should end, dependence on the relationship may increase. For example, women tend to live longer than do men, and they typically marry someone older, more educated, better employed, and taller. Imagine the challenge that a 50-year-old brain surgeon has in finding an eligible partner when she is interested in a romantic relationship. Her pool of eligibles (an older, more educated, better employed male) would be quite small.

Commitment

Sometimes commitment to marriage alone sustains marriages. The point at which people become permanently committed to the relationship changes across cultures. Some cultures permit only three dates before a commitment is made; others are committed at the time of first sexual intercourse after the marriage (often called consummation); still others are committed only after a first child is born; and some are never fully committed.

Marriages that are performed in places of worship, in front of friends and family, tend to have more barriers to dissolution than do those marriages performed in a roadside "chapel" in Las Vegas. There can be many reasons for this. Marriages performed in places of worship often contain a belief that marriage is a sacrament, and

Wedding chapels may provide the thrill of spontaneity, but a formal wedding in front of family and friends provides a greater chance for stability.

that the commitment is to God, each other, and the community "until death do we part." Also, when marriage is performed in front of a community, the couple declares an intention to enter into a contract, and the community agrees to support the union ("If anyone has any reason why this couple should not be joined, speak now or *forever* hold your peace."). The commitment extends beyond personal satisfaction, with the awareness that there are times in marriage when it is not rewarding, but also that the experiences of other members of the family and community are dependent on the couple to do what they can to keep their marriage working. The married couple, like Chief Executive Officers of major corporations, establish the climate and stability of the family system. To dissolve a marriage affects the lives of many people, and through commitment the couple can remain stable and grow through their difficulties rather than giving up.

With that acknowledged, it must be added that there are situations in which one member or both partners behave in ways that prohibit the couple from being able to maintain a commitment to marriage. Physical or emotional abuse, substance abuse, infidelity, or other such difficulties in the marriage can necessitate dissolution. Such difficulties force the most committed partner to make the choice to end the relationship.

Final Thoughts

After the couple has put in all of the work and preparation it can to develop and sustain a healthy relationship, it is the work of the social network to support the couple's efforts, to provide guidance and encouragement during difficult times, and to be responsible enough to prevent interference in the couple's ability to sustain the relationship. If it takes a village to raise a child, it takes a nation to protect and nurture healthy relationships.

Relationships are the most enjoyable and challenging of all endeavors in life. They may also be, depending on your worldview, the primary purpose of life. Most people, when they look back over their lives, will feel like a success or a failure primarily by assessing the quality of their marriage and family relationships. Many also believe that the family is the foundation of each nation and marriage is the foundation of the family. With so much riding on our marriages, it seems curious that more attention and effort are not put into helping people be successful at this relationship. Consider all the effort that must go into getting a driver's license or a license to practice as a lawyer, a beautician, a plumber, or a physician, yet in most states all that has to go into getting a marriage license is a few signatures and two forms of identification. In fact, very few people ever have a high school or college course on learning to be successful at making relationships work. You, however, have now completed at least one course on relationships and perhaps you are better prepared to avoid some of the common pitfalls of marriage. We're hoping that this text has provided you with one possible map to achieving healthy, rewarding, and stable marriage for yourself and for others in your life.

References

Ainsworth, M. D. S., & Bell, S. M. (1970). Attachment, exploration, and separation: Illustrated by the behavior of one-year-olds in a strange situation. *Child Development, 41,* 49–67.

Albom, M. (1997). *Tuesdays with Morrie.* New York: Doubleday.

Amato, P. R. (2001). Children of divorce in the 1990s: An update of the Amato and Keith (1991) meta-analysis. *Journal of Family Psychology, Special Issue, 15,* 355–370.

Amato, P. R., & Keith, B. (1991). Parental divorce and the well-being of children: A meta-analysis. *Psychological Bulletin, 110,* 26–46.

Amato, P. R., Loomis, L. S., & Booth, A. (1995). Parental divorce, marital conflict, and offspring well-being during early adulthood. *Social Forces, 73,* 895–915.

Aponte, H. (1982). Foreword. In M. McGoldrick, J. K. Pearce, & J. Giordano, *Ethnicity and family therapy.* New York: Guilford Press.

Axinn, W. G., & Barber, J. S. (1997). Living arrangements and family formation attitudes in early adulthood. *Journal of Marriage and the Family, 59,* 595–611.

Bartlett, J. (1937). *Familiar quotations* (11th ed.) (p. 431). Boston: P. F. Collier and Son.

Bengston, V., Rosenthal, C., & Burton, L. (1990). Families and aging: Diversity and heterogeneity. In R. H. Binstock and L. George (Eds.), *Handbook of aging and the social sciences* (3rd ed.). New York: Academic Press.

Berg, J. (1984). Development of friendship between roommates. *Journal of Personality and Social Psychology, 46,* 346–356.

Berg, I. K., & Jaya, A. (1993). Different and the same: Family therapy with Asian-American families. *Journal of Marital and Family Therapy, 19*(1), 31–38.

Bernard, J. (1972). *The future of marriage.* New York: World.

Bernard, M. L., & Bernard, J. L. (1983). Violent intimacy: The family as a model for love relationships. *Family Relations, 32,* 283–286.

Berry, R. E., & Williams, F. L. (1987). Assessing the relationships between quality of life and marital income satisfaction: A path analytic approach. *Journal of Marriage and the Family, 49,* 107–116.

Berscheid, E. (1983). Emotion. In H. H. Kelley, E. Berscheid, A. Christensen, J. H. Harvey, T. L. Huston, G. Levinger, E. McClintock, L. A. Peplau, & D. R. Peterson (Eds.), *Close relationships* (pp. 110–168). New York: W. H. Freeman.

Bettelheim, B. (1987). *A good enough parent.* New York: Vintage Books.

Blinn-Pike, L. (1999). Why abstinent adolescents report they have not had sex: Understanding sexually resilient youth. *Family Relations, 48,* 295–301.

Blumstein, P., & Schwartz, P. (1983). *American couples: Money, work, sex.* New York: William Morrow.

Boss, P. (1988). *Family stress management.* Newbury Park, CA: Sage Publications.

Braiker, H. B., & Kelley, H. H. (1979). Conflicts in the development of close relationships. In R. Burgess & T. Huston (Eds.), *Social exchange in developing relationships* (pp. 135–168). New York: Academic Press.

Bride's magazine. (2001). Retrieved on 9/15/01 from Emerald Weddings: www.emeraldweddings.com.

Burns, D. (1999). *Feeling good, the new mood therapy: A clinically proven drug-free treatment for depression* (rev. ed.). New York: HarperCollins.

Busby, D. M. (2000). *Physical and sexual abuse in the family: Filling knowledge gaps for therapists.* Iowa City, IA: Geist & Russell.

Busby, D. M., Holman, T. B., & Taniguchi, N. (2001). RELATE: Relationship evaluation of the individual, family, cultural, and couple contexts. *Family Relations, 50,* 308–316.

Busby, D. M., & Preece, J. C. (2000). Parenting quality and familial stress as mediators of the psychological and interpersonal adjustment of incest survivors. In D. M. Busby (Ed.), *Physical and sexual abuse in the family: Filling knowledge gaps for therapists.* Iowa City, IA: Geist & Russell.

Busby, D. M., & Smith, G. L. (2000). Family therapy with children who are victims of physical violence. In C. E. Bailey (Ed.), *Children in therapy: Using the family as a resource.* New York: W. W. Norton.

Busby, D. M., & Taniguchi, N. (2000). *Expanding Gottman's model into the family and individual realms.* A paper presented at the Annual Conference of the National Council on Family Relations, Minneapolis, MN.

Buss, D. M. (1990). International preferences in selecting mates: A study of 37 cultures. *Journal of Cross-Cultural Psychology, 21,* 5–47.

Buss, D. M., & Barnes, M. (1986). Preferences in human mate selection. *Journal of Personality and Social Psychology, 50,* 559–570.

Carlson, R. (2001). *The don't sweat guide for couples.* New York: Hyperion.

Cate, R. M., Henton, J. M., Koval, J. E., Christopher, F. S., & Lloyd, S. A. (1982). Premarital abuse: A social psychological perspective. *Journal of Family Issues, 3,* 79–90.

Chadwick, B. A., & Heaton, T. (1992). *Statistical handbook on the American family.* New York: Oryx Press.

Christopher, S., & Sprecher, S. (2000). Sexuality in marriage, dating, and other relationships: A decade review. *Journal of Marriage and the Family, 62,* 999–1017.

Cole, C. L., & Cole, A. L. (1999). Marriage enrichment and prevention really works: Interpersonal competence training to maintain and enhance relationships. *Family Relations, 48,* 273–275.

Coleman, M., Ganong, L., & Fine, M. (2000). Reinvestigating remarriage: Another decade of progress. *Journal of Marriage and the Family, 62,* 1288–1307.

Cuber, J. F., & Haroff, P. B. (1971). Five types of marriage. In A. S. Skolnick & J. H. Skolnick (Eds.), *Families in transition.* Boston: Little, Brown.

Cummings, E. M. (1987). Coping with background anger in early childhood. *Child Development, 58,* 976–984.

DeBecker, G. (1997). *The gift of fear: Survival signals that protect us from violence.* New York: Little, Brown.

Doherty, W. J. (2002). *Take back your marriage.* New York: Guilford Press.

Dossey, L. (1999). *Reinventing medicine: Beyond mind-body to a new era of healing.* New York: Harper San Francisco.

Doxey, C., & Holman, T. (2001). Social contexts influencing marital quality. In T. B. Holman (Ed.), *Premarital prediction of marital quality or breakup* (pp. 119–140). New York: Plenum.

Edler, R. (1995). *If I knew then what I know now.* New York: Berkley Books.

Ekman, P. (1984). Expression and the nature of emotion. In K. R. Scherer & P. Ekman (Eds.), *Approaches to emotion* (pp. 319–344). Hillsdale, NJ: Lawrence Erlbaum Associates.

Frey, W. H., Abresch, B., & Yeasting, J. (2001). *A field guide to the U.S. population, America by the numbers* (p. 125). New York: The New Press.

Friedman, H. S., Schwartz, J. E., Tomlinson-Keasey, C., & Martin, L. R. (1995). Psychosocial and behavioral predictors of longevity. *American Psychologist, 50,* 69–78.

Gilbert, L. A. (1994). Reclaiming and returning to context: Examples from studies of heterosexual dual-earner families. *Psychology of Women Quarterly, 18,* 539–558.

Glenn, N., & Marquardt, E. (2001). *Hooking up, hanging out, and hoping for Mr. Right: College women on dating and mating today.* New York: Institute for American Values.

Goodwin, R. (1990). Sex differences among partner preferences: Are the sexes really very different? *Sex Roles, 23,* 501–513.

Gordon, L. H. (2001). *PAIRS: If you really loved me.* Dallas, TX: PAIRS Foundation.

Gottman, J. M. (1994). *What predicts divorce? The relationship between marital processes and marital outcomes.* Hillsdale, NJ: Lawrence Erlbaum Associates.

Gottman, J. M. (1999). *The marriage clinic: A scientifically based marital therapy.* New York: W. W. Norton.

Gottman, J., & Declaire, J. (1997). *Raising an emotionally intelligent child: The heart of parenting.* New York: Simon and Schuster.

Gottman, J. M., & Declaire, J. (2001). *The relationship cure: A five-step guide for building better connections with family, friends, and lovers.* New York: Crown.

Gottman, J., & Katz, L. (1989). Effects of marital discord on young children's peer interaction and health. *Developmental Psychology, 57,* 47–52.

Gottman, J. M., & Notarius, C. I. (2000). Decade review: Observing marital interaction. *Journal of Marriage and the Family, 62,* 927–947.

Guralnik, D. B. (Ed.). (1982). *Webster's new world dictionary of the American language.* New York: Simon and Schuster.

Harvey, J. H., Wells, G. L., & Alverez, M. D. (1978). Attribution in the context of conflict and separation in close relationships. In *New directions in attribution research* (Vol. 2, pp. 235–260). Hillsdale, NJ: Lawrence Erlbaum Associates.

Heatherington, E. M. (1992). Coping with marital transitions: A family systems perspective. *Monographs for the Society for Research in Child Development, 57,* 6–10.

Heller, P. E., & Wood, B. (1998). The process of intimacy: Similarity, understanding and gender. *Journal of Marital and Family Therapy, 24*(3), 273–288.

Hill, C. T., Rubin, Z., & Peplau, L. A. (1976). Breakups before marriage: The end of 103 affairs. *Journal of Social Issues, 32*(1), 147–168.

Holman, T. B., & Associates. (2000). *Premarital prediction of marital quality or breakup: Research, theory, and practice.* New York: Plenum.

Holman, T. B., Busby, D. M., Doxey, C., Klein, D. M., & Loyer-Carlson, V. (1997). *The RELATionship Evaluation (RELATE).* Provo, UT: Marriage Study Consortium.

Holman, T. B., & Jarvis, M. O. (2000). *Replicating and validating Gottman's couple conflict types using survey data.* Paper presented at the annual meeting of the National Council on Family Relations, Minneapolis, MN.

Holman, T. B., Larson, J. H., & Harmer, S. L. (1994). The development and predictive validity of a new premarital assessment instrument: The PREParation for marriage questionnaire. *Family Relations, 43,* 46–52.

Holman, T., & Linford, S. (2001). Premarital factors and later marital quality and stability. In T. B. Holman (Ed.), *Premarital prediction of marital quality or breakup: Research, theory, and practice* (pp. 1–28). New York: Plenum.

Horn, W. F. (2000, December 22). Abusive parents; unhappy marriages. *The Washington Times.* p. E1.

Huber, J., & Spitze, G. (1989). Trends in family sociology. In N. J. Smelser (Ed.), *Handbook of sociology* (pp. 425–448). Newbury Park, CA: Sage Publications.

Johnson, D. W. (2000). *Reaching out: Interpersonal effectiveness and self-actualization* (97th ed.). Boston: Allyn & Bacon.

Kelley, H. H. (1979). *Personal relationships: Their structures and processes.* Hillsdale, NJ: Lawrence Erlbaum Associates.

Kelly, E. L. , & Conley, J. J. (1987). Personality and compatibility: A prospective analysis of marital stability and marital satisfaction. *Journal of Personality and Social Psychology, 52,* 27–40.

Killian K., & Busby, D. M. (1996). Premarital physical abuse of women by male partners. In D. M. Busby (Ed.) *The impact of violence on the family: Treatment approaches for therapists and other professionals.* Boston: Allyn & Bacon.

Laner, M. R., & Russell, J. N. (1998). Desired characteristics of spouses and best friends: Do they differ by sex and/or gender? *Sociological Inquiry, 68,* 186–202.

Larson, J. H. (2000). *Should we stay together? A scientifically proven method for evaluating your relationship and improving its chances for long-term success.* San Francisco: Jossey-Bass.

Larson, J. H., & Holman, T. B. (1994). Premarital predictors of marital quality and stability. *Family Relations, 43,* 228–237.

Lasswell, M., & Lasswell, T. (1991). *Marriage and the family* (3rd ed.) (p. 7). Belmont, CA: Wadsworth Publishing.

Lerner, H. (2001). *The dance of connection*. New York: HarperCollins.

Leslie, L. A., Huston, T. L., & Johnson, M. P. (1986). Parental reactions to dating relationships: Do they make a difference? *Journal of Marriage and the Family, 48*, 57–66.

Levine, L. B., & Busby, D. M. (1997). Co-creating shared realities with couples. *Contemporary Family Therapy, 15*, 405–421.

Levinger, G., & Rands, M. (1985). Compatibility in marriage and other close relationships. *Compatibility and compatible relationships* (309–331). New York: Springer-Verlag.

Levinger, G., & Snoek, J. D. (1972). *Attraction in relationships: A new look at interpersonal attraction.* Morristown, NJ: General Learning Press.

Linamen, K. S. (2001). *Sometimes I wake up grumpy . . . and sometimes I let him sleep.* Grand Rapids, MI: Fleming H. Revell.

Long, E. C., Angera, J. J., Carter, S. J., Nakamoto, M., & Kalso, M. (1999). Understanding the one you love: A longitudinal assessment of an empathy training program for couples in romantic relationships. *Family Relations, 48*, 235–242.

Long, E. C., Cate, R. M., Fehsenfeld, D. A., & Williams, K. M. (1996). A longitudinal assessment of a measure of premarital sexual conflict. *Family Relations, 45*, 302–308.

Mackellar, F. L., & Yanagishita, M. (1995). *Homicide in the United States: Who's at risk.* Washington, DC: Population and Reference Bureau.

Markman, H., Stanley, S., & Blumberg, S. L. (1994). *Fighting for your marriage.* San Francisco: Jossey-Bass.

Massachusetts Wedding Guide. (2001). Retrieved on 9/05/01 from Massachusetts Wedding Guide: *www.maweddingguide.com.*

McGoldrick, M., Preto, N. G., Hines, P. M., & Lee, E. (1991). Ethnicity and family therapy. In A. S. Gurman & D. P. Kniskern, *Handbook of family therapy: Vol. 2* (pp. 546–582). New York: Bruner/Mazel.

McHale, S. M. (1993). Challenges to healthy development: Protective factors for at-risk children and adolescents. In V. L. Loyer-Carlson & F. K. Willits (Eds.), *Youth at risk: The research and practice interface* (pp. 31–37). University Park, PA: Northeast Regional Center for Rural Development.

McKenry, P. C., & Price, S. (1991). Predictors of single, noncustodial fathers' physical involvement with their children. *The Journal of Genetic Psychology, 153*, 305–319.

McRae, S. (1999). Cohabitation or marriage? In G. Allan (Ed.), *The sociology of the family* (pp. 172–173). Malden, MA: Blackwell Publishers.

Media life. (1999). Retrieved on 9/15/01 from Media Life: http://www.64.154.21.227/news1999/june99/news3629.html.

Meredith, D. B., & Holman, T. B. (2001). Breaking up before and after marriage. In T. B. Holman (Ed.), *Premarital prediction of marital quality or breakup: Research, theory, and practice.* (pp. 47–78). New York: Plenum.

Miller, B. C., & Benson, B. (1999). Romantic and sexual relationship development during adolescence. In W. Furman, B. B. Brown, & C. Feiring (Eds.), *The development of romantic relationships in adolescence* (pp. 99–121). Boston: Cambridge University Press.

Miller, B. C., Norton, M. C., Curtis, T., Hill, E. J., Schvaneveldt, P., & Young, M. H. (1997). The timing of sexual intercourse among adolescents: Family, peer, and other antecedents. *Youth & Society, 29*, 54–83.

Miller, J. B., & Stiver, I. P. (1997). *The healing connection: How women form relationships in therapy and in life.* Boston: Beacon.

Newman, B. M., & Newman, P. R. (1995). *Development through life: A psychosocial approach* (p. 533). Pacific Grove, CA: Brooks/Cole.

Olson, D. H. L. (1989). *Families, what makes them work.* Newbury Park, CA: Sage Publications.

Olson, D. H. L., Russell, C. S., & Sprenkle, D. H. (1989). *Circumplex model: Systemic assessment and treatment of families.* New York: Haworth Press.

Perli, R., & Bernard, J. M. (1993). Making multiculturalism relevant for majority culture graduate students. *Journal of Marital and Family Therapy, 19*(1), 5–16.

Popenoe, D., & Whitehead, B. D. (2000). *What's happening to marriage?* (p. 1). New Brunswick, NJ: The National Marriage Project at http://www.marriage.rutgers.edu.

Reifman, A., Villa, L. C., Amans, J. A., Rethinam, V., & Telesca, T. Y. (2001). Children of divorce in the 1990s: A meta-analysis. *Journal of Divorce and Remarriage, 36,* 27–36.

Rice, F. P. (1995). *Human development: A life span approach* (pp. 611–612). Upper Saddle River, NJ: Prentice Hall.

Riley, M. W., Foner, A., & Waring, J. (1988). Sociology of age. In N. J. Smelser (Ed.), *Handbook of sociology* (pp. 243–290). Newbury Park, CA: Sage Publications.

Roche, J. P. (1998). Premarital sex: Attitudes and behavior by dating stage. In M. E. Muuss (Ed.), *Adolescent behavior and society: A book of readings* (5th ed.) (pp. 235–243). New York: McGraw-Hill.

Rogers, C. (1965). Dealing with psychological tensions. *Journal of Applied Behavioral Science, 1,* 6–25.

Roosa, M. W. (1993). Youth at risk: The family as a contributor to child resiliency and as a focus for intervention. In V. L. Loyer-Carlson & F. K. Willits (Eds.), *Youth at risk: The research and practice interface* (pp. 39–47). University Park, PA: Northeast Regional Center for Rural Development.

Rosenblum, L., & Pauley, G. (1984). The effects of varying envioronmental demands on maternal and infant behavior. *Child Development, 55,* 305–315.

Rubin, L. B. (1983). *Intimate strangers.* New York: Harper & Row.

Rubin, L. B. (1976). *Worlds of pain: Life in the working-class family.* New York: Basic Books.

Ruiz, D. M. (1997). *The four agreements.* San Rafael, CA: Amber-Allen.

Sabatelli, R. M. (1987, November). Social exchange and the mediators of relationship commitment, courtship progress, and relationship stability. Paper presented at the meeting of the National Council on Family Relations, Atlanta, GA.

Schnarch, D. (1991). *Constructing the sexual crucible.* New York: W. W. Norton & Company.

Schnarch, D. (1997). *Passionate marriage: Keeping love and intimacy alive in committed relationships.* New York: Henry Holt.

Seidman, S. N., Mosher, W. O., & Aral, S. D. (1989). Predictors of high-risk behavior in unmarried American women: Adolescent environment as a risk factor. *Journal of Adolescent Health, 15,* 126–132.

Sheppard, J. A., & Strathman, A. J. (1989). Attractiveness and height: The role of stature in dating preference, frequency of dating, and perceptions of attractiveness. *Personality and Social Psychology Bulletin, 15,* 617–627.

Sherman, R., Oresky, P., & Rountree, Y. (1991). *Solving problems in couples and family therapy: Techniques and tactics.* NewYork: Brunner/Mazel.

Simon, S. B., Howe, L. W., & Kirschenbaum, H. K. (1972). *Values clarification: A handbook of practical strategies for teachers and students.* New York: Hart Publishing.

Sonenstein, F. L., Pleck, J. H., & Ku, L. C. (1989). Sexual activity, condom use, and AIDS awareness among adolescent males. *Family Planning Perspectives, 21,* 152–258.

Stahmann, R. F., & Hiebert, W. J. (1997). *Premarital and remarital counseling.* San Francisco: Jossey-Bass.

Stayton, W. R. (1996). Sexual and gender identity disorders in a relational perspective. In F. Kaslow (Ed.), *Handbook of relational diagnosis* (pp. 357–370). New York: John Wiley & Sons.

Tang, S., & Zuo, J. (2000). Dating attitudes and behaviors of American and Chinese college students. *The Social Science Journal, 37,* 67–78.

Thibaut, J. W., & Kelley, H. H. (1959; 1986). *The social psychology of groups.* New Brunswick, NJ: Transaction, Inc.

Thompson, E. H., Jr. (1991). The maleness of violence in dating relationships: An appraisal of stereotypes. *Sex Roles, 24,* 261–278.

Thornton, A. (1990). The courtship process and adolescent sexuality. *Journal of Family Issues, 11,* 239–273.

Waite, L. J., & Gallagher, M. (2000). *The case for marriage: Why married people are happier, healthier, and better off financially.* New York: Doubleday.

Wallerstein, J., Lewis, J., & Blakeslee, S. (2000). *The unexpected legacy of divorce: A 25 year landmark study.* New York: Hyperion.

Walters, M., Carter, B., Papp, P., & Silverstein, O. (1988). *The invisible web: Gender patterns in family relationships.* New York: Guilford.

Wamboldt, F., & Reiss, D. (1989). Defining a family heritage and a new relationship identity: Two central tasks in the making of a marriage. *Family Process, 28,* 317–336.

Waters, E., Vaughn, B. E., Posada, G., & Kondo-Ikemura, K. (1995). Caregiving, cultural, and cognitive perspectives on secure-base behavior and working models: New growing points of attachment theory and research. *Monographs of the Society for Research in Child Development, 60*(2–3, Serial No. 244).

Weigel, D. J., & Ballard-Reisch, D. S. (1999). How couples maintain marriages: A closer look at self and spouse influences upon the use of maintenance behaviors in marriages. *Family Relations, 48,* 263–269.

Whitbeck, L. B., Conger, R. D., Simons, R. L., & Kao, M. Y. (1993). Minor deviant behavior and adolescent sexual activity. *Youth & Society, 25,* 24–37.

Wile, D. B. (1993). *After the fight: A night in the life of a couple.* New York: Guilford.

Wright, J. W. (Ed.) (2000). *The New York Times 2001 Almanac.* New York Times, pp. 489–490.

Zill, N., Morrison, D. R., & Coiro, M. J. (1993). Long-term effects of parental divorce on parent-child relationships, adjustment, and achievement in young adulthood. *Journal of Family Psychology, 7,* 91–103.

Index